SPYING

IN

AMERICA

SPYING

IN

AMERICA

Espionage from the Revolutionary War
to the Dawn of the Cold War

MICHAEL J. SULICK

Georgetown University Press
Washington, DC

Library of Congress Cataloging-in-Publication Data

Sulick, Michael J.
 Spying in America : espionage from the Revolutionary War to the dawn of the Cold War / Michael J. Sulick.
    p. cm.
 Includes bibliographical references and index.
 ISBN 978-1-58901-926-3 (hbk. : alk. paper)

1. Espionage—United States—Case studies. 2. Espionage—United States—History. 3. Spies—United States—Biography. 4. Spies—United States—History. 5. United States—History—Civil War, 1861-1865—Secret service. 6. Espionage, German—United States—History—20th century. 7. Spies—Communist countries—History—20th century. 8. Military intelligence—United States—History. I. Title.

 UB271.U5S85 2012
 327.120973—dc23

                        2011052068

15 14 13 12   9 8 7 6 5 4 3 2 First printing

To Shirley, my beloved wife and best friend, for her unswerving support and patience

CONTENTS

CONTENTS

ILLUSTRATIONS

PREFACE

This book was written from the perspective of a career intelligence officer. During my twenty-eight-year career at the Central Intelligence Agency (CIA), I served as its chief of counterintelligence and later as director of the National Clandestine Service, which is responsible for the collection of intelligence through espionage and the coordination and evaluation of clandestine operations in the US intelligence community. While I was chief of counterintelligence, I often gave presentations in the intelligence community about espionage and drew from many historical examples. I consulted several of the many excellent books on espionage in specific periods of American history and on individual spy cases. I searched in vain for a study that included them all in one compact volume—so, when I first retired, I decided to write one myself.

A book of this scope on a topic so broad, covering more than thirty spies through 180 years of American history, can serve as little more than an introduction to the history of espionage in America. Throughout this long period there were far more incidents of espionage against the United States than can be included here. My selections are based on the importance of the particular case or its relevance to a host of issues regarding espionage in American history. The intent of the book is to spark the interest of laypeople and students who are increasingly interested in the field of intelligence, and provide them with a starting point to begin exploring in greater depth the threat of espionage as illustrated throughout American history. I would also venture that even veteran intelligence officers, preoccupied as they must be with the press of current threats, might learn something new about the history of their chosen profession from the spy stories presented here. To assist those who are interested in delving more deeply into espionage by Americans, I have included an extensive bibliography as a guide to the literature available on individual spy cases and on espionage in specific periods of American history.

I would like to express my thanks both to those who encouraged me to publish this book and assisted me in doing so, especially Doug Hubbard, Mark Lowenthal, David Major, Keith Melton, Jim Olson, and Hayden Peake. Their own writings on intelligence have inspired me, and their advice made my own work a much-improved product. Most of all, I would like to thank my colleagues at the CIA and in the intelligence community for all they taught me over the years and for their unheralded dedication and tireless devotion to protecting this nation.

All statements of fact, opinion, or analysis are those of the author and do not reflect the official positions or views of the CIA or any other US government agency. Nothing in the contents should be construed as asserting or implying US government authentication of information or the CIA's endorsement of the author's views. The material in this book has been reviewed by the CIA to prevent the disclosure of classified information.

Abbreviations

CIA   US Central Intelligence Agency

CPUSA   Communist Party of the United States of America

FBI   US Federal Bureau of Investigation

GRU   Glavnoe Razvedyvatel'noe Upravlenie (Main Intelligence Directorate). The GRU is the foreign military intelligence directorate of the General Staff of the Armed Forces of the Russian Federation and collects intelligence overseas on military issues related to Russian national security. During the Soviet era, the GRU belonged to the Soviet Army General Staff of the Soviet Union.

KGB   Komitet Gosudarstvennoy Bezopasnosti (Soviet Committee of State Security), 1954–91.

NKGB   Narodnyy Komissariat Gosudarstvennoy Bezopasnosti (People's Commissariat for State Security), February 1941–July 1944; April 1943–March 1946.

NKVD   Narodnyy Komissariat Vnutrennych Del (People's Commissariat for Internal Affairs), July 1934–February 1941; July 1941–April 1943.

OGPU   Ob"edinennoe Gosudarstvennoe Politicheskoe Upravlenie (Joint State Political Directorate), 1923–34.

THE PERIL OF DISBELIEF

To counter espionage, you must first understand it. To do this,
you must be aware of its history

MARK LLOYD, *Guinness Book of Espionage*

Can you keep a secret? Maybe you can, but the US government cannot. Nations both large and small, from Russia and China to Ghana and Ecuador, have stolen the most precious secrets of the United States since the country's birth. During the Cold War, the Soviet Union and its allies acquired American military secrets that would have jeopardized the nation's defense if the two superpowers had clashed in open warfare.

The Soviet Union spied on America by various means—such as satellite reconnaissance, electronic eavesdropping, and code breaking—but its greatest achievements in espionage stemmed from its collaboration with American spies inside the US government. Thanks to one Cold War spy, naval warrant officer John Walker, the Soviets knew every move of America's nuclear submarine fleet, which was considered the most invulnerable leg of the nation's land, air, and sea defense triad. Fortunately, however, the superpowers never triggered a nuclear war. Yet even if the superpowers had only engaged in a conventional war in Europe, the Soviets would still have had a distinct advantage—a spy in the US Army, Sergeant Clyde Conrad, had given their Hungarian ally NATO's complete defense plans for the continent.

All nations have been victims of espionage, but the United States has proven to be particularly vulnerable to spies who endangered the national defense during the Cold War. By the time the Cold War ended, spies in the US government included Americans from every agency involved in national security and every branch of the armed forces except the coast guard.[1] However, although many Americans associate espionage with the superpower rivalry between the United States and the Soviet Union, the betrayal of US government secrets by spies is hardly a Cold War phenomenon.

The Soviet intelligence services and their allies in the Soviet Bloc were certainly aggressive in spying against the United States, but America's vulnerability to espionage was more deeply rooted in the nation's past. America's susceptibility to the threat of espionage in the Cold War and thereafter developed, ironically, from the very qualities that catapulted the nation to superpower status and made it a symbol of democracy: an exceptional geography and a tradition of individual liberties. These attributes shaped American attitudes toward national security and bred both disbelief about the threat of espionage and a distrust of countering it at the expense of these cherished liberties.

America's exceptional geography blessed the country with abundant natural resources, a thriving economy, and the natural border of two oceans that comfortably separated it from squabbling European nations to the east and emerging Asian powers to the west. For more than a century after its birth, the United States was rarely challenged by security threats from abroad and thus felt little need for vigilance against espionage. For the first 120 years of US history, the only major conflicts in the nation involved citizens who spoke the same language, shared the same heritage, and even worked side by side in the same fields and factories. The lack of a serious threat from foreign aggressors in the nineteenth century only reinforced America's disbelief that its citizens in positions of trust would spy for another nation.

This disbelief spawned a "national capacity for naiveté," as former Central Intelligence Agency (CIA) counterintelligence chief Paul Redmond dubbed it, which surfaced as early as the American Revolution.[2] George

Washington feared British espionage, but even he was shocked that Benedict Arnold, one of the era's greatest military commanders, could betray his country. However, the British were actively trying to persuade high-level colonial officers to defect, and rumors had circulated that a top patriot general was collaborating with the British. Washington's intelligence chief, Benjamin Tallmadge, had also received information about a highly placed spy inside the colonists' ranks. Arnold, however, remained above suspicion, even though he was involved in shady business deals and had grumbled loudly about his unfair treatment by the Continental Congress. Americans from the commander in chief down simply refused to believe that a general of Arnold's caliber and achievements could betray the cause.

American disbelief regarding espionage has persisted throughout the nation's history. A century and a half later, during the Great Depression, Americans disillusioned with capitalism were lured by the utopian promises of communism and swelled the ranks of the Communist Party of the United States (CPUSA). The Soviet intelligence services seized the opportunity by forming an underground network in the CPUSA to recruit Americans as spies and, within a decade, they were running the most colossal espionage operation against the United States in its history. Communist sympathizers attracted by Franklin D. Roosevelt's New Deal policies flocked to work in the new administration and willingly supported the Soviet cause by passing government secrets. When irrefutable proof of widespread Soviet espionage eventually surfaced, the highest levels of the US government still refused to believe that senior officials of Roosevelt's administration were Soviet spies.

American efforts to thwart espionage were also influenced by the nation's passionate insistence on the primacy of individual freedoms. As a result, Americans developed a highly suspicious distrust of government efforts to combat enemy spying, viewing them as intrusiveness and even persecution of its citizenry. This distrust regarding the impact of counterespionage on civil liberties also harked back to America's earliest days.

Espionage was an important tool in the statecraft of eighteenth-century Europe, where monarchs sought information about their rivals to increase their power. However, many colonists had fled to the New World to escape the oppression, injustice, and poverty associated with these royal intrigues. Espionage, in their view, was alien to the spirit of democracy and guarantee of civil liberties promised in the New World. Despite this national distaste for spying, the nation was eventually compelled to confront the dilemma between the need for security and the guarantee of individual liberties as world wars loomed and foreign intelligence services increased their efforts to steal American secrets.

Maintaining the delicate balance between security and freedom proved to be difficult. American efforts to counter espionage by hostile intelligence services were often crippled, not only by the disbelievers who refused to see spies anywhere, but also by misguided zealots who saw spies everywhere. These zealots, unfortunately, only increased the country's suspicion of counterespionage by committing the very excesses Americans feared.

During the Civil War, one of the two Union counterespionage agencies was led by Lafayette Baker, a former vigilante who was hired because of his harsh stance on Confederate subversion. Baker's National Detective Police was supposedly established to discover Confederate espionage, but Baker's zealous pursuit of spies led to lawless persecution and abuses of citizens' rights. The National Detective Police rounded up hundreds of alleged subversives, dragging them out of their homes in the middle of the night, holding them without any due process, and brutally interrogating them. In the end, Baker's massive raids snared few real spies.

Baker's excesses would be repeated in the future whenever America felt threatened by foreign philosophies. After World War I Attorney General Mitchell Palmer sounded alarms about vast conspiracies to overthrow the government. The alarm rang true—anarchists had, in fact, orchestrated labor strikes and sent letter bombs to government officials, including Palmer himself. Palmer launched his infamous Red Raids to root out subversives and detained hundreds of suspects. The scope of alien subversion, however, proved far less than his shrill warnings predicted, and he was ultimately discredited once his widespread abuse of citizens' rights was revealed.

Because of these abuses, counterespionage became synonymous with persecution, and fears of an American Gestapo led to the dismantling of the few government organizations involved in countering espionage. Spy mania would erupt at other critical periods after World War II and lead to the same abuses. Actions taken during these periods of spy mania surfaced no real espionage operations jeopardizing national security, but the practice of finding them was viewed with suspicion.

This distrust of counterespionage also contributed to the absence of a central organization in the government to combat enemy spying for the first 160 years of the nation's existence. The United States did not establish a central counterespionage authority until President Roosevelt, who was frustrated by bureaucratic turf wars and was worried about looming US involvement in a world war, assigned the task to the Federal Bureau of Investigation (FBI) in 1939. Before that, Americans only established institutions in wartime to counter enemy spying and collect information through espionage.

Once the colonists went to war against the British to win their independence, they quickly cobbled together capabilities to steal enemy secrets and catch enemy spies. George Washington cleverly used intelligence to even the odds against a professional British force that outgunned his inexperienced, ragtag army. But once their independence had been won, the Americans disbanded their wartime organizations for espionage and counterespionage, a pattern that was repeated for the next century and a half. In peacetime Americans retreated to their comfortable security and again grew complacent about the threats from potential enemies. As a result, the capabilities that developed during wartime atrophied. Those who had gained experience moved on to other pursuits, grew old, and died; and thus the next generation had to confront new espionage threats from scratch, without any institutional knowledge that might have been developed in a professional counterespionage organization.[3]

Although Washington was concerned about British espionage, he never organized a unified colonial response to the need to ferret out spies. The only counterspy service during the Revolutionary War was John Jay's Committee on Detecting and Defeating Conspiracies, which successfully rooted out Tory spies but operated only in the New York region. The committee was dissolved after the colonies gained their independence, and Americans on both sides of the Civil War had to build counterespionage capabilities anew.

The Civil War witnessed the first instance of interagency rivalries that would plague American efforts to combat espionage for the next seventy years. At one point, the Union was served by two separate organizations to catch Confederate spies, one headed by Allen Pinkerton and the other by Lafayette Baker. These two organizations not only operated independently but, like the Keystone Cops, sometimes arrested each other's operatives.

Both organizations were dissolved after the Civil War, and so the United States entered World War I with a hodgepodge of federal agencies thrashing about to find enemy spies. The State Department, Justice Department, the Secret Service, and the military services at various times all assumed counterspy responsibilities and bickered with each other over jurisdiction. By the late 1930s the FBI had proven to be relatively more effective against foreign spies and subversives than its sister agencies and already had the legal authority to investigate federal crimes, including espionage. In 1939 President Roosevelt assigned the FBI responsibility for counterespionage and thus finally established a central organization to neutralize spying by foreign agents and the American citizens who collaborated with them.

This book presents the stories of those operations by hostile intelligence services and the spies who collaborated with them from the Revolutionary War to the early days of the Cold War. These stories provide the foundation for understanding America's vulnerability to espionage in the Cold War and up to the present. Throughout this long period, there were far more incidents of espionage against the United States than could be included here, and the selections given in the chapters that follow are based on the importance of the particular case or its relevance to a host of issues regarding espionage in American history. Incidents of spying increased from the Cold War to the present day, but espionage and US efforts to combat it changed dramatically. Revelations about widespread Soviet espionage and the onset of the superpower conflict finally prompted the United States to develop formidable counterespionage capabilities in the FBI domestically and the CIA overseas. The Soviets and their bloc allies, and also other nations, were still successful in spying against America, but those stories merit separate treatment in a subsequent volume because of evolving US attitudes and responses to espionage.

The stories presented here focus on six fundamental elements of espionage: the motivations that drove Americans to spy; their access and the secrets they betrayed; the tradecraft used by the intelligence services that controlled them—that is, the techniques of concealing their espionage; the exposure of the spy operations; the punishment meted out to the spies; and, finally, the damage these espionage operations inflicted on America's national security.

Espionage in specific periods of American history and the individual stories of these spy operations have been treated in more detail in other works, which I cite throughout this book. This study treats each of these stories briefly but, in doing so, illustrates the common threads in those spy operations and the evolution of American attitudes toward espionage leading up to the Cold War. Hopefully, the stories will pique the reader's interest to delve further into the history of espionage against America.

All these Americans spied for their own unique reasons. Some spied out of pure greed, whereas others supported a cause or country at odds with the United States. None of these Americans, however, spied in a vacuum. Their espionage was often shaped by the political, economic, and social dynamics of the era in American history when they committed their crimes. Their stories, unique though they may be, mirror the dynamics at play in American society at critical junctures in the nation's history.

The motives that have driven Americans to commit espionage are the same ones that have impelled people around the world to betray their countries for centuries: money, ego, revenge, romance, simple thrills, ideological sympathy, and dual loyalties. Hostile intelligence services have capitalized on these motives and on American complacency about espionage to undermine the nation's security. Money has historically been the primary motive behind espionage, and American spies have been no exception. America's first spy, Benjamin Church, a prominent Massachusetts patriot, sold secrets to the British to support a mistress and a lavish lifestyle. Benedict Arnold also demanded hefty payments from the British, but money was only one among a tangled web of motives that drove him to betray his country. He suffered from a monumental ego and believed that his compatriots had denied him the recognition he merited for his military exploits. The payments that the British made to Arnold for his espionage were, to some degree, both an acknowledgment of his self-worth and a means to avenge the perceived injustice done to him.

Although money has been the primary motive behind most American espionage, some citizens have spied for purely ideological reasons. In one of the unique chapters in the annals of espionage, during the 1930s and 1940s the largest collective of spies in US history betrayed their nation's secrets almost solely because of ideological sympathy with communism. Few of the major American spies of the era accepted a penny for their secrets and, in fact, some were insulted when the Soviet intelligence services tried to offer them payment.[4]

The motives of all these spies were less important to their intelligence service masters than their access. As Allen Dulles, one of the early directors of the CIA, notes, "The essence of espionage is access."[5] The stories presented here include Americans inside the inner circle of power, like Benedict Arnold, the highest-ranking military officer to spy against the United States, and Harry Dexter White, a top Treasury Department official under President Roosevelt. They include lower-ranking spies who sat at the right hand of power, like Edward Bancroft, an aide to Benjamin Franklin, or who worked as junior analysts on files full of classified information, like Judith Coplon in the Justice Department. But the stories also include spies who never held a government job with access to secrets but ran extensive networks of sources who did. Among them were two spinsters, Elizabeth Bentley, who oversaw a ring of Soviet spies in the 1930s and 1940s, and Elizabeth Van Lew, who ran a network of similar scope to protect the Union during the Civil War. And, finally, the stories include scientists who plundered the most vital secrets of American military weaponry on behalf of their masters in Nazi Germany and the Soviet Union.

Stealing these secrets proved relatively easy in an open society where espionage threats were largely ignored. Communicating the secrets, however, entailed far more risk. As the historian John Keegan notes, "Real agents are at their most vulnerable when they attempt . . . to reach their spymasters. The biographies of real agents are ultimately almost always a story of betrayal by communications failure."[6] To counter these risks and to communicate with their spies, intelligence services employ "tradecraft"— the full range of techniques to hide clandestine intelligence operations from the enemy, including codes, secret writing, and "dead drops," that is, concealed caches of information planted in areas where they are not likely to be found by passers-by.

Spy tradecraft has evolved over centuries because of technological advances in communications, but time-tested techniques have remained in use. One of the earliest American spies, Edward Bancroft, worked for Benjamin Franklin in Paris, where the venerable patriot was orchestrating

French covert assistance to the colonies. Bancroft's British spymasters communicated with him via an elaborate system that worked effectively—the spy was never discovered during his lifetime. Two centuries later, Soviet intelligence operatives still used a remarkably similar system to communicate with their spies in the US government.

Although these measures may seem overly elaborate, spies and spymasters who ignore tradecraft do so at their peril. Tradecraft blunders have led to the discovery of legions of spies throughout history. Though the Germans had some successes spying against the United States before and during both world wars, overall their attempts at espionage and sabotage were foiled because of their own shoddy tradecraft and security. Insufficient evaluation of their own officers and the Americans they recruited ultimately resulted in the exposure of key intelligence operations and wrecked their espionage networks in the United States.

One of the more glaring cases of inadequate tradecraft in the United States was the exposure of the Soviet spy networks in the 1940s. The KGB struggled to impose discipline on its ideologically committed spies and urged them to follow basic tradecraft instructions. Many of its espionage rings, however, had sprung from Marxist discussion cells and had never abandoned this coffee klatch approach in their spying activity. Members of a ring often knew the identities of their fellow spies, a cardinal violation of basic security practice that enabled defectors from the communist cause to identify entire espionage networks to the FBI.

Once American spies were caught, their punishment varied depending on a host of factors, many of which reflected the dynamics of the era when they committed their crimes. Sentences for convicted spies throughout American history have ranged from execution to no punishment at all. During the Revolutionary War, the Continental Congress was in a quandary when America's first spy, Benjamin Church, was arrested because there was no espionage law on the books applicable to civilians. Congress hastily established the death penalty for espionage, but the law could not be applied retroactively against Church. During the Civil War, minor spies on both sides were simply released to spare the expense of feeding them in prison. More damaging spies were sometimes hung, not on the basis of jury trials but simply on the whim of the commander in the area where the spy was caught.

This haphazard approach to dealing with arrested spies ended when Congress enacted the Espionage Act of 1917 right after America's entry into World War I. The Espionage Act, however, covered a range of subversive activities besides spying, and the majority of Americans tried under the law were accused of crimes other than espionage. President Wilson urged passage of the law because of his fears of German American subversion, which were widely shared but exaggerated throughout the country as citizens burned German books and outlawed teaching of the language in schools. As the historians Henry Steele Commager and Samuel Eliot Morison noted, "In 1917–19 the people of the United States abandoned themselves to a hysteria of fear of German conspiracies, . . . and the government indulged in greater excesses than at any previous crisis of our history."[7]

After World War II, American liberals believed a new "hysteria of fear" about communism was epitomized by the conviction and execution of Julius Rosenberg and Ethel Rosenberg for espionage. Their case is one of the best illustrations of how the sociopolitical dynamics of an era influenced the punishment meted out to spies. The Rosenbergs were arrested and tried in the tense early years of the Cold War. The pendulum of public opinion had swung dramatically since the end of World War II—a country where some people had once flirted with communism now feared and despised it.

By the time of the Rosenberg trial, the Soviets had installed puppet regimes in Eastern Europe, Mao Zedong's communists had seized power in China, and North Korean communists had invaded their neighbor to the south. The Soviets had also developed and tested their own atomic bomb years ahead of schedule—thanks, in part, to the secrets they obtained from Julius Rosenberg.[8] The Rosenbergs had not only spied for a country that was spreading its totalitarian philosophy around the world but had also given it the weapon to challenge the postwar hegemony of the United States. In the rabidly anticommunist climate of the early 1950s, the Rosenbergs were sentenced to death and remain today the last American civilians executed for espionage.

The damage to national security from Julius Rosenberg's espionage has been debated for decades. However damaging Rosenberg's espionage may have been, he was still only one of many Soviet spies inside America's most secret military project of World War II. Cumulatively, the information passed by all these spies enabled the Soviet Union to develop its own atomic bomb more quickly than its scientists would have done on their own. As a result, some historians conclude, Joseph Stalin felt emboldened to challenge the United States and approved North Korea's invasion of its neighbor to the south, launching a conflict that ended with 4 million casualties and the deaths of more than 35,000 US servicemen.[9]

Ironically, however, the overall damage to national security from espionage has reinforced America's disbelief about spying and suspicion of counterespionage. Although the United States has been riddled with spies throughout its history, the nation still stands. As John Keegan points out, "Intelligence in war, however good, does not point out unerringly the path to victory."[10] Benedict Arnold passed secrets to the British, but his plans for West Point went awry and the colonies still won their independence. The Union was preserved after the Civil War despite Confederate spying, and the United States emerged victorious in two world wars despite enemy espionage. A confluence of other political, military, and economic factors proved far more decisive than espionage in resolving the nation's conflicts with its enemies. Nonetheless, although espionage may not be the decisive factor in winning wars, these stories illustrate that, as in the atomic bomb case, it can affect the course of events in ways that damage national interests, including the loss of American lives.

The stories presented here are just part of the history of espionage against America because they tell only of known spies and intelligence service operations. Some of these known spies escaped justice and were not discovered for years. Edward Bancroft's espionage during the American Revolution only came to light sixty-eight years after his death. Another story concerns Theodore Hall, a brilliant young scientist at Los Alamos who passed atomic bomb secrets to the Soviet Union. Although he was identified as a Soviet spy, he escaped prosecution because of a lack of evidence that could be used in court. Another spy, George Koval, also escaped to the Soviet Union, and his espionage inside the atom bomb project was only revealed six decades later. And there have undoubtedly also been other truly successful spies against America who have never been identified and have eluded justice.

Perhaps one of you reading this is among these unknown spies. You snicker as you read how other spies like you spent too much money, talked too much, or made some other blunder that led to their arrest. You live comfortably and perhaps have already retired, and so your spying days are over and your name, if even known to your handlers, is buried deep in dusty files in some foreign capital. You followed instructions from your spymasters to the letter, you never cut corners, and you spent your spy money well but wisely. As you sink into a plush easy chair, a modest purchase from your ill-gotten gains, you watch the news on TV, knowing that you played some part in world events unknown to your friends and colleagues, secure in your belief that you have hoodwinked the entire counterespionage apparatus of the US government.

But you can never be at peace. You must live with your conscience. Besides, at some time, somewhere, you may have made a mistake—a thought that constantly gnaws at you. And you will never know when some spy in that foreign capital will approach the United States and provide that nugget of information that will pinpoint you. Your story may yet be told.

PART **1**

THE
REVOLUTIONARY
WAR

ESPIONAGE AND
THE REVOLUTIONARY WAR

There is one evil I dread, and that is their spies.

GEORGE WASHINGTON, *March 24, 1776*.
Quoted by US Central Intelligence Agency, *Intelligence*.

Espionage played a crucial role in the turbulent conflicts of eighteenth-century Europe, where ruthlessly ambitious monarchs clashed over trade, territory, and religious differences. Among European nations, Great Britain had few rivals in espionage, and it had developed an effective intelligence service two centuries earlier under Francis Walsingham, Queen Elizabeth I's spymaster. By the mid-1700s, Walsingham's successors had seeded spies inside the royal courts of Britain's European neighbors to protect its empire, which had become the major economic and military power on the globe.

Before the Revolution, the British were too preoccupied with threats from European rivals to spy on their American colonies and had little need to do so. The relationship between the Crown and its subjects across the Atlantic was mutually beneficial for both sides. The British were content to let the colonies govern themselves as long as trade flourished and the Crown benefited. The colonies purchased half the ironware, cotton, and linen produced in Britain, which in turn was the major consumer of raw materials from its New World subjects. From 1700 until the Revolutionary

War, colonial exports to Britain grew sevenfold, and trade between the colonies and the mother country increased from £500,000 to £2.8 million.[1]

The British economy, however, began to suffer from the heavy costs of defeating France in the Seven Years' War (1756–63). To recover their losses, King George III and his Parliament imposed a series of taxes on the colonies. Tensions between the Crown and its subjects escalated from protest to covert resistance and finally erupted into armed conflict in Massachusetts, the hotbed of colonial opposition to the taxes. Britain's stubborn refusal to compromise and its rejection of appeals for negotiations only drove the colonists further along the road to revolution.

Despite British intransigence, colonial support for independence was hardly unanimous even after the harsh taxes were imposed. Even the most vocal opponents of the king's taxes, including founding fathers like John Adams and Benjamin Franklin, initially opposed independence and simply sought a colonial voice in Parliament regarding any decisions to tax the colonies.

Even after the first salvos of the war in Lexington and Concord in 1775, the Second Continental Congress advocated negotiations to reconcile with London. The assemblies of two colonies, New Jersey and Pennsylvania, instructed their delegates to Congress to oppose any move to secede from the British Empire. As John Adams later claimed, before the war one-third of the colonial population supported independence, one-third opposed it, and the remaining one-third was neutral.[2]

These divided loyalties facilitated espionage by both sides. Recruiting spies was a relatively simple task because the colonists, whether Tory or revolutionary, spoke the same language and shared the same heritage. Espionage swiftly became as important to the British in the colonies as it was in the royal courts of Europe. To suppress the independence movement, the British relied on spies to gauge levels of colonial unrest, troop strength, and stockpiles of munitions and supplies. The Crown spared little expense to fund this espionage effort. Within a few years after the first shots of the American Revolution were fired, the budget of British intelligence chief William Eden doubled.[3]

Espionage was even more important to the Revolutionary cause. The colonials faced a better-armed and more experienced enemy, and colonial commander in chief George Washington realized that intelligence on British troop strengths and movements could even the odds. As the intelligence historian Thomas Powers notes, espionage played a central role in the American Revolution: "The American cause was born in secrecy in the coffeehouses of Boston, it was nurtured in secrecy in the Committees of Correspondence, it was pressed by citizens disguised as Indians who dumped tea in Boston harbor. . . . Behind the pageant lay all the hidden web of espionage, propaganda, secret diplomacy. In truth, it was the clandestine arts as much as American armies which won American independence."[4]

Espionage, in fact, was the spark that ignited the war. General Thomas Gage, the royal governor of Massachusetts and commander of British forces, received a report from a spy that New England colonists were hiding stockpiles of weapons because they feared the British would seize them.[5] Gage decided to march into Concord to capture the weapons before the colonists could use them against his troops. On the revolutionary side, Boston patriots learned of Gage's plan of attack from their own spies in the king's ranks. Paul Revere, chief of Boston's amateur intelligence service, alerted two leading figures of the local resistance, John Hancock and Samuel Adams, that Gage intended to arrest them. Revere's renowned "Midnight Ride" to warn these two founding fathers was perhaps the first delivery of timely threat information to key policymakers by American intelligence.

Revere, a silversmith by trade, was chosen by the Massachusetts Provincial Congress to conduct intelligence activities as part of the establishment of the Committee of Safety to protect the colony. He assembled a band of about thirty amateur spies who were dubbed the Mechanics because, like Revere, they were all artisans.[6] Their professions gave them natural pretexts to move about Boston and spy on Gage's troops. They often acquired useful information in alehouses by eavesdropping on British soldiers who talked indiscreetly after quaffing a few brews.[7]

The Mechanics also tried to ferret out British spies among Boston's Tory citizens but found the task more difficult than collecting intelligence. The shared language and heritage that facilitated espionage complicated the discovery of spies. The average colonist strolling about the town square in his waistcoat, ruffled sleeves, and distinctive tricornered hat or quaffing ale in the local tavern could be a Tory or a patriot. Distinguishing one from another was even difficult within families: Benjamin Franklin's son William was an ardent loyalist and the Crown's governor of New Jersey. He spied on his father and reported on his activities to the British. William was later imprisoned by the Continental Congress and, after his release, organized raids against revolutionary forces in New York.[8]

Because of the blurred lines between Tory and patriot, George Washington left counterespionage to individual colonies and local commanders who would be better equipped to identify spies among their townsfolk.[9] As a result, although Washington may have dreaded British spies, he never established a central counterespionage unit to thwart British espionage. However, he did play a role in establishing a fledgling counterspy service in one of the colonies. New York, unlike Massachusetts, was heavily populated by Tories and was occupied by British forces in 1776. In June 1776 Washington convinced the New York Congress to establish the Committee on Detecting and Defeating Conspiracies (CDDC) to "close the regular channels of intelligence from the city."[10] He chose John Jay, who would later become the first chief justice of the United States Supreme Court, to head the CDDC, which in effect became the nation's first counterespionage service. Because of Jay's work on the CDDC, in 1997 the US Central Intelligence Agency honored him as the father of American counterintelligence.[11]

Jay was the first in a long line of American spy hunters with a penchant for absolute secrecy. He often disagreed with Washington's desire to publicize some intelligence successes for morale-building purposes.[12] Even after the war, Jay related to his close friend, James Fenimore Cooper, the exploits of his master spy in the CDDC but refused to provide his agent's name. Based on Jay's tales, Cooper wrote *The Spy*, a novel in which the hero, Harvey Birch, spies on the British for George Washington.

PAINTING OF JOHN JAY by Gilbert Stuart. *Library of Congress*

The character of Birch was largely based on Enoch Crosby, a shoemaker from Danbury, Connecticut, who left the Continental Army because of war injuries but later reenlisted in New York. Crosby befriended a British sympathizer in Westchester County, New York, who, believing that the shoemaker shared his views, introduced him to a Tory spy ring. After exposing the ring to the CDDC, Crosby rejoined his new Tory comrades in time to be arrested with them and then engineered his own escape. Jay was so impressed with this operation that he recruited Crosby as a permanent counterspy and provided him with the hefty budget of one horse and $30 for the task.[13]

Crosby was a master in eliciting information and winning the trust of Tory spies, who were duped by his humble demeanor. He was, after all, a mere shoemaker, wandering from town to town to eke out a living by cobbling shoes. He was the quintessential little gray man, shy, taciturn, only 5 feet, 3 inches tall, which was slight even by eighteenth-century standards. To protect his cover, he was often arrested along with the spies he exposed but repeatedly escaped. On one occasion he was taken prisoner and brought to Jay's house. Fortunately, a witting house servant recognized Crosby and treated his guards with enough whiskey to put them to sleep and enable him to slip away and rejoin his British confederates.

Crosby's cumulative counterespionage achievements were significant, but he and his colleagues in the CDDC never exposed any major British spies. As the intelligence historian John Bakeless noted, "No amount of counterintelligence could catch all the British agents" operating in the colonies.[14] Among them were three highly placed agents in the inner councils of the American cause whose spying could have altered the course of the Revolution.

THE FIRST SPY

BENJAMIN CHURCH

In the Fall of 1774 and Winter of 1775, I was one of upwards of thirty, chiefly mechanics, who formed ourselves into a Committee for the purpose of watching the Movements of the British soldiers, and gaining every intelligence of the Movements of the Tories. We held our meetings at the Green Dragon Tavern. We were so careful that our meetings should be kept secret that every time we met, every person swore on a Bible, that they would not discover any of our transactions, but to Messrs. Hancock, Adams, Doctors Warren, Church, and one or two more.

PAUL REVERE, letter

More than 230 years have passed since the American Revolution, and Benedict Arnold still towers over all other spies against America as the most infamous traitor in US history. Arnold, however, was not the first major spy against America. That dubious honor belongs to Dr. Benjamin Church. Although Church remains an obscure figure in the history of the Revolutionary War, he was the most highly placed civilian spy in the British espionage network. Because he was trusted with the most important secrets of the colonies, he could have inflicted significant damage on the revolutionary cause.

Church was among the leading patriots in the highly patriotic colony of Massachusetts. In December 1773 he participated in the Boston Tea Party, when colonists disguised as Indians dumped chests of tea on a British ship overboard to protest the king's tax. Church was also a propagandist who penned several pamphlets supporting the revolutionary cause. He was elected to the Massachusetts Provincial Congress and was chosen by his peers to present the colony's defense plans to the Second Continental Congress and seek aid for the colony's militia.[1]

A physician by profession, Church treated wounded revolutionaries at the Battle of Bunker Hill and was eventually appointed chief surgeon of the Continental Army. As Paul Revere's comments indicate, Church was also in the inner council of Boston revolutionaries who swore on a Bible at the Green Dragon Tavern to protect the colonists' most guarded secrets. His revolutionary credentials were impeccable.

Church was also a highly paid spy in the espionage network of the British general Thomas Gage. Gage needed intelligence on the plans, intentions, and capabilities of the upstart Massachusetts revolutionaries. After the Boston Tea Party, King George III decided to crack down on the mutinous colony. He appointed Gage commander of British Forces in North America and royal governor of Massachusetts to quell the increasing defiance of his colonists. Soon after his arrival, Gage began to satisfy the monarch's wishes by closing Boston Harbor to ships from overseas and other colonies, effectively cutting Massachusetts' economic lifeline. He also restricted many of the self-governing authorities of the colony and reduced the jurisdiction of its courts. Gage realized that colonial opposition to his harsh measures was quickly mounting, so he infiltrated spies to discover Massachusetts' progress in building a militia and stockpiling weapons and supplies.

Paul Revere was convinced that one of Gage's spies had penetrated the Sons of Liberty, an underground organization of colonists dedicated to subverting royalist rule in America. One of Revere's informants told him that Gage knew details of a secret Sons of Liberty meeting held in the Green Dragon Tavern the day after it occurred.[2] Church, however, was beyond reproach, despite hints of some suspicious activities. In one instance, Revere was advised that Church had been spotted entering Gage's quarters in Boston and appeared "more like a man that was acquainted than a prisoner."[3] Church later claimed that he had been detained but set free in a few days. Revere dismissed the incident.

Revere was not alone in ignoring disturbing signs about his Sons of Liberty colleague. Church was married but had taken a mistress and begun living a lavish lifestyle, although his colleagues were aware that he had been in dire financial straits. He was living well beyond his means as a physician, a profession that hardly netted the income modern doctors command (his salary as surgeon general was $4 a day, which was relatively small compensation for a physician of that stature even by eighteenth-century standards).[4] Despite this unexplained wealth, the notion of a

BENJAMIN CHURCH was a prominent and trusted patriot in Massachusetts during the Revolution, but he turned out to be a spy for Britain. *National Guard Bureau, Army Heritage Education Center*

dedicated revolutionary like Church spying for the enemy was simply inconceivable and foreshadowed the endemic blindness of Americans to glaring indicators of espionage throughout American history. Church was only the first of many Americans who committed espionage out of greed and whose newfound riches were ignored by colleagues and counterspies.

Church's espionage might never have been detected if he had not made a serious tradecraft blunder in communicating with the British. Communications is the riskiest element of espionage. At some point, the spy and his handler must communicate for one to receive information and for the other to receive his espionage tasks and money. As former Central Intelligence Agency director Allen Dulles noted, "there is no single field of intelligence work in which the accidental mishap is more frequent or more frustrating than in communications."[5] In Church's case the mishap proved to be his undoing.

Church's greed led to the tradecraft blunder. Church had been dispatched to the Continental Congress in Philadelphia and was thus out of contact with Gage. Meanwhile, he received a letter from his Tory brother-in-law pleading with him to renounce his rebellion against Britain. His brother-in-law asked him to respond via a British naval commander in Newport named Captain James Wallace. Church may have suspected that the letter was a veiled attempt by the British to renew contact with him, so he wrote a letter in response that included some juicy intelligence in hopes of earning further profits from his lucrative spying. Because he was unable to travel to Newport himself, he made the cardinal error of entrusting the compromising letter to his mistress.

Church's mistress went to Newport and appeared at the door of her former boyfriend, a baker named Geoffrey Wenwood whom she mistakenly thought was a Tory. She asked him to arrange a meeting with Captain Wallace. Pressed by Wenwood, she claimed that she had a letter to deliver by hand to Wallace, but Wenwood finally convinced her to give him the letter and he would see to the matter. Wenwood, a colonial patriot, showed the envelope to a friend. They opened it and found three pages of text, all in code. Writing letters in primitive code was common practice in the eighteenth century when correspondents wanted to ensure privacy. Although their interest was piqued, Wenwood and his friend simply dropped the matter, and the baker buried the envelope in his desk. Two months later Wenwood received a letter from his old girlfriend asking why he had not delivered the letter as he had promised. At this point Wenwood and his friend sought advice and were rushed with the enciphered letter to General Nathaniel Greene, the commander of Rhode Island's patriot troops. Suspecting espionage, Greene immediately showed the letter to George Washington.

Once Washington saw that the letter was addressed to a British major on Gage's staff, he immediately confronted the woman. In spite of his relentless questioning, the woman claimed not to know the contents of the encrypted letter and would not divulge the name of the person who had asked her to deliver it. Finally, faced with Washington's threat of harsh punishment, she relented. She confessed that Dr. Benjamin Church had given her the letter.

Washington was appalled and ordered that Church be apprehended and brought to him. Confronted by Washington, Church confirmed the woman's story but claimed that the enciphered text was a simple letter to his brother-in-law. At the same time Church offered no plausible explanation for why he had sent the letter through a British naval commander. Still, this was hardly proof of espionage. Washington had Church's home searched, but his troops found neither the cipher key nor any incriminating papers. As it turned out, another Gage spy had apparently reached Church's home first and had removed any evidence of espionage.

Washington has been acknowledged by the CIA as the father of American intelligence, but the Church case should have earned him the same honor in American cryptography. Without any concrete evidence of Church's guilt, Washington arranged for two independent attempts to decipher the text of his letter. One decryption was done by the Reverend Samuel West, an amateur cryptanalyst who also happened to be a Harvard classmate of Church. The other was done by the team of Colonel Elisha Porter of the local militia and Elbridge Gerry, a member of the Massachusetts Congress who would later become the fifth vice president of the United States. These three men planted the first seeds of American cryptography that sprouted two centuries later into the National Security Agency.

Both teams successfully deciphered the message, a damning one for Church. The letter contained statistics about troop strength, artillery, and supplies in various colonies and information about the unity and determination of the Continental Congress. Confronted with the deciphered text, Church tried to bluff his way out. He claimed that he was deceiving the enemy to assist the revolutionary cause by intentionally exaggerating colonial capabilities in hopes of discouraging British military action. Church would be the first in a line of American spies confronted with evidence of their treachery who would claim that they had passed bogus information to deceive the enemy.

Despite Church's desperate attempts to save himself, other incriminating comments in the letter sealed his fate. In one plaintive sentence, the writer claimed that he was "out of pay and determined to be so until something comes my way" and asks the British to "make use of every precaution or I perish."[6] Church's concerns about money and security belied his allegation that he was a self-styled double agent deceiving the British.

At the same time, the figures Church provided to the British were truly inflated. Was his information really inaccurate? This is difficult to imagine, given his place in the inner councils of the patriots. Did he intentionally inflate the figures to deceive the British while collecting their spy fees, perhaps his internal compromise to lessen his guilt? Besides this, Church apparently did not reveal to Gage the identities of his fellow conspirators at the Green Dragon. None of Revere's Mechanics was ever exposed as a spy, and Revere himself was only detained once during his famed "Midnight Ride" and immediately released. The possibility exists that Church might have attempted to gain the best of both worlds by supporting his lavish life-style with spy payments yet providing inaccurate intelligence to maintain his allegiance to the Revolution. We will probably never know. Until his death, Church denied that he was a spy; but no evidence has ever surfaced to prove his innocence.

However, further details confirming Church's espionage did emerge more than a century later among General Gage's archives, which were given to the University of Michigan's Clements Library. In a May 1775 letter to Gage found among the papers, the anonymous author provides a wealth of military information about colonial fortifications in Massachusetts.[7] The writer then adds a marginal comment about his mission as an envoy to the Continental Congress in Philadelphia, which pinpoints Church, the only one given the task. Church's financial motivation was also highlighted in one of his reports to Gage: "The 25th of this month finishes a quarter"—a gentle reminder that his British masters owed him his thirty pieces of silver.[8]

Although the full extent of the secrets Church passed to the British remains unknown, his damage to the revolutionary cause was minimal because he was neutralized early in his spy career. The National Counterintelligence Center, in its multivolume *Counterintelligence Reader,* argues convincingly that Gage failed to exploit Church's potential as a spy.[9] Gage, a military commander, was primarily interested in tactical information that would enable him to win battles against the rebels. Church, however, offered far more intelligence value. Through his access to the Continental Congress, he was privy to the highest-level policy deliberations not only in Massachusetts but in all the colonies. As a member of the Sons of Liberty and participant in meetings of the Mechanics, Church also had access to the colony's intelligence and counterespionage activities and could have betrayed a number of patriot spies to the British.

In October 1775 Washington convened a war council to decide Church's fate. The council determined that Church was guilty but could not sentence him for spying because the Continental Congress had passed no law against espionage. At most, under the military "Articles of War," Church would receive thirty-nine lashes, a fine of two months' pay, and dismissal from the army for criminal correspondence with the enemy.[10] The revolutionaries moved quickly to correct the oversight and appointed a committee, which included John Adams and Thomas Jefferson, to recommend espionage legislation. The Continental Congress accepted their recommendation and enacted America's first espionage law in November 1775, which mandated the death sentence for spying. Fortunately for Church, the law was passed after his conviction and he escaped the gallows.

Others did not. In June 1776, about seven months after the law was passed, Sergeant Thomas Hickey, a member of Washington's own guard, was found guilty of plotting a Tory uprising in New York and was hung. Washington himself ordered the hanging four days after the court-martial and made a public spectacle of the ghastly execution as a warning to other soldiers with sedition on their minds. Another Tory spy, Edmund Palmer, was caught by the troops of General Israel Putnam in August 1777. The British governor of New York appealed for clemency but was rebuffed. Putnam's response underscored colonial resolve in implementing the new espionage law: "Sir, Palmer, a lieutenant in your King's service, was taken in my camp as a spy. He was tried as a spy. He was condemned as a spy and, you may rest assured, sir, he shall be hanged as a spy."[11]

Although Church escaped the same fate, the Continental Congress did imprison him. He narrowly escaped a lynch mob that besieged the prison, and his home was ransacked by an angry mob. Finally, in 1780 Church was released to be exiled to the West Indies, but he never reached his new home. His ship was presumably lost at sea. His wife returned to Great Britain, where she was provided with a pension by King George III, "tacit admission of the services rendered the Crown by her late husband."[12]

The Benjamin Church affair has all the earmarks of espionage cases that would plague US national security for the next two centuries: spying for money, unfettered access to valuable national security information, the spy's rationalization of espionage when caught, compromise by shoddy tradecraft, the failure to recognize indicators of espionage, and, finally, the impact of an individual spy case on the development of espionage legislation.

Just as Church's Revolutionary War colleagues ignored the signs of his espionage, their counterparts during the next two centuries would continue to ignore the possibility that their trusted civil and military servants would betray the nation's secrets. For years in the mid-1980s, the CIA would suffer a string of serious operational compromises as it lost valuable agents in the Soviet Union. The organization refused to believe that one of its own, the elite of American intelligence and front line of defense in the Cold War, would commit espionage for the Soviet Union until the head of the Soviet counterintelligence branch, Aldrich Ames, was unmasked as a KGB spy. Less than a decade later, the Federal Bureau of Investigation would suffer the same fate when one of its own, Special Agent Robert Hanssen, turned out to be a longtime Soviet mole. Just as revolutionary-era Americans ignored the signs of Church's espionage, his association with known Tories, and his unexplained wealth, their twentieth-century counterparts would fail to see similar indicators.

Unlike many of the major spies against America, however, Church was discovered before his espionage could hinder the patriots' quest for liberty. Another spy against America was far more fortunate, because his espionage only came to light sixty-eight years after his death.

THE UNDETECTED SPY

EDWARD BANCROFT

It is impossible . . . to prevent Being watch'd by Spies.

BENJAMIN FRANKLIN
Charlevois, "Nothing to Hide."

The Revolutionary War was fought against the backdrop of eighteenth-century European rivalries, particularly the bitter conflict between France and Great Britain. France had lost Canada to Great Britain in the Seven Years' War and was eager to exploit British conflicts with the colonies to counter the defeat. At the same time, France could not risk another war with Great Britain by openly supporting the American cause. Covert support, however, offered an attractive alternative.

The American colonies sorely needed arms and supplies to fight the King's Army, and the Continental Congress had established a Committee on Secret Correspondence to seek military assistance and win political support for the colonies among Great Britain's adversaries in Europe. In December 1775 the French foreign minister dispatched a merchant, Julien de Bonvouloir, to approach Benjamin Franklin about a secret channel between the Continental Congress and France. Bonvouloir and Franklin agreed that, in exchange for American commodities, France would open its ports to American ships and covertly provide arms and military supplies through a front company.[1]

The Continental Congress sent Silas Deane, a Connecticut delegate, to Paris as liaison for the covert effort. Deane had never traveled abroad, spoke no French, and was out of his depth amid the foreign intrigues of Paris. To assist him, Franklin highly recommended Dr. Edward Bancroft, an American-born resident of London who the venerable patriot had befriended and mentored during his years as the colonies' representative in Britain. Deane, coincidentally, had been Bancroft's tutor at a Connecticut high school and agreed with Franklin's suggestion. He sent a letter to Bancroft in London and enlisted the young doctor to assist him in his efforts with the French. Bancroft was also enlisted soon after by British intelligence to spy against America.

The Bancroft spy case was marked by the same elements that would characterize future espionage operations against America. Like other spies to follow, Bancroft professed that he was motivated by purely ideological motives although he was paid handsomely for his information. In a surprisingly revealing letter written on September 17, 1784, he asked the British foreign secretary for payment of compensation due him for his espionage and detailed his motivations and spying activities for Great Britain. He claimed that he had agreed to cooperate primarily to thwart a Franco-American alliance and achieve reconciliation between the Crown and the colonies.[2] Although he emphasized in the letter that he initially sought no compensation, he readily accepted the Crown's offer of payment. His self-professed ideological motivation was far overshadowed by his subsequent complaints about delayed salary payments in other correspondence. At the time of his recruitment by the British, he was experiencing serious financial difficulties as a result of an unsuccessful business enterprise to sell dyes made from South American tree bark.[3] He was also a notorious gambler and speculator on the London stock market, an issue that would have a considerable impact on his spy career.

Bancroft's clandestine relationship remained undetected until 1889, when documents detailing his espionage, including the September 1784 letter, were found among papers opened by the British National Archives. Like Benjamin Church and other American spies, Bancroft's occasionally suspicious activities were largely ignored by his colleagues. He also communicated with his British handlers using clandestine tradecraft methods that other intelligence services have also used throughout history to collect secrets from American spies. Most curiously, he escaped detection as a spy in his lifetime but he may have been a pawn in a grand American deception of the British by Benjamin Franklin—the answer still remains a mystery today.[4]

Bancroft was born in Westfield, Massachusetts, in 1745 and moved to Connecticut after his father's death. Like Benjamin Church, Bancroft was a physician. He worked as a plantation doctor in Dutch Guiana, where he became an expert on the flora and fauna of the region and subsequently wrote an extensive study of its people and its plant and animal life.[5] He then returned to London to continue his study of medicine and wrote a political treatise on British relations with the colonies. His work brought him to the attention of Franklin, who sponsored him for membership in the Royal Society. Bancroft later returned to South America to assist in improving crop production at plantations in Suriname owned by Paul Wentworth, a New Hampshire native from a wealthy family who had resettled in Britain. This relationship proved to be a turning point in Bancroft's life.

Wentworth contacted his old friend Bancroft after British intelligence intercepted Deane's letter of invitation to the young doctor. A staunch loyalist, Wentworth ran a British spy network targeted against Americans in France, and Bancroft's new position with Deane could provide a unique opportunity to uncover Franco-American machinations against the Crown. In August 1776 Bancroft met with Wentworth and agreed to spy on America. He eventually signed a contract with the British, which paid him a handsome £500 bonus (roughly $80,000 to $100,000 by today's standards), a £500 annual salary, and a lifetime £200 annual pension.[6]

Bancroft shuttled back and forth between London and Paris to meet his American colleagues and British spymasters. On the one hand, he passed Deane tidbits of political information that, though accurate, did little damage to the British cause but enhanced his credibility with his American counterparts. On the other hand, Bancroft provided the Crown with significant inside information about French covert aid to the colonies. Deane not only shared details about French aid with Bancroft but also enlisted him on occasion to interpret for meetings with his French interlocutors and translate French documents.[7]

As the war progressed, the Continental Congress grew increasingly eager to sign a treaty with France and sent Franklin himself to Paris to head the American mission accompanied by Arthur Lee, an irascible Virginian who was both a physician and lawyer. Franklin, far more versed in the intricacies of European politics than his colonial counterparts, proved a shrewd master at manipulating the French relationship to America's advantage (because of his activities in France, Franklin was acknowledged by the Central Intelligence Agency in 1997 as the father of American "covert action").[8] To stir up French public opinion against Britain, Franklin released forged documents that supposedly proved the British were paying Native Americans for the scalps of Americans murdered in the colonies. In 1778, the British initiated peace overtures to Franklin. His insistence on complete independence scuttled any hope of reconciliation, but he told the French about the overtures and hinted that negotiations to end the war were imminent. If Britain concluded a peace agreement with the colonies, prospects for increased French trade with America would diminish and the British could also turn their guns against France. Franklin hoped his disinformation would persuade France to ally with the colonies as quickly as possible. The ruse worked.

After his arrival in Paris, Franklin increased Bancroft's involvement with the American commission. Because of these new duties, Bancroft became a treasure trove of intelligence for the British. He was privy to the correspondence of Franklin's commission with the Continental Congress and the French. He provided the British not only with information about progress on colonial alliances with France and Spain but also with insider knowledge of Franklin's strategies to move France toward a treaty. He gave the British the identities of colonial spies and the names, cargoes, and travel dates of ships transporting aid from France to the colonies. He also passed copies of several documents, including a draft of the proposed Franco-American treaty. When the final version of the treaty was signed in February 1778, King George III had a copy on his desk two days later, thanks to Bancroft.[9]

Bancroft was such a valuable spy that the British used the full panoply of clandestine tradecraft methods to ensure the security of the operation. French counterspies and foreign agents swarmed around Paris, so the British could only risk direct contact with Bancroft on rare occasions. If French surveillance had spotted Bancroft in touch with anyone even remotely associated with British authorities, the French would have advised Franklin and possibly compromised the Crown's best source in France. In addition to clandestine meetings with Wentworth in France, the British resorted to impersonal communications to contact Bancroft, using techniques designed to enable communications between spy and handler without risky face-to-face meetings. These same methods were used by their successors in British MI-6 and the CIA during the Cold War to evade KGB scrutiny in Moscow, and the KGB in turn used them to communicate with their most productive spies in the US government.

Bancroft wrote his messages to British intelligence using both ciphers and secret ink. The encoded messages were written with the secret ink between the lines of "cover letters," real text on innocuous subjects that would arouse no attention if scrutinized by censors or counterespionage investigators. Bancroft addressed the letters to an alias provided by the British, signed them as "Mr. Edwards," and wrote boring texts on, ironically, the topic of gallantry.

To transmit his messages Bancroft was instructed to use a "dead drop," a preselected site known to spy and handler in an obscure location that would attract no attention from a casual observer. Bancroft went every Tuesday night under cover of darkness to a popular Paris park, the Tuileries Garden, where he stuffed his messages into a bottle and inserted them into the deep hollow of a tree. A British intelligence officer later came to the same site and retrieved the bottle by tugging on a piece of twine tied to it. The British officer left any communications in the same bottle for retrieval by Bancroft later the same night. This simple technique, still in use more than two centuries later by intelligence services, apparently worked. There is no indication that Bancroft's communications with the British were ever discovered.[10]

Despite these measures, Bancroft was still nervous about detection, so the British took other steps to protect him. He was sent by Franklin and Deane on occasional trips to London to ferret out information, which also provided him the opportunity for face-to-face meetings with his British spymasters. To allay any suspicions about his activities in enemy territory, he continually complained to Franklin and Deane about the risks of going to London. His British handlers also devised a clever scheme to "arrest" him during one of his trips to Britain, allegedly for aiding the colonies. His quick release raised no eyebrows among the

Americans, and Franklin and Deane instead apologized to him for his "harrowing experience."[11]

In spite of all these British measures to protect Bancroft, he was still at risk. Although spies are most vulnerable in communications with their handlers, they are also jeopardized when the governments for which they spy act on their information. In Bancroft's case, the details he provided on the movements of ships with arms and supplies bound for the colonies provided the British ambassador in Paris with accurate data to protest French violations of neutrality. Although several spies operating at ports in France could have supplied the information, the French government suspected a higher-level leak and alerted the Americans that their information was turning up in London. Franklin, however, ignored this warning.

One American, however, did suspect Bancroft. Arthur Lee, the curmudgeonly third member of the Paris legation along with Franklin and Deane, claimed that he had irrefutable evidence that Bancroft had met with British officials when in London. Lee even confronted Bancroft with the accusation, almost provoking a duel.[12] Lee, however, was considered cantankerous and malicious, especially by Franklin. Lee's information was also poorly sourced, and Bancroft, enraged by the accusation, was easily able to disprove the story. Lee's allegation was thus dismissed as the grumblings of a misanthrope. Any suspicion of Bancroft was further dispelled when, ironically, Lee's own secretary was exposed as a British agent. In response to French protests over the case, Lee was eventually recalled to America and Bancroft continued to spy without raising any further suspicion.

Bancroft's espionage went undiscovered for years, and his reports to the British were "more numerous, more detailed and more accurate than those of any other agent."[13] Despite this, Bancroft's spying had little impact, partly because the top British policymaker, King George III himself, was skeptical about the intelligence from his prize agent and refused to act on it. Ironically, Bancroft was held in higher regard by the Americans he betrayed than by the British monarch for whom he spied.

King George was aware that Bancroft was gambling heavily on the London stock market and was concerned that his spy may have been fabricating or, at the very least, embellishing intelligence to line his pockets. Bancroft, in fact, was an active speculator on the market and had even shared the information about the Franco-American treaty with his business partner so they could sell off stocks before the anticipated plunge in the market. Bancroft, however, was not alone in this "insider trading," which was common practice among leading patriots. Revolutionary leaders received little or no remuneration and required income to support their families, and ethical restrictions on such practices were years away. As commonplace as the practice may have been, King George was bitterly opposed to it and thus was naturally disinclined to believe a stock-manipulating spy. In a letter to his prime minister, Lord North, the king claimed "no faith can be placed in his [Bancroft's] intelligence" because the spy was trying to convince the British that the French were close to joining the war on the side of the colonies.[14]

King George's skepticism about Bancroft's reporting resulted as much from ego as from his moral qualms about stock market speculation. The monarch, as one observer wryly noted, was "averse to accepting any information that he deemed unpleasant."[15] He believed intelligence reports that touted British successes but distrusted those that reflected unfavorably on the Crown's efforts or prospects. The king especially refused to believe that the French would challenge him by signing a treaty with his own colonies, so he dismissed Bancroft's information as the drivel of a shady stock speculator. And the king was not the only ruler who disregarded intelligence that did not fit the preconceived notions of an overweening ego. Almost two centuries later, a Soviet spy in Japan, Richard Sorge, would receive solid information about a planned Nazi surprise attack against the Soviet Union. Joseph Stalin, who had signed a nonaggression pact with Hitler two years before, refused to believe the Nazi ruler would have the audacity to violate the treaty. He was wrong.

King George III was not the only skeptic about Bancroft's information. British government officials were also suspicious about his reporting on France's objectives in considering an alliance with the colonies. Bancroft had reported that France was only interested in increased trade with America and not in recapturing its lost territories in the New World. Even his friend and spy handler, Paul Wentworth, doubted the French would enter an alliance merely for better commercial relations.[16] Despite these British doubts, there is no evidence that Bancroft fabricated this or any other intelligence, and letters discovered a century later show that the information he provided to the Crown accurately reflected America's collaboration with the French.

Despite his accurate reporting, Bancroft ultimately did little damage to the revolutionary cause. Aside from British skepticism about his reporting, the Crown was in many respects powerless to act on the information. Even though the British received detailed information from Bancroft about ships carrying war matériel to America, the seizure or destruction of vessels sailing under the French flag or with French seamen could have sparked a military conflict, and the British were too overstretched to fight battles both in the colonies and in Europe. Also, even though the British were fully informed about Franklin's progress toward an alliance with France, there was little they could do to stop it. When the British lost the last battle of the war at Yorktown in 1781, almost half the force that defeated them consisted of French troops.[17]

Franklin was undoubtedly aware of the Crown's dilemma about a Franco-American alliance. At the same time, he appeared blissfully unaware of Bancroft's suspicious behavior. Bancroft's frequent travel to London, his quick release after his alleged arrest, his leaks of information about ship movements, and Lee's purported evidence about his meetings with British officials were all alarm bells that Franklin ignored. Franklin's failure to recognize a spy in his midst has been blamed for "one of the most egregious penetrations in the history of espionage."[18] Franklin has also been accused of practicing shoddy security himself, leaving his most sensitive papers lying around for all to see. Franklin, already in his seventies while in Paris, had perhaps grown senile and had been bamboozled by the young British spy: "Of all the dupes of history, surely none can best his record in the Bancroft case."[19]

Was Franklin so easily duped? His shrewd diplomacy with the French makes it difficult to believe that he had grown senile. The British ambassador in Paris, exasperated with Franklin's machinations against the Crown, called him a "veteran of mischief." Moreover, though Franklin disliked the querulous Lee, he would have hardly disregarded evidence of Bancroft's meeting British officials in London.

But there is yet another possibility that puts the Bancroft case in a different light. According to some historians, Franklin was well aware that Bancroft was a spy and used him for his own purposes. Franklin hinted at his views about such informants in his midst in a letter to an acquaintance who had warned him to beware of British spies: "I have long observed one

Rule which prevents any Inconvenience from such Practices. It is simply this, to be concern'd in no affairs that I should blush to have made publick, and to do nothing but what Spies may see & welcome. When a Man's action are just and honourable, the more they are known, the more his Reputation is increas'd and establish'd. If I was sure, therefore, that my Valet de place was a spy, as probably he is, I think I should not discharge him for that, if in other Respects I lik'd him."[20]

Reading between Franklin's cryptic lines, as the hypothesis goes, he knew that Bancroft was a spy and, instead of firing him, used him to deceive the British and manipulate the Crown's policy toward the colonies. The more the British learned about the growing relations between the French and Americans, the more Franklin could foment conflict between the two European nations that might lead to a decreasing number of British forces in the colonies. The more the British knew about French arms deliveries, the more they would realize that the Americans could not be defeated and the more likely they might be to grant independence without further bloodshed. This theory certainly fits Franklin's penchant for subterfuge, as evidenced in the intentional leaks, forgeries, and fabrications he orchestrated to hamper British efforts against the colonies.

Considering the importance of French support, Franklin may well have decided that it was more valuable to exploit Bancroft than to expose him. As one proponent of this theory put it, "In fact, had Edward Bancroft not existed, Franklin might have had to invent him."[21] We may never know the truth, but if this hypothesis is accurate, Franklin may have been one of the greatest masters of deception of his time.

Edward Bancroft and Benjamin Church were two civil servants with significant access who betrayed their country by spying for the enemy. The colonial military was also not immune to espionage, and one of its proudest members would embark on a spying career that made his name forever synonymous with treason.

THE TREASONOUS SPY

BENEDICT ARNOLD

Let his name sink as low in infamy as it was once high in our esteem. On this stage all good men will unite in execrating his memory. . . . Even villains less guilty than himself will not cease to upbraid him and, though they approve the treason, they will despise the traitor.

LIEUTENANT COLONEL ELEAZAR OSWALD, *private secretary to Benedict Arnold, in a letter to Colonel John Lamb, December 11, 1780.*
Quoted by Wallace, *Traitorous Hero.*

After more than two centuries, Benedict Arnold remains the most vilified spy and traitor in American history. He remains the highest-ranking American official, military or civilian, to betray his country. And his treachery went far beyond espionage. Besides passing military secrets, he was on the verge of enabling the British to capture West Point, a key American military base, at a critical juncture in the Revolutionary War. Considering the strategic importance of West Point to colonial defense, his betrayal, in modern terms, would have been equivalent to an American general handing over the Strategic Air Command to the Soviets during the Cold War.

If this was not sufficient cause for Arnold's preeminence among American spies, after his escape and defection to the British, he took up arms against the colonies and attacked his former compatriots in Virginia and in his home state of Connecticut. In September 1781 his troops slaughtered the defenders of Groton and pillaged and reduced the entire town of New London to rubble after crushing its outmatched defenders.

Arnold's treachery seems all the more paradoxical if one considers his battlefield achievements for the American Revolution. Before he betrayed his fellow revolutionaries, he had won some of the most significant victories of the war and, even in defeat, he wreaked havoc that foiled the British strategy to subdue the colonies. He was an accomplished seaman, and he was also unique among military commanders in American history in leading combat in major battles both on land and at sea.

Off the battlefield, however, Arnold was a brooding, hot-tempered egotist with a soul in constant turmoil with itself and with others around him. These conflicting drives simmered below the surface for years until a convergence of unfortunate events—some beyond his control, others of his own making—lit the final spark that exploded into his treason.

The conflicts that would haunt Arnold throughout his life already emerged in childhood. He was born in 1741 to the middle-class family of a sea captain turned merchant in Norwich, Connecticut. Scrappy and solidly built, young Benedict was a natural leader among his boyhood mates and was always ready to fight older boys to defend them. At the same time, these early glimmers of leadership masked a darker side that surfaced in sordid incidents of childhood cruelty, in which he tortured animals and threw broken glass on the dirt streets of Norwich to cut his playmates' feet.[1]

The family moved to New Haven and sent Benedict off to the prestigious Canterbury School. His father, a heavy drinker, began to spend more time in local taverns than at work and went bankrupt. Without money for tuition, Benedict returned to New Haven to become a fourteen-year-old apothecary's apprentice. His withdrawal from the school and his father's bankruptcy were humiliating, the first reversal of fortune in the pendulum swing of successes and failures that would mark the rest of his life.

Arnold found an outlet for these frustrations in the military. At the age of eighteen years, he enlisted to fight in the Seven Years' War but deserted to visit his ailing mother. He joined another unit a year later and served a short hitch before returning to finish his apprenticeship. After the war, his parents died, and he returned to New Haven with his sister Hannah, where he experienced perhaps the calmest period in an otherwise tempestuous life. He prospered after opening his own apothecary shop and married the local sheriff's daughter, Margaret Mansfield, who bore him three sons.

Margaret died suddenly after the pair had been married only five years, and Arnold's sister Hannah immediately filled in as surrogate mother to raise his sons. To overcome his grief, he immersed himself in buying ships and sailing them to trade in the West Indies. He finally gained the respectability and recognition that had eluded him after the Canterbury School humiliation. He had become a successful merchant

A PORTRAIT OF BENEDICT ARNOLD by John Trumbull. Arnold, who eventually rose to major general in the Continental Army, is the most notorious turncoat in American history. *Library of Congress*

and was also elected captain of the local militia in December 1774.

Arnold was swept up in the revolutionary spirit that was spreading through the colonies. Being volatile by nature, he was drawn more to fighting for the cause than pamphleteering. After he learned of the Boston Massacre in March 1770, he wrote a letter to a friend urging immediate retaliation against the British: "Are the Americans all asleep, and tamely yielding up their liberties or are they all turned philosophers, that they do not take immediate vengeance on such miscreants?"[2]

Arnold's reaction was more than mere bravado. After the first shots of the Revolution were fired, he rallied his New Haven militia and led them to Massachusetts, where he convinced the local Committee of Safety that he could seize Fort Ticonderoga, a critical gateway to the north, strategically located on the main route between Canada and the Hudson Valley. He insisted that the capture of the fort would halt a British advance and also entail the capture of cannons that could be used to defend Boston. The committee appointed Arnold a Massachusetts colonel and provided him with written instructions to take Ticonderoga. Ironically, the instructions were signed by Benjamin Church.

Arnold's assault on Fort Ticonderoga would launch a brilliant military career but would also highlight serious character flaws that would plague him for years and eventually lead him down the path to espionage and treason.

Arnold arrived on the outskirts of Ticonderoga only to discover that the Connecticut Assembly had independently dispatched its own force to take the fort. Connecticut's troops, the Green Mountain Boys, were a ragtag bunch of soldiers from Vermont led by Ethan Allen, a swaggering, hard-drinking, irreverent frontiersman. At 6 feet, 4 inches, he towered over the 5-foot, 9-inch, Arnold, but their feisty spirits and hot tempers were evenly matched. The clash between the two commanders was almost as heated as the attack on the fort. Arnold, eager for fame and glory on a mission he had conceived himself, waved his written orders in Allen's face; but the rugged frontiersman cared little for paper authority. Ultimately, Arnold and Allen curbed their stubborn pride and reluctantly compromised on a joint command. Together, they easily captured Fort Ticonderoga.

Arnold and Allen were celebrated as heroes after the victory, but both were then relieved of command because of a political dispute over jurisdiction at the newly conquered fort. Arnold was livid and initially refused to turn over command but was forced out. He emerged from the Fort Ticonderoga battle in the eyes of his military superiors and the Continental Congress as a brilliant military tactician who was also an egotistical, insubordinate troublemaker.

Arnold's confrontational style was exacerbated by financial problems. Like other military commanders of the era, he was compelled to pay and supply his troops from his own pocket because the financially strapped colonial legislatures were slow and tightfisted in dispensing funds. The Massachusetts Congress reimbursed him a meager $195 for his expenses, a sum so miserly that the Continental Congress later voted him an additional $819.[3] Even more galling to Arnold's already wounded pride, the Massachusetts Congress decided to investigate allegations of his shoddy accounting procedures. The investigation continued for years and remained a constant thorn in his side.

Ironically, Arnold could only find peace when he was at war. After he returned home from Fort Ticonderoga, he was stricken with a severe case of gout and struggled to rebuild his flagging business. To escape his problems, he eagerly responded to the call to play a leading role in the Continental Army's plan to invade Canada. The campaign for Canada involved a two-pronged approach, an attack on Montreal led by General Richard Montgomery and another on Quebec led by Arnold. In September 1775 Arnold led 1,100 volunteers on an arduous two-month trek up the Kennebec River in Maine toward Quebec. Bitter cold, heavy snow, and soaking rain cursed the expedition, but Arnold's perseverance prevailed in the end. He drove the haggard troops onward despite tremendous losses of boats, food, and medical supplies. At times the troops only survived with soup made from boiling the leather from their moccasins.[4] By the time Arnold reached Canada, half of his original force had perished.

Montgomery easily captured Montreal and joined Arnold for the assault on the impregnable fortress of Quebec. British forces had concentrated their strength in Quebec and far outnumbered the patriots. Despite Arnold's bravery on the battlefield, the Americans were overwhelmed. Montgomery was killed in the battle, and Arnold's leg was severely wounded. Arnold ultimately had to retreat as the British began to drive the revolutionaries out of Canada. Always setting an example for his troops, Arnold was the last American to leave Canadian soil, with British troops hot on his heels. For his bravery, he was promoted in January 1776 by Congress to brigadier general. Once again, however, his heroic achievements were tarnished as new rumors surfaced about looting by his troops in Montreal.

The British counteroffensive was designed not only to drive the Americans out of Canada but also to continue moving south to break the back of colonial resistance in New England. The British general, William Howe, would move north from New York City to join General Guy Carleton, who would march south from Canada to squeeze the Continental Army in a vise. To accomplish this, the British had to proceed across Lake Champlain to retake Fort Ticonderoga.

Arnold was chosen to counter the British offensive by defending Lake Champlain. He quickly cobbled together a makeshift fleet of galleys and gunboats and anchored them off Valcour Island in the middle of the lake. But his fleet was far outnumbered by British warships, and he lost it—but his delaying tactics cost the British dearly. With winter rapidly approaching, the British were forced to abandon the plan to link their two armies. As one historian noted, "Arnold, by his splendid leadership, had frustrated the

British plan to divide the colonies and may have thereby saved the Revolution."[5] Arnold had gained valuable time for patriot forces to regroup for 1777, the year in which France would join the fight for American independence and the British would be defeated in the Battle of Saratoga, the turning point of the Revolutionary War.

Once again Arnold's military achievement was overshadowed by another career setback. Although Arnold's exploits at Lake Champlain frustrated British plans to divide the colonies, the Continental Congress passed over him and instead promoted five of his colleagues to the rank of major general in February 1777. His overbearing arrogance and rumors of his inaccurate ledgers and plundering in Montreal had scuttled his promotion. However, this latest snub still did not deter him from serving the revolutionary cause. Soon after his return to New Haven, the British launched an attack in Connecticut and Arnold marshaled about five hundred militia to resist a force four times larger that had surrounded the town of Ridgefield. Arnold narrowly escaped death in the battle when a bullet pierced the collar of his coat as he stood on the ramparts leading the outnumbered defenders.

After the Connecticut battle, George Washington protested the congressional slight so adamantly that Arnold finally received his promotion, but with a hitch. Congress still refused to make Arnold's ascension to major general retroactive, and the other five promoted generals, whose exploits paled in comparison with his, remained senior to him. Instead of the retroactive promotion, Congress threw him a bone, which perhaps was more insulting than giving him nothing at all, by awarding him a "fine horse, properly caparisoned."[6]

After he was passed over, Arnold, citing the "ingratitude of his countrymen," submitted his resignation to Washington, who then convinced him to reconsider. Arnold then resigned a second time over continued disputes about his accounting from the Quebec campaign. He pled his case directly with Congress, but his blustering rankled the lawmakers and he was rebuffed. Little by little, each setback, each humiliation was fueling Arnold's resentment against his compatriots. Congressional demands for meticulous bookkeeping seemed especially niggling when commanders were otherwise engaged on the battlefield, and few commanders had been as active as Arnold. He had led an exhausting march through the Maine wilderness, fought a losing battle against overwhelming odds in Quebec, executed a dangerous retreat through enemy territory, and still managed to launch a seaborne counteroffensive that may have saved the Revolution.

Despite these setbacks, Arnold was once again persuaded by Washington to rejoin the fray. The British had revived their strategy to isolate and crush New England in a vise, and they were concentrating their forces in upstate New York against the northern army of General Horatio Gates. Washington sent Arnold to lead troops under Gates's command; but upon his arrival in New York, the temperamental war hero immediately clashed with the general and was restricted to quarters.

Although the impatient Arnold now had no command and no authority, he was not about to sit by idly. The British commander, General John Burgoyne, had built solid entrenchments on Bemis Heights, the hills overlooking Saratoga, and launched an attack from there against Gates's army. Arnold, acting without orders, rounded up a detachment, galloped into the fray against the advancing British troops, and drove them back to Bemis Heights. Burgoyne was forced to keep retreating until he finally surrendered at Saratoga. The resounding rout of Burgoyne's army reinvigorated the patriots after a string of defeats and, more important, convinced the French to enter the war against King George.

During the battle, Arnold's thigh was struck by a musket bullet, the second time his right leg had been wounded in the war. After his latest display of heroism, Arnold's seniority was restored by Congress, but his leg wounds incapacitated him for further combat. In May 1778 Washington appointed him military commander in Philadelphia after British forces had withdrawn from the city.

The assignment of Arnold to Philadelphia was perhaps Washington's worst personnel choice in the war, one for which he would later pay dearly. The post played to none of Arnold's talents and all his flaws. Philadelphia was in postoccupation turmoil when Arnold arrived. Patriots who had suffered under British occupation resented and distrusted not only Tory sympathizers but also the neutrals who had benefited under the king's rule. Tensions also flared between the revolutionaries on the Pennsylvania Council and the Continental Congress, and Arnold's arrival as military commander inflamed jurisdictional disputes even more. The job of military commander in the fractured city required diplomacy, tact, and patience, traits alien to Arnold's pugnacious and volatile nature.

Frustrated by Philadelphia's Byzantine politics, Arnold turned his attention to his ailing finances. By the time he arrived in Philadelphia, he had almost no business revenues, no property except his small New Haven house, and no resolution of his accounting woes. To reverse his fortunes, he began lining his pockets through shady commercial ventures, which enabled him to live a lavish lifestyle in the departed British commander's elegant home. Eager for acceptance into Philadelphia high society, Arnold courted prominent Tories and revolutionaries alike and invited them to elaborate parties at his home. His posh parties, however, prompted rumors among grumbling Philadelphians about the source of his newfound wealth and whispers behind his back about his Tory sympathies.

These rumors reached Joseph Reed, the head of the Pennsylvania Council, who found Arnold's ego insufferable and continually clashed with the new military governor. Reed persuaded the Pennsylvania Council to charge Arnold with eight counts of public malfeasance because of his questionable business dealings. Most of the charges were unsubstantiated and were dismissed when referred to the Continental Congress. Reed, however, insinuated to the Congress that its relations with Pennsylvania would sour unless some action was taken against Arnold. To avoid conflict with a key colony, Congress directed Arnold's superior, George Washington, to court-martial him on some of the charges.

For Arnold this accusation was yet another insult heaped upon a mound of humiliating affronts. Arnold was by no means a reflective man and, sidelined in Philadelphia by his leg wounds, he began to brood about his fate. Reed's accusations came at a critical juncture in Arnold's life. He had led some of the most decisive battles of the war and was at the height of his popularity as a military hero. He had risen meteorically through the ranks from captain to major general in just three years. His personal life, however, was another matter. His business had been neglected, and he was struggling to raise three motherless sons with the help of his sister. He felt cheated by Congress on promotions and finances, and his accountings were still unsettled and stuck in a bureaucratic quagmire. His honor had been impugned, and he had been denied the recognition he craved. He had become "pathologically sensitive to criticism," and his resentment was festering under the surface at these perceived injustices, which, in his black-and-white view of reality, were in no way his fault.[7]

Amid these gloomy reflections, however, there was one ray of sunshine. In the summer of 1778 Arnold met Peggy Shippen, a young socialite half his age. As was typical of Philadelphia society, the Shippen family included both Tories and revolutionaries. During the occupation, Peggy's father, Edward Shippen, often hosted British officers in his home, who were perhaps drawn there more because of his three daughters than their father's political leanings. Peggy was enthralled by the British officers and became friendly with one of them, Major John André, who would play a significant role in Arnold's espionage. Although Peggy considered the colonials to be yokels, she fell in love with their hero, Benedict Arnold, and he became equally enamored. They shared a love for the luxurious trappings of high society, and Peggy represented for Arnold the social status he had craved since childhood.

They married in April 1779. Soon after, Arnold volunteered to the British. Espionage was hatched in courtship, and "before the end of the honeymoon Arnold was ready to give up the cause of America."[8] Although no concrete evidence exists of Peggy Arnold's collaboration, she undoubtedly played a role in her husband's decision to betray the colonies. She admired British ways and had extensive contacts with Tories and British officers. If she was not instrumental in the decision, she would certainly have shared and even encouraged her husband's resentment against the colonies. Years later, after Arnold and his family resettled in England, King George awarded Peggy a pension of £500, perhaps another indication of her role in the plot.[9]

Peggy Arnold became the first of many American wives who would play critical roles in their spouse's espionage. Two centuries later, during the Cold War, Central Intelligence Agency officer Aldrich Ames, also resentful of his superiors' neglect of his talents, married an avaricious woman eager for creature comforts a government salary could not provide. Rosario Ames learned of her husband's spying and assisted him willingly, even badgering him at times for his sloppy tradecraft. She was arrested and convicted with her husband, but she received a light sentence of five years' imprisonment in exchange for his cooperation.

Also during the Cold War, US Navy warrant officer John Walker had a different experience. Walker, one of the most damaging spies in American history, passed the Soviets cryptographic information that could have turned the tide against the United States in the event of war with the USSR. But after years of abuse by Walker, his wife, Mary, finally informed the Federal Bureau of Investigation about his espionage, sparking an investigation that led to the arrest of her husband and his other accomplices.

Arnold's wife may have cured him of any lingering doubts about his impending decision to betray his country, but they were certainly dispelled when Washington postponed his court-martial. The postponement was the last straw for Arnold, who was longing to vindicate himself. Moreover, in spite of his many setbacks, he had always answered Washington's call to return to service. If Arnold had even a drop of loyalty left for anyone in the colonies, it was to Washington. Now Arnold was convinced that even Washington had turned on him. In response to the decision, Arnold wrote Washington an almost hysterical letter begging for the trial and, if need be, execution. Arnold's comments showed that he was fraying at the edges:

> If your Excellency thinks me criminal for heaven's sake let me be immediately tried and, if found guilty, executed. I want no favour; I ask only Justice. . . . Let me beg of you, Sir, to consider that a set of artful, principled men in office may misrepresent the most innocent actions and, by raising the public clamor against your Excellency, place you in the same situation I am in. Having made every sacrifice of fortune and blood, and become a cripple in the service of my country, I little expected to meet the ungrateful returns I have received from my countrymen; but as Congress have stamped ingratitude as a current coin, I must take it. . . . I have nothing left but the reputation I have gained in the army. Delay in the present case is worse than death.[10]

That same month, Arnold made his first approach to the British. Arnold was a "write-in," that is, a variation of a "walk-in," a term in modern intelligence jargon for a volunteer offering secret information. Volunteers often approach official representatives or facilities of the enemy to offer these services, but in Arnold's case the risk of detection was too high for an officer with his profile to contact a British official directly. Philadelphia, however, was rife with Tories who could convey a message on his behalf, and Arnold chose as his intermediary Joseph Stansbury, a crockery merchant known to be a British sympathizer. Peggy Arnold knew Stansbury well and may have suggested him to her husband as an avenue to reach her friend, John André, who was head of British intelligence for the colonies. In a letter discovered years later, Stansbury confirmed his role as the go-between: "Arnold . . . communicated to me, under a solemn obligation of secrecy, his intention of opening his services to the commander in chief of the British forces."[11]

Arnold's motives in volunteering to the British were a muddy brew of greed and revenge for a litany of real and perceived slights. Many of Arnold's complaints were justifiable and not of his making, but he often exacerbated his problems because of his arrogance and stubbornness. But because Arnold's judgment was clouded by his monumental ego, he was convinced that everyone else was responsible for his woes.

Arnold was the first of many American traitors who rationalized their crime by claiming that they spied for nobler political motives. Many spies would follow him who argued that they did not spy against America but for some cause that ultimately served the nation's interest. In Arnold's opinion, the Continental Congress, the army, and even his close friend George Washington had all proven that they were unworthy of leading the colonies in independence. Because of their inability to govern, Arnold decided that the colonies must remain in the British Empire and "contended that he could best serve the country by betraying it."[12] Arnold, a Protestant, also despised the colonists' alliance with heavily Catholic France (ironically, his exploits at Saratoga contributed to the victory that convinced the French to openly side with the colonies).

Although Arnold rationalized his treason with a patina of ideological motives, there is no evidence that he ever voiced any pro-British sympathies before his espionage. As Carl Van Doren notes, "In spite of Arnold's later claim that he had been opposed to independence and the French alliance, he seems never to have put a syllable of dissatisfaction on record anywhere before May 1779. Whatever political motives he then had, he gave no sign of being actuated by any but personal ones."[13]

In his first letter to the British, Arnold hinted at his supposed ideological motives. For security reasons, he signed the letter with an alias, "Monk," which referred to General George Monk, who rebelled against the Cromwellian Parliament to help restore Charles II to the throne. Monk was thus a traitor who, from the Crown's perspective, was really a patriot. The British undoubtedly appreciated the reference and welcomed the overture. They also did not miss an additional hint in the analogy. Monk had received a dukedom in return for his loyalty to the Crown, and Arnold clearly expected similar compensation.

The timing of Arnold's approach to the British squared perfectly with the British war strategy. Major John André, who had befriended Peggy during his frequent visits to the Shippen house, became intelligence chief to British commander in chief, Sir Henry Clinton, in May 1779. One of André's primary tasks was to identify disaffected high-ranking American officers who might be induced to spy for the Crown or defect for propaganda purposes. Arnold should have been a prime target. Any professional intelligence officer would have spotted the potential and pursued this promising catch. As one historian noted, "The dossier would record: a middle-class background, vigorous entrepreneur, prewar captain of a superior company of militia, early in the war the brains of the seizure of Ticonderoga, energetic admiral who swept Lake Champlain. . . . Undoubtedly, however, Arnold's dossier would also record his present ill repute with Congress, . . . acute financial embarrassment, and the probable Tory leanings of his young bride Peggy."[14]

Even though Arnold may have been a prize catch, his offer to the British generated a flurry of correspondence for sixteen months as both sides negotiated the terms of his treachery. Impersonal communications such as Andre's correspondence with Arnold are difficult enough for the passage of secret information and infinitely more cumbersome for protracted negotiations. Initially, the British asked Arnold to spy in place until they could gain some significant advantage from his defection. Arnold agreed but, ever the haggling merchant, demanded a lump sum payment of £10,000 and indemnification for losses if he were to be caught.[15]

The British proved to be equally hard bargainers. They reminded Arnold that he had resigned his command in Philadelphia and that his access to secrets was also presumably limited because of his tarnished reputation. The British would pay him £10,000 but only for concrete information in response to specific questions that they had provided to him and for guarantees that he could accomplish their objectives.

The communications were also frustrated by a series of blunders. André had practiced solid tradecraft by providing the potential spy with a cipher code and secret inks for correspondence and, for further security, insisted that the topics of the correspondence must concern business transactions. Although the communications were secure, old responses crossed with new ones, doubletalk even in the enciphered text was misunderstood, and some letters were simply lost. Once the wrong codebook was used, and another time the message was indecipherable because the secret ink ran. Other times Arnold just pouted over British intransigence and delayed in responding.

Today's intelligence officer, even in this age of rapid communications, would sympathize with André's plight. Spy handlers must exercise some degree of control to keep an agent productive and responsive to tasks. Managing a relationship with a spy demands a mixture of tact and firmness, an ability to gauge nuances and continually assess the spy's moods, to praise when he is productive and to prod when he is not. High-ranking spies of Benedict Arnold's stature present even more challenges. They may have the best access to secrets but are also far less pliant to an intelligence officer's control. They are accustomed to barking orders, not taking them. They know what is best and are used to their subordinates acknowledging their seniority; they make demands commensurate with their rank, even if unwarranted, and they expect these demands to be met. Arnold not only exhibited all these traits but also was inherently a difficult and combative character with whom to cope in any relationship. Conducting a clandestine relationship with him face-to-face, let alone through the eighteenth-century postal system, was a far more daunting task.

André initially manipulated this long-distance relationship with skill. Even though negotiations reached an impasse over payment, Arnold still provided the British in his letters with secret information in response to their questions, even though he had not received a pence in return. Although the information was of some value and was probably the best the British could receive without face-to-face meetings, André gently coaxed Arnold to obtain better intelligence when he urged his spy in one letter to "permit me to prescribe a little exertion."[16]

The British ultimately decided on a specific task, which André included in a letter to Arnold: "Join the army, accept a command, be surprised, be cut off—these things may happen in the course of manoeuvre, [so you will not] be censured or suspected. A complete service of this nature involving a corps of five or six thousand men would be rewarded with twice as many thousand guineas."[17]

Arnold and the British finally agreed that he should seek the command of West Point, a key fortress for colonial defense against the Crown's plan to isolate New England. Arnold, however, still insisted on increased sums of money and indemnification that would be paid to him in the event of his capture. However, plagued by mounting debt, he finally relented and acquiesced to the British offer of £20,000 in exchange for West Point and its three thousand troops but without any indemnification if the plot failed. It was the first, and hopefully last, time in American history that anyone had agreed to sell an entire military base to the enemy.

Meanwhile, the court-martial convened and determined that Washington should reprimand Arnold on one charge. Washington reluctantly issued a mild reprimand, which he did not even deliver to Arnold but instead buried in the day's general orders, hoping to mollify his boldest commander and lure him back to the fight. Washington offered Arnold the command of a wing of the northern army and was surprised when Arnold, normally unhappy as a chairborne ranger, rejected the combat assignment because he had not recovered from his leg wounds. Instead, Washington reluctantly granted Arnold's request for the less arduous command of West Point.

West Point was of vital strategic importance. The British could control the entire Hudson River Valley by seizing West Point, a pivotal goal in their strategy to divide the colonies. If the British controlled West Point, the Continental Army would need to retake the fortress, a struggle that would delay its planned campaign in Virginia. The loss of West Point, combined with the defection of the legendary military commander Arnold, would also be a crushing blow to the colonies' morale and might also force the French to reconsider their covert support for the American cause.

André wisely decided that the delivery of West Point could never be executed through their current communications by mail and urged a personal meeting with Arnold to work out the complicated details of the conspiracy. The meeting would also enable André to debrief Arnold more fully on intelligence questions of interest to the British. At the same time, a meeting between two high-profile combatants was a hazardous enterprise and required the best tradecraft possible to escape detection.

Although Arnold had little experience in intelligence, he tried to exert control by requesting that the venue be on colonial territory and that André be disguised as a civilian. General Clinton categorically rejected the demand as too risky. If André was captured behind enemy lines as a civilian, he would be executed as a spy instead of treated as a prisoner of war. Clinton thus insisted that André had to wear his uniform, meet on neutral ground, and not carry any incriminating documents from Arnold.

To obey his commander's orders, André developed an alternate plan for the dangerous meeting that would provide him with some protection.

Arnold would meet under a flag of truce with Colonel Beverly Robinson, a local British commander, ostensibly to discuss the disposition of Tory property in the area. Robinson would be ferried to Arnold on a British gunboat and accompanied by André. On the American side, Arnold arranged for a safe conduct pass for "John Anderson," André's alias, and, as an extra layer of security, he wrote to Washington's intelligence chief, Benjamin Tallmadge, to request that "John Anderson" be brought safely under escort to him at West Point in the event that André needed to cross American lines.

André restricted knowledge of the operation to a handful of colleagues, a wise security move that unfortunately backfired during his first attempt to meet Arnold. The meeting was aborted when a British patrol boat, the *Vulture,* unaware of the arrangements, fired on Arnold's barge as it rowed out to meet the party. The conspirators tried again on the night of September 21, 1780. In uniform, André sailed with Robinson on the *Vulture* and was dropped off downriver from West Point. A Tory associate of Arnold, Joshua Smith, who was not told about André's identity, picked André up and took him to the general. Arnold and André plotted throughout the moonlit night in a wooded grove until about 4 a.m. Arnold provided André with documents and sketches of West Point and discussed plans for the fort's surrender and his compensation. Dawn broke as Arnold took André to a farmhouse to await his rowboat for return to the *Vulture.*

Suddenly, they heard the boom of artillery in the distance. The Americans monitoring the *Vulture's* movement began shelling the British warship, which hastily retreated. Arnold left André, now stranded, in the hands of the unwitting Smith to make their way back to British lines by land. He gave André the safe conduct pass in the alias "Anderson" and convinced him to disguise himself as a civilian and carry the documents back. There were six documents in all, five of them written in Arnold's hand. André stuffed the documents in his boot, took off his uniform, and threw on a beaver hat and burgundy coat.

At this point André committed cardinal tradecraft blunders by acceding to his agent's requests instead of exercising control over the operation. By donning civilian clothes and carrying incriminating documents through enemy lines, André was not only disobeying Clinton's orders but was also exposing himself to incredible risk. He had lingered too long in the pre-dawn hours with his spy to return by his original route to safety. After sixteen months of negotiations with Arnold, André presumably wanted as much time as possible now that he was face-to-face with the potentially valuable spy. As Carl Van Doren notes, "André was as eager to buy West Point as Arnold was to sell it."[18]

Arnold rode back to West Point and André hid until the next night, when the intermediary, Joshua Smith, escorted him part of the way back to British lines. They had a tense moment passing one American checkpoint but finally reached an area where colonial patrols no longer operated, roughly fifteen miles from a British outpost near White Plains. Smith left André to make his way through a "genuine no man's land."[19]

This no man's land was not patrolled by British or American troops but was prowled by Tory "cowboys" and colonial "skinners," who were more highway robbers than soldiers. Three bushwhackers came upon André and confronted him. One of them wore a stolen British uniform, so André mistakenly assumed that they were British and admitted that he was an officer of His Majesty's Army. One of the brigands found the documents while searching André and told his companions "this is a spy."[20] They immediately took him to the nearest American outpost. After the entire affair was over, one of them admitted that, if André had shown his safe conduct pass, they would have released him. The three bandits were later given lifetime annuities and medals from Washington for capturing André.[21]

The commander of the outpost, Lieutenant John Jameson, decided to forward the documents to Washington and to send André under guard to Arnold with a letter about the arrest. Tallmadge appeared at the outpost later that evening and learned about the André arrest from Jameson. Tallmadge immediately recognized the alias "Anderson" from Arnold's earlier request. Once Tallmadge heard from Jameson that André had admitted that he was a British officer and had suspicious documents regarding West Point, he knew that Arnold was a spy. He implored Jameson to stop the message to Arnold, but the outpost commander stubbornly refused.

In one of the many bizarre twists that day, Washington was on his way to visit Arnold at West Point just as the traitorous spy received the letter from Jameson at his home. Realizing his plot was foiled, Arnold knew he had to flee immediately. After telling his aides he was going to the fortress to prepare for the visit, Arnold quickly informed Peggy about the disas-

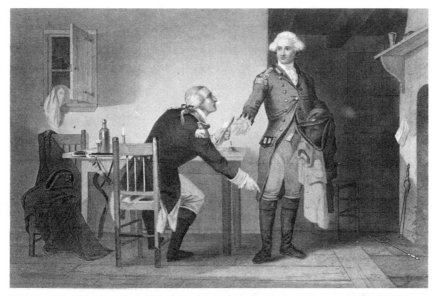

TREASON OF ARNOLD by C. F. Blauvelt. Benedict Arnold (seated) persuades his British handler, Maj. John Andre, to conceal the documents and sketches of West Point in his boot. *Library of Congress*

trous developments and bade her farewell just before Washington arrived. He raced to the river and ordered his bargemen to row him to the *Vulture*. Continuing his treason, Arnold had his bargemen taken prisoners by the British. His hasty escape had worked more smoothly than the unfortunate André's.

Washington was shocked when he learned of Arnold's treachery. He went alone into a room in Arnold's house and sat silently on a couch. "This was," as Thomas Allen notes, "the first time anyone had seen Washington cry."[22] Washington's tears must have changed to a scowl when he received a hypocritical letter from Arnold, who was now safely in British hands: "The heart which is conscious of its own rectitude cannot attempt to palliate a step which the world may censure as wrong. I have ever acted from a principle of love to my country, since the commencement of the present unhappy contest between Great Britain and the colonies. The same principle of love to my country actuates my present conduct, however it may appear inconsistent to the world, who very seldom judge right of any man's actions."[23]

Washington quickly convened a trial for André, who won the sympathy of his captors with his sincerity and professionalism. The suggestion of trading

Arnold and André arose, but the British reluctantly rejected any spy trade, even though they were sealing the fate of their intelligence chief. If the British were to trade Arnold back, they would have little hope of inducing any other American officers to defect. Washington, despite the personal admiration he quickly developed for André, ordered his execution. André, after all, had been caught as a spy, not in uniform, and with American secrets in his possession.

Meanwhile, Arnold was taken to Clinton and showed more concern for his own plight than André's. Clinton, who had already come to loathe Arnold for his haggling over money, felt that he had traded a good major for a vilified general.[24] Because of Arnold's manipulation of André, Clinton held his new defector responsible for his intelligence chief's execution. But Clinton was stuck with the traitor and, to encourage other defections, he had to mollify Arnold, who was awarded his compensation and appointed a brigadier general in the British army.

The American patriots had averted a catastrophe because Arnold's grand plan had been derailed by a series of seemingly trivial mishaps. However, although his information about West Point—the number of troops, ordnance, sketches, and possible attack approaches—never reached the British, Arnold had provided a significant amount of information in his correspondence with them over a sixteen-month period.

Arnold, in his letters, passed André details of French assistance to the colonies, American information about British deployments, and Washington's movements and plans. Just before his fateful meeting with André, Arnold learned that Washington would stay overnight in Peekskill en route to meet the French general Jean-Baptiste-Donatien de Vimeur, comte de Rochambeau, in Hartford. Arnold passed the information to the British in case they wanted to kidnap the American commander in chief. In one ironic twist, Arnold had also told the British about a planned American–French invasion of Canada. He was unaware that the information was a clever deception designed by Washington to divert the British from an offensive to seize New York. In his efforts to impress the British, Arnold had unwittingly helped the very cause he was betraying.

How much did Arnold's espionage damage the revolutionary cause? Ironically, the most vilified spy in American history did very little damage. The intelligence he gave to the British clearly did not turn the tide against the colonies. His information about a French invasion of Canada was part of a deception operation conceived by Washington. Other information about French assistance to the colonies was undoubtedly accurate, but, as illustrated in the Bancroft case, Franklin may have been intentionally feeding similar information to the British.

From the propaganda perspective, Arnold also accomplished little. He envisioned a mass defection of troops after his own, but few Americans switched sides. In fact, his defection may have stiffened the backs of the colonials. News of Arnold's treachery spread like wildfire throughout the colonies. He was condemned in the colonial press and was burned in effigy in several towns, and a mob desecrated his father's tombstone in Connecticut.

Arnold's primary contribution to the British would have been West Point, but British intelligence never even received his documents about the fort, let alone the fort itself. One of the many motives that drove Arnold to espionage, his supreme arrogance, in the end destroyed him. Because of his arrogance, he developed a hasty, amateurish plan to exfiltrate André once his planned return to the *Vulture* went awry. He also requested a safe conduct pass from Washington's intelligence chief, Tallmadge, a move that enabled the patriot spymaster to realize immediately that Arnold was a traitor. Arnold's arrogance along with André's failure as an intelligence officer to control the situation and plan for contingencies ultimately compromised the operation. The most celebrated spy case in American history involved only a single meeting, which was an utter failure.

The Americans were lucky that Arnold's arrogance and a series of mishaps unmasked a major spy before he inflicted significant damage to the revolutionary cause. But should Arnold have been discovered earlier? Were there early warning signs that could have enabled the Americans to thwart Arnold's espionage? The National Counterintelligence Center, in its multivolume history of American counterintelligence, expresses a belief that this is so: "Effective CI [counterintelligence] awareness and countermeasures should have detected Arnold's protracted negotiations and data sharing with the British commander in chief General Henry Clinton."[25]

Tallmadge had received intelligence reports about a very senior traitor inside the Revolutionaries' camp along with vague rumors that a top patriot general had crossed over to the British. Arnold should certainly have been on any list of suspects. He demonstrated the classic indicators of espionage: a need for money, a thirst for recognition, and resentment against his government. However, throughout American history, many public servants have exhibited the same signs but never crossed the line into espionage. Arnold, moreover, was beyond suspicion. He had risked his life in battle and was acknowledged by many as "easily the outstanding battlefield officer of the Revolution."[26] And, although his contemporaries were unaware of the depth of his resentment, he made little effort to conceal his grievances. His indignation at perceived slights was blustery, and his counterattacks were loud and public.

To put Arnold's situation in context, he may have been the most vocal but he was certainly not the only officer who quarreled with the Continental Congress. Other officers were disenchanted with the lack of financial support from Congress, and the inevitable disputes between field commanders and politicians arose not only during the Revolution but also throughout history. Almost two centuries later, other bold military commanders like George Patton and Douglas Macarthur would clash with their political masters, but they would not vent their opposition by committing espionage.

In hindsight, of course, there were glaring signs that should have at the very least singled out Arnold for scrutiny. Arnold's unexplained wealth in Philadelphia should have been one of the obvious signs, even if he was hardly the only officer who enriched himself in a system where Congress barely compensated its military. But his shady business dealings were so egregious that louder alarm bells sounded. One officer, Lieutenant Colonel John Brown, claimed in 1777 that "money is this man's God and to get enough of it he would sacrifice his country."[27] Arnold thought that Brown was incompetent and had refused to promote him years before, so the colonel's persistent attacks were dismissed as pure vindictiveness. Another officer in Philadelphia, Major Allan McLane, directly warned Washington about Arnold's dubious business practices, but the general also ignored him. Even Washington's closest aides at West Point grew increasingly suspicious of Arnold's activities during the final stages of his espionage but assumed he was involved in illicit commerce.

Once he embarked on his path to espionage, Arnold committed other indiscretions that should have alerted the revolutionaries. On one occasion, he tried to pass a letter to the British through the risky method of an intermediary. The courier in this case gave the letter to a Connecticut general who thought it was a simple business letter and filed it away. Arnold also pressed two of his colleagues, General Lafayette and General Howe, for the names of all their agents in New York to assist him in his new post commanding West Point. Fortunately, both refused, but they simply thought him overzealous in doing his job and never reported the obvious probe for secret information.

Lieutenant Jameson, commander of the outpost where André was taken with Arnold's secret documents, refused to believe the worst, even in the face of overwhelming evidence. As in the Church case, he and other revolutionary leaders could not believe that a hero of Arnold's stature, no matter how disgruntled, would become a turncoat. This pattern would continue throughout American history. US government leaders would dismiss evidence of Soviet spy networks in the uppermost levels of the government in the 1930s and 1940s, and the CIA and FBI would turn a blind eye to the possibility of spies in their own organizations during the Cold War.

Arnold ultimately suffered the dismal fate of most unmasked spies. After his defection, he probably did his greatest damage by taking up arms against his former compatriots. He mustered a loyalist regiment that attacked towns in Virginia and later in his native Connecticut, where his troops devastated New London and massacred American defenders in Groton.[28] At the same time, he lived in constant fear because the revolutionaries made numerous plans to kidnap and execute him. In 1781 he left America for the safety of Great Britain and spent the rest of his life shuttling between there and Canada. He received £6,000 for his treachery, half pay for life, and a plot of land, but he had the gall to appeal to the US government for his back pay from the colonial army.[29]

Arnold squandered his spy pension on a series of failed business ventures. Aside from his financial woes, he was also despised by the British, who considered him a double traitor, one who had been disloyal first to the Crown and then to the Americans. Arnold died in Britain, poor, embittered, and scorned by both countries. The Revolutionary War general Nathaniel Greene summed up Arnold's fate in this scathing epitaph: "The love of parade and thirst for gold proved his ruin. How black, how despised, loved by none, and hated by all. Once his country's idol, now her horror."[30]

Benedict Arnold betrayed his solemn military oath in wartime, gave secrets to the enemy, almost sold an entire strategic military base, and took up arms against those he had betrayed. He pales before all the other spies who were to come after him in both the audaciousness of his treachery and the heights of glory from which he fell. As Richard Sale notes in *Traitors,* "the spies who follow him are no more his size than fleas on a bear."[31] And there were many spies to follow.

PART **2**

THE CIVIL WAR

ESPIONAGE AND THE
CIVIL WAR

*There was probably more espionage in one year in any medieval
Italian city than in the four-year War of Secession.*

ALLEN DULLES, *The Craft of Intelligence*

In the decades after the Revolution, the United States still faced threats
from European nations jockeying for territory in the uncharted expanse of
the New World. Americans, however, retreated into a self-imposed isolation, a precedent that would characterize their postwar experience for the
next two centuries. They also dissolved institutions created during wartime
to collect intelligence and catch spies. The capabilities developed in these
key national security arenas eroded, and their leading practitioners went
off to other pursuits. After the Revolutionary War, John Jay's Committee
for Detecting and Defeating Conspiracies was disbanded and Jay went on
to become chief justice of the Supreme Court. Benjamin Tallmadge became
a successful businessman and served sixteen years as a US representative
from Connecticut. Enoch Crosby returned home to work the family farm in
Carmel, New York, and serve as a justice of the peace.

Intelligence collection fared slightly better than counterespionage.
Among his first acts as president, George Washington established the Con-

tingency Fund for the Conduct of Foreign Intercourse, a bland euphemism for monies to support clandestine intelligence activities. A few of his successors made ample use of these secret funds. Thomas Jefferson, for example, authorized the Lewis and Clark expedition to gather intelligence on the western United States, and James K. Polk dipped into this same pot of money to discover Mexico's secret intentions regarding Texas and California.[1]

In spite of these presidential missions, American intelligence collection capabilities were still largely neglected. The nation's intelligence exploits in the War of 1812 were undistinguished; and few generals, with notable exceptions like Andrew Jackson, devoted much effort to developing the capability that Washington had honed during the Revolution. As the intelligence historian Nathan Miller notes, "Virtually no intelligence or espionage activities of any importance were conducted at any level during the war. The United States was so unprepared with respect to war-related intelligence that maps of the Canadian border areas were unavailable, even though the conquest of Canada was a major objective of the conflict."[2] Three decades later, the United States still remained without an established intelligence service in the Mexican-American War, when "no move was made to establish a permanent intelligence capability, . . . either in the fighting or in the peace that followed. [General Zachary] Taylor ignored intelligence almost to the point of dereliction in his invasion of northern Mexico."[3]

The counterespionage front was even more dismal. Foreign espionage against the United States continued after the Revolution as European powers sought to protect their remaining possessions in the Americas or carve out new territory. Before the War of 1812, Great Britain ran an extensive network of spies in North America under the control of the royal governor in Canada. During this conflict, no significant spies in American ranks were uncovered, primarily because no counterespionage service existed to ferret them out. Espionage against the United States was ignored until the first shot of the Civil War was fired at Fort Sumter in 1861.

The Civil War was fought on both sides by average citizens, doctors, lawyers, teachers, clerks, and farmers. The United States only had a small professional army of about 16,000 men when the conflict began, one that was to be split into the Union Army and the Confederate States Army. To wage a major war, both sides had to incorporate state militias, draft thousands of citizens, and quickly train them. The US Army had a small cadre of professional officers, although more than three hundred of them left to lead the Southern military. Some, however, were well past their prime. Winfield Scott, the commanding general of the Union Army, was seventy-four years old at the outbreak of the war, and his age and tremendous girth prevented him from even mounting his horse.

The situation was far bleaker in the intelligence and counterespionage arenas. Without a central organization on either side, commanding officers of individual units ran local networks of spies that paled in comparison with the rings run by George Washington. All these efforts were uncoordinated and, even in individual units, time and energy were wasted on duplication of effort and spies of marginal value. Information was rarely shared among units, and, with few exceptions, little attempt was made to analyze the scattered tidbits of knowledge. Communications were also painfully slow, and actionable intelligence was often useless by the time it reached the battlefield commander.

Neither the Union nor the Confederacy made concerted efforts to recruit well-placed spies inside each other's key government and military institutions. Neither side had sources with the insider access of Benjamin Church, Edward Bancroft, or Benedict Arnold. Most intelligence was gathered from scouts, deserters, and prisoners of war, and often from newspapers, which flagrantly published secret information. General Robert E. Lee reportedly pored over every available Northern newspaper for intelligence, and another Confederate general once kept his troops in position when he learned from a *New York Times* article about Union plans to trick him into moving his army.[4]

As in the Revolutionary War, the common language and heritage shared by the North and the South facilitated intelligence collection but complicated the jobs of spy hunters. Identification of friend or foe was an extraordinary challenge that was even more daunting because of varying loyalties to the cause on both sides. As in the Revolution, support for the war was not unanimous in either the North or the South. The South was initially unified because of its feverish advocacy of slavery, but as the Confederacy began losing battles, some supported peace negotiations while the more headstrong wanted to fight to the bitter end. In the North, President Abraham Lincoln had to cope, on one hand, with abolitionists violently opposed to slavery and, on the other, with those who would not support a war fought solely for this cause.

Even families were divided as brother literally fought against brother. At the top of the Union government, the president's wife, Mary Todd Lincoln, was a Kentuckian with a brother and three half brothers fighting in the Confederate Army. Abraham Lincoln's sister-in-law also smuggled sorely needed quinine behind rebel lines for ailing Confederate troops. Two former secretaries of war in the decade preceding the Civil War left the Union to join the Confederacy.

Given the passions on both sides of the conflict, almost all the major spies of the Civil War were motivated by patriotic devotion to their respective causes and not by the financial motives that would drive Americans to spy in the next century. Besides, both sides faced financial woes throughout the conflict. The North and the South could barely feed their troops, let alone fund espionage networks. One Union spy, Elizabeth Van Lew, financed her own spy network and died penniless as a result. Civil War penny-pinching on espionage was reflected in an anecdote about a Union accountant quibbling with an agent because of "a dispute regarding repaying $28.50 to a federal woman spy . . . for buying men's clothing to use as a disguise."[5]

Counterespionage at first was far more difficult for the Union. Although the North had more manpower, money, and industrial might, the South had distinct advantages in gathering intelligence. When war broke out, the Union capital of Washington was essentially a Southern city, and security was notoriously lax. Southern sympathizers were already working in the War Department, the Union Army, and other Union institutions. The Confederates had at their disposal an established force of "stay-behinds" not only with cover to live and move about Washington but also with direct access to enemy secrets by virtue of their jobs.[6]

Although the Confederates had advantages in gathering intelligence, they proved inept at catching spies. John Winder, the provost marshal of the Southern capital of Richmond, was given responsibilities to combat Union espionage, but he was so overburdened by other duties that he devoted little effort to the job. His own slapdash approach to security rivaled that of his careless Union counterparts. He kept a blackboard in his office so he could retrieve information easily. Among the items chalked on his board was a complete list of the regiments defending the Confederate capital, which were left in plain sight for any visitor to jot down and pass to Union spies. By the time the Confederates established a counterespionage service in 1864, the war was almost over.[7]

The Union created two rival counterspy organizations, one led by Allan Pinkerton, who would later gain fame as head of a prominent American detective agency, and the other by Lafayette Baker, a shadowy and corrupt dilettante in intelligence. Pinkerton and Baker referred to their respective organizations as "the US Secret Service" even though neither one, in fact, was bestowed with government-wide authorities. Pinkerton's unit was not even a government entity but was contracted by General George McClellan to perform intelligence and counterintelligence functions for the Army of the Potomac that he commanded. The unit never had a title except, perhaps, for the innocuous-sounding Headquarters City Guard, Provost Marshal Office, the rubric under which its intelligence reports were conveyed to McClellan.[8] Baker's organization, which he christened the National Detective Police, operated under the War Department and was responsible for countering Confederate subversion, not collecting intelligence.[9] Both services, if they can even be called such, operated independently of the other and, in some comic episodes, even investigated and arrested each other's officers. Still, the Pinkerton and Baker organizations introduced basic investigative and intelligence techniques into counterespionage, a discipline that had been largely ignored since the Revolutionary War. However primitive and flawed they were, these two organizations formed the first institutional counterespionage capability in the United States.

Any study of Civil War espionage is a daunting task. Few records survive, and many of the spies and the field commanders who hired them were understandably reluctant to discuss their activities even after the war. At the same time, some Civil War spies and spy catchers surpassed even their modern counterparts in publicly touting their exploits. Pinkerton and Baker wrote their memoirs, and a legion of spies on both sides of the war published their own stories after the Civil War. Most of these accounts are of little historical value. The memoirs of Pinkerton and Baker are self-serving defenses of their records, and the other tales have been dismissed as melodramatic fiction, more "moonlight and magnolias" than history.[10]

Despite these embellished accounts, enough evidence emerges from Civil War histories to show that espionage, though bumbling and unprofessional, was occasionally marked by flashes of amateur brilliance. If the soldiers who fought the war were primarily average citizens, so were the spies. The amateurs of Union and Confederate espionage demonstrated considerable daring and ingenuity in their quest for secrets. Spies on both sides displayed a natural flare for shaping cover and donning clever disguises that enabled them to penetrate enemy lines, gather information, and evade spy catchers. Newsboys, actors, doctors, wandering peddlers, and the members of any other profession with a natural pretext to move through enemy lines were all deployed to discover enemy secrets. Spies also used race, gender, and even physical handicaps as cover on reconnaissance missions and at times leveraged their enemies' own prejudices to their advantage.

As one example, both North and South cleverly used female spies to exploit male gallantry. When the rebel spy Rose Greenhow was arrested by Pinkerton, her chivalrous captors gave her enough freedom so that she was able to continue conveying secrets to the Confederacy even while in detention. The North also took advantage of Southern prejudices by using slaves both as couriers and intelligence collectors. The second-class status of slaves in the eyes of Southerners ironically put them above suspicion; they were simply considered too uneducated and intellectually inferior to gather secret information.

The spies also made ingenious use of disguise. A Union spy, Emma Edmonds, disguised herself as a young man to join the army and then spied for the North under a dazzling array of guises, posing in turn as a male slave, a female nanny, a white female Irish immigrant, and a Southern gentleman—all effective covers to avoid suspicions and gain access to enemy lines. A Confederate male spy, Benjamin Stringfellow, who was slight in figure and had delicate features, dressed as a woman and learned from his male dance partner at a Northern ball that Ulysses S. Grant would be the new commander of the Union Army.[11]

Physical and mental handicaps also arouse little suspicion and were used by Civil War spies to collect information. A Union spy working for Pinkerton, Dave Graham, feigned stuttering and epileptic fits as he wandered through Confederate lines posing as a peddler.[12] A Confederate spy, John Burke, would often take his glass eye out for disguise purposes.[13]

The Union and Confederacy also used spies from professions that were considered above suspicion. Doctors had natural cover to travel unimpeded through enemy lines at any hour. The Confederates established an elaborate courier system of doctors supposedly on house calls to relay information and overcome the normally tortoise-like communications of the times. Documents were carried in the physician's traditional black bag, an item unlikely to be searched.[14] Stringfellow, in addition to posing as a Union belle, also worked as a dentist's apprentice. He received intelligence from spies who posed as patients, and one victim of a severe toothache informed him about the Union Army's plans to advance against the rebels at Manassas.

The resourcefulness of these amateur spies and the lack of a professional counterespionage capability allowed spies on both sides to operate at will in the early days of the Civil War. The Union, which faced more difficult challenges countering the Confederate espionage threat, was the first to realize that drastic action had to be taken. Its first attempt to do so was primitive in many ways and clownish at times, but ultimately sowed the seeds for an American counterespionage service.

ALLAN PINKERTON
AND UNION
COUNTERINTELLIGENCE

What a strange time it was! Who knew his neighbor? Who was a traitor and who a patriot? The hero of to-day was the suspected of tomorrow. . . . There were traitors in the most secret council-chambers. Generals, senators, and secretaries looked at each other with suspicious eyes. . . . It is a great wonder that the city of Washington was not betrayed, burned, and destroyed a half-dozen times.

MARY ELIZABETH WILSON SHERWOOD,
Epistle to Posterity, "On Spying."

Allan Pinkerton was born in Scotland into the family of a Glasgow corrections officer. After he and his wife emigrated to America, he entered the Chicago Police Department and became its first detective at thirty years of age. He then established his own private detective agency, which was hired by railroad companies to thwart increasing incidents of train robberies. While on assignment for a railroad in 1861, he was tipped off to a secessionist plot to assassinate newly elected President Lincoln while he traveled by train to his inauguration in Washington. Pinkerton's detectives infiltrated the cabal and safely arranged Lincoln's clandestine travel to the inauguration.

Pinkerton had worked for the Illinois Central Railroad and had befriended its president, George McClellan, a former military officer. After war broke out, McClellan returned to service to command the Army of the Ohio and hired Pinkerton to gather intelligence for him. After the Union's crushing defeat at Bull Run in July 1861, Lincoln appointed McClellan commander in chief of the Union Army, and Pinkerton joined him in Washington as his intelligence chief.

Pinkerton was given dual responsibility by McClellan for combating espionage in pro-rebel Washington and obtaining intelligence on the Confederate army. Although Pinkerton only worked for the army and had no government-wide authority, he simply assumed responsibility for both missions throughout the Union. In his memoirs, which he wrote after the war, he dubbed himself "the chief of the United States Secret Service." His office was buried in the army provost marshal's office and its reports were submitted under the letterhead of the Headquarters City Guard, an innocuous cover title to mask its clandestine activities.

A year later, Secretary of War Edwin Stanton would launch a rival service under Lafayette Baker to combat espionage in Washington. Pinkerton and Baker shared one common trait, their mutual proclivity toward romantic fiction. Both spy hunters wrote memoirs after the war to justify their wartime intelligence activities, but the accounts were seriously marred by lack of facts and self-promoting yarns of derring-do. Pinkerton's memory of events could not be challenged by any records because all his files were destroyed in the Chicago fire of 1871.

Pinkerton undoubtedly felt the need to defend his record because he was severely criticized for his failure in intelligence collection. His staff of about eighteen men and women was made up of police officers like Pinkerton who were steeped in criminal investigations but inexperienced in intelligence gathering.[1] Most just fanned out behind enemy lines to scout Confederate troops and elicit information from unsuspecting rebels. By the end of 1861, the first year of the war, only five of Pinkerton's men were actually in enemy territory; the rest of his intelligence collectors were focusing on interrogations of prisoners, whose information was woefully outdated.[2] Pinkerton's unit failed to recruit a single spy in the Confederate government with direct access to information on Southern plans and intentions.

Pinkerton's primary flaw as an intelligence collector was pandering to McClellan by shaping the low-level intelligence he received to conform to the general's preconceived views. McClellan was a notoriously cautious commander, prone to act only when he believed he had overwhelming forces to engage the enemy. At one point, an exasperated President Lincoln sarcastically noted, "If McClellan is not using the army, I would like to borrow it."[3] McClellan's decisions to avoid combat were reinforced by Pinkerton's grossly inflated reports of enemy troop strengths. In one instance Pinkerton "analyzed" his agent's reports to advise McClellan that Robert E. Lee had almost 100,000 troops in his Army of Northern Virginia, more than double the actual number.[4]

In another case McClellan received an unexpected treasure trove of intelligence not from Pinkerton's agents but from a mistakenly discarded Confederate document. In September 1862 Union soldiers discovered three cigars in a field in Frederick, Maryland. Wrapped around the cigars was a sheet of paper that turned out to be "Special Order 191," Robert E. Lee's detailed military plan for an offensive against the North beginning with the capture of a Union garrison at Harper's Ferry.[5] The paper was rushed to McClellan, who advised President Lincoln that Lee's division of his forces to execute the plan was a "gross mistake" that now provided the Union with an exploitable opportunity.[6] McClellan, however, still believed the faulty intelligence overestimating Lee's troop strength. As a result, instead of fully capitalizing on the information in the special order, he dallied as always. This intelligence led McClellan to Sharpsburg, Maryland, where Union forces were able to stop the Confederate offensive into the north at the Battle of Antietam. But McClellan's delay allowed the scattered Confederate forces to recombine during the course of the battle, which prevented what might have been an even more significant Union victory. Lincoln finally grew so frustrated with McClellan's timidity that he replaced him with General Joe Hooker in November 1862. After McClellan left, Pinkerton's "secret service" was disbanded.

Hooker took a historic step to improve Union intelligence by creating a special unit to collect and analyze information from every type of source. In 1863 Colonel George Sharpe of the 120th New York Volunteers was tabbed to lead the new Bureau of Military Information. Sharpe made sure that the bureau received information from a wide variety of sources: scouts, desert-

ALLAN PINKERTON at the Battle of Antietam, 1862. *Library of Congress*

ers, agents, newspapers, and the most innovative collection method of the time, balloonists, a Civil War precursor of today's reconnaissance satellites. Sharpe's staff molded this hodgepodge of information into what is today called all-source intelligence in order to give a comprehensive picture of the plans, intentions, and tactics to the president and his military commanders.[7] The Union commanders began to receive more accurate assessments of enemy troop strength and artillery.[8]

Although Sharpe surpassed Pinkerton's intelligence collection and analysis capabilities, Pinkerton proved far more adept at counterespionage. Given his background as a detective, Pinkerton was the first American counterspy to introduce law enforcement techniques into espionage investigations, and he fully integrated these techniques with analytic and intelligence collection methods. And though Sharpe may have been the first to establish an all-source intelligence capability, Pinkerton was the father of the all-source counterintelligence approach that the US government uses today.

In a city where the most sensitive war secrets were carelessly left out on desks, Pinkerton insisted on operational security and compartmentation. In a long letter to McClellan outlining his counterintelligence philosophy, Pinkerton began by emphasizing that knowledge of his unit must be limited to "as few persons as possible."[9] Pinkerton also refused to divulge the names of his agents and would only provide their initials, a practice that irritated government bookkeepers. Pinkerton himself used the alias "Major E. J. Allen."

Beyond operational security, Pinkerton articulated in his letter to McClellan the vital importance of penetrating enemy spy networks.[10] Just as his staff had infiltrated the secessionist cell plotting Lincoln's assassination, Pinkerton focused on infiltrating rebel spy organizations in Washington. Pinkerton's systematic approach was all-encompassing, attacking the target from a host of various entry points. His operatives would be infiltrated on every level of society and profession to encircle the target, from upper-class socialites to menial laborers. Information from these sources would be supplemented by other investigative techniques, especially surveillance. Pinkerton's service would be the first in the United States to use surveillance as a tool in unmasking a high-level spy.

One of the key points in Pinkerton's letter to McClellan is his intent to use penetration not only to arrest spies and conspirators but also "for the purposes of learning, if possible, the plans of the rebels."[11] As a former counterintelligence expert at the Central Intelligence Agency, Kenneth Daigler notes in his study of Civil War Washington, "This is pure counterintelligence targeting and analysis of an enemy organization, rather than an internal security/law enforcement approach of penetrating an organization and arresting its membership."[12]

Pinkerton's integration of counterintelligence and law enforcement was still unable to halt the rampant espionage in the Union capital, but his operatives rounded up a number of Confederate spy networks in the city. One of his best operatives was Timothy Webster, who, like his boss, was a police officer turned counterspy. Webster's career came to a tragic end, ironically, because of Pinkerton himself.

THE CHAMELEON SPY

TIMOTHY WEBSTER

I die a second death.

TIMOTHY WEBSTER *at his execution.*
Quoted by Markle, *Spies and Spymasters,* 147.

Timothy Webster possessed uncanny abilities to adopt a persona, ingratiate himself in any company, and adapt instinctively to any circumstances—especially in a crisis. All these abilities made him an ideal candidate for the murky and hazardous world of Civil War espionage, and he was, before his untimely death, undoubtedly among the best spies of the war.

Webster was born in England in 1821 and emigrated to the United States with his parents at the age of thirteen years. After serving as a New York City policeman, he worked for Pinkerton's detective agency and followed his boss to serve in his new security service in Washington. On his first mission Webster posed as a fanatic rebel and infiltrated the Baltimore secessionists plotting Lincoln's assassination. After the conspiracy was unmasked with Webster's help, Pinkerton dispatched him to penetrate rebel subversives in Kentucky and Tennessee before summoning him back to Baltimore.[1]

After returning to Baltimore, Webster posed as a wealthy socialite and plied locals with rounds of whiskey to convince them of his Confederate sympathies. He was accepted into the Knights of Liberty, a rebel organization dedicated to subverting the Union. One night, while Webster was regaling patrons in a Baltimore saloon, one of them fingered him for exactly what he was, a Union spy, and accused him in front of the other customers. Webster did not flinch. He seized the offensive with righteous indignation, called his accuser a liar, and goaded him into a fistfight. He was a physically imposing figure, and flattened his accuser with a punch. His accuser scrambled to his feet, knife in hand, ready to strike until Webster whipped out a cocked pistol and held it to the gentleman's head. No one again challenged Webster's Confederate credentials after the fight.[2]

His cover was so well established with rebel subversives that a new Pinkerton agent, tipped off by a source about Webster's Confederate activities, arrested him in Baltimore. Pinkerton's unit was so tightly compartmented that his new operative had no idea of Webster's true identity, and Pinkerton himself had to arrange his "escape," an exploit that once again enhanced the Union spy's standing among the rebels.

Webster's career as a counterspy skyrocketed when he became a Confederate courier between Baltimore and Richmond. Because his reputation was impeccable among rebel sympathizers in Baltimore, he volunteered his services as a spy to Confederate secretary of war Judah Benjamin. Charmed as Webster's other targets were, Benjamin entrusted him with batches of documents to carry to Richmond, including military plans and valuable counterespionage information about Confederate spies in the Union ranks. In return Webster provided marginal feed information about the Union that was supplied by Pinkerton.

On one of his courier trips, Webster contracted rheumatism, which was later to play a key role in his demise. While en route to Richmond, he sought refuge from a rainstorm in an isolated cabin. His muscles ached from trying to sleep on the cold, damp floor of the cabin, and he spotted an oilskin packet on the floor and opened it. The packet contained maps of Union Army deployments, and he arranged to send the material to Pinkerton, which led to the arrest of a Confederate spy working as a clerk in the War Department.

Webster's fourth trip as a courier to Richmond proved to be his last. His rheumatism afflicted him so much that he was bedridden in Richmond for weeks and out of contact with Pinkerton. Worried about his best spy, Pinkerton dispatched two agents, Pryce Lewis and John Scully, to find him. In his concern for his prize agent, Pinkerton committed a major tradecraft error. Lewis and Scully had investigated and conducted searches in the homes of suspected Confederate sympathizers in Washington, and the possibility existed that some of these sympathizers could be visiting or living in Richmond and could identify them as Union agents.

This tradecraft blunder proved fatal. The two agents were indeed identified by one of their earlier targets, a Richmond resident who owned a house in Washington that the pair had searched. Confederate counterespionage agents surveilled Pinkerton's duo, who, disregarding basic security measures, found Webster's room and simply knocked on his door, now linking them directly to the Union's master spy. Scully and Lewis were arrested and sentenced to hang. Faced with death, Scully broke and admitted that Webster was a spy, and in return, he and Lewis served only two years in prison. Webster was immediately arrested and sentenced to the gallows. As testimony to Webster's importance, President Lincoln agreed with Pinkerton's request to appeal to the Confederacy to spare him.

This appeal fell on deaf ears. Minor spies in the Civil War had been routinely exchanged or simply released merely by promising not to resume their spying. Neither side had adequate jail space or food for arrested spies. Webster's case, however, was a different matter. Webster had gained the trust of the Confederate secretary of war, who was now supremely embarrassed by the Union counterspy's trickery. Webster had also carried key documents about Confederate military plans and agents, all of which were now in Union hands. Considering the gravity of Webster's espionage, clemency was out of the question. On April 29, 1862, Webster ascended the gallows. In a gruesome twist, the rope around his neck snapped as the trapdoor opened and he had to be hung a second time.

Allan Pinkerton, who established America's first organized counterespionage service, was ultimately responsible for the death of his most effective operative. His dispatch of two agents who themselves made elementary security blunders and whose identities were known to Confederates in Richmond highlighted the primitive state of American counterespionage. But Pinkerton rebounded from this setback and embarked on an investigation that would lead to the arrest of one of the Confederacy's most fascinating spies.

THE SPY IN
THE UNION CAPITAL

ROSE GREENHOW

*I am a Southern woman, . . . born with revolutionary
blood in my veins!*

ROSE GREENHOW, *a Confederate spy*
My Imprisonment, Kindle edition, location 707.

No one epitomized the Confederate advantage of "stay-behinds" in pro-Southern Washington more than Rose O'Neal Greenhow. Although she had no direct access to secrets, "Rebel Rose," her moniker among Southern sympathizers, ran a network of spies for the Confederacy that included sources from every level of Union society.

Greenhow's motivation for espionage was purely ideological. She was born to slaveholding parents in Maryland, and her hatred of abolitionists was forged at an early age when her father was murdered by a slave. Her proslavery views were nurtured in childhood by John Calhoun, the former US vice president who was a frequent visitor to her home and one of the most ardent defenders of slavery and states' rights.[1]

Rose O'Neal married Robert Greenhow, a State Department lawyer of considerable financial means, and she soon became a popular Washington socialite. After her husband's untimely death, the widow Greenhow attracted male admirers who helped extend her influence in the capital. Invitations to her parties were coveted in Washington society, and prominent figures like Secretary of War William Seward and Senator Stephen Douglass were regular attendees. Even James Buchanan, the only unmarried president, was often a late-night visitor, which set tongues wagging in the capital. One of Greenhow's closest contacts was Senator Henry Wilson, chairman of the Military Affairs Committee, and his letters to Rebel Rose hint at a romance with Washington's most popular hostess. Wilson, who was undoubtedly one of her unwitting sources of information, went on to become vice president of the United States under Ulysses S. Grant.[2]

Greenhow's support for the Southern cause and her connections in Washington made her an ideal candidate for recruitment by the Confederacy. Another Confederate "stay-behind," Captain Thomas Jordan, spotted her early in the war and easily persuaded her to join the cause. Jordan was serving as an assistant quartermaster in the Department of War in Washington and remained in the job when the war broke out in order to organize a rebel spy network inside the enemy capital. Like many Confederate officers, he was a graduate of West Point, where his roommate was William Tecumseh Sherman, who would later become the Union general who would devastate the city of Atlanta during the war's final throes. Once Jordan had organized his Washington spy ring, he was commissioned a colonel in the Confederate Army and became intelligence chief for General Pierre Beauregard, whose army was deployed across the Potomac River from the Union capital. Greenhow became his principal agent, and he provided her with an alias to use in communications with him and a simple cipher to encrypt information.

Although some historians believe that Greenhow caused extensive damage to the Union, Edwin Fishel, a preeminent scholar of Civil War espionage, claims that her exploits have been exaggerated and that the impact of her spying has been grossly overrated.[3] Even Fishel, however, credits her contribution to the Confederate victory in the first major battle of the war at Bull Run. In July 1861 Greenhow sent messages to the Confederates warning of Union general Irvin McDowell's plan to advance against the rebel army through Fairfax, Virginia. She provided details about McDowell's troop strength, the date of his intended march, and his plan to cut the Winchester–Manassas railroad line to prevent reinforcements from reaching Beauregard's ranks.

This alert gave Beauregard time to reinforce his army and hand the Union an unexpected defeat. Beauregard credited his victory to Greenhow's information, and Colonel Jordan also sent her a secret message acknowledging her role: "Our President and our General direct me to thank you. We rely upon you for further information. The Confederacy owes you a debt."[4]

Greenhow sent one of the messages about Bull Run through Betty Duvall, a fetching social butterfly who was also sympathetic to the Confederacy. Duvall concealed the message in her hairdo and stunned Beauregard's aide when she unpinned her chignon and let the information fall from her shiny black curls—

ROSE GREENHOW, prominent Washington hostess and Confederate spy. *Library of Congress*

yet another example of the advantages women had in Civil War espionage.[5]

Emboldened by her reporting on Bull Run, Greenhow turned her attention to gathering intelligence on Union troops in the capital itself. The Union, however, suspected that espionage could have played a role in its defeat at Bull Run. Allan Pinkerton, who was by now the Union's chief of intelligence, was asked to investigate Greenhow, whose sympathy for the Confederacy was well known in Washington. In his investigation, Pinkerton employed the full array of counterespionage measures he had outlined in his letter to McClellan (see chapter 6). However, as events unfolded, Pinkerton's counterespionage philosophy proved at times to be more effective in theory than in practice.

First, Pinkerton arranged surveillance of Greenhow's residence to monitor visitors who might be spies delivering Union information to the widow. In one comic episode, which Pinkerton himself relates in a rare moment of self-deprecation in his memoirs, the spy catcher participated in the surveillance himself one rainy night and, playing a Peeping Tom, shed his shoes and stood on the shoulders of one of his surveillants to peer through the blinds of Greenhow's house.

Pinkerton spotted a Union officer inside passing documents to Greenhow. As the officer left, the shoeless Pinkerton rushed after his prey. But his bizarre surveillance was easily spotted by the officer, who worked at the War Department. The officer eluded Pinkerton and ordered Union soldiers to arrest him on the street. Pinkerton eventually got a message through to his colleagues, who then arranged his release. He ordered the suspect officer's arrest, but the spy had already fashioned an alibi for his nocturnal visit to Greenhow. This incident, however, had now convinced Pinkerton that Greenhow was spying for the Confederacy.

In August 1861 Pinkerton closed in on Greenhow and set off a chain of investigative blunders that almost damaged his case. He arrested Greenhow outside her house as she returned from a morning walk. But Greenhow, making a prearranged warning signal, took out a handkerchief to alert an associate on the street. As Pinkerton's men quickly searched the house for evidence, Greenhow's young daughter climbed a tree outside and shouted to passers-by about her mother's arrest, thereby warning any potential visitors from the spy network to avoid the house.[6]

Other blunders followed. Because they were victims of their cultural values, Pinkerton's chivalrous men allowed Greenhow to change her clothes when she feigned heat stroke on the muggy Washington summer day. And while she was alone in her boudoir, she crumpled up and swallowed her cipher code and hid incriminating information in her skirt. Pinkerton's men, again treating the respectable lady in a gingerly fashion, had also not searched her and were thus unaware that she was armed with a pistol. When one of Pinkerton's men realized the mistake of leaving her alone, he entered the room. Greenhow was on the verge of shooting him, but fortunately she decided not to do so.[7]

Pinkerton kept Greenhow under house arrest and soon also incarcerated a few other female spies in the house, which thus was dubbed "Fort Greenhow." Despite her imprisonment, Greenhow still managed to communicate secrets to the Confederacy. She outwitted her guards by surreptitiously receiving information from those visitors who were allowed to see her and also passing information to them. She was also allowed to send letters, in which she buried hidden messages in innocuous texts complaining to friends about her plight. She embroidered to pass the time, and in her later autobiography she called her finished products a "vocabulary of colors" with intelligence information.[8] She was finally transferred to the Old Capital Prison in 1862, where she allegedly continued her spying, sometimes by signaling from her cell window to agents or by throwing her daughter's rubber balls out the window with messages wrapped around them.

Even though Pinkerton's men committed mistakes in their detention of Greenhow, her spy tradecraft was equally atrocious. Although she was operating in the heart of the enemy's capital, she left incriminating documents in her house that were discovered by Pinkerton's men. Many of them were unencrypted plain text and contained glaring evidence of her espionage. Others were enciphered, but the code was so simple that Pinkerton's men easily decoded the messages. Some observers suggest that Pinkerton allowed Greenhow to communicate in order to entrap other spies and, given his avowed penchant for double agent operations, he would have likely exploited her communications for his own purposes.[9] But in the end it was a moot point. Greenhow's Confederate handler, Thomas Jordan, was highly skeptical of any messages she sent after her imprisonment and did not respond to her overtures for continued communications.

Pinkerton also faced political challenges in detaining Greenhow. Despite the strong suspicions of her espionage, she still enjoyed considerable influence in Washington's corridors of power, which may have led Pinkerton to initially keep her under house arrest rather than detain her in prison. Aside from political considerations, Pinkerton was also on shaky legal ground. In the chaotic bureaucracy of the early war years, Pinkerton detained Greenhow without any warrant and only on the oral authority of his superiors in the War Department, and soon powerful voices in the capital began grumbling about violations of her constitutional rights.[10]

The Union finally disposed of the Rose Greenhow case by deporting her to the South. On the basis of her notoriety as a spy, the Confederacy sent her as an envoy to Europe to promote the rebel cause. After her diplomatic missions, she returned to live in the South in 1864. Forever loyal to the cause, Rebel Rose smuggled gold bars for the Confederacy aboard a blockade runner that ran aground in a storm. Fearing arrest by the Union, she hopped in a rowboat to flee, but the craft capsized in the squall. Rose O'Neal Greenhow drowned, dragged to the bottom of the sea by the weight of the gold she carried for her beloved Confederacy. Her body washed up on shore days later, and she was buried in Richmond with all the honors of an official state funeral.

Although Greenhow was deified by the Confederacy for her spying exploits, the actual damage she did to the Union cause was highly questionable. The information she passed to Confederate agents before her arrest, according to Edwin Fishel, was of marginal value.[11] Aside from her early warnings before Bull Run, her reports, in Fishel's assessment, were exaggerated or inaccurate. She also never indicated her subsources in her reports, and so the Confederates had no means to assess the reliability of the information.

The myth surrounding Rose Greenhow's spy exploits is largely woven of her own cloth in her autobiography. Like many memoirs written by spies on both sides of the Civil War, her account is a fanciful blend of fact and fantasy. Among her alleged triumphs, she claimed to have acquired General McClellan's war plans and the minutes of Lincoln's cabinet meetings, although there is absolutely no evidence that she obtained either.[12]

Ironically, Pinkerton also enhanced the importance of Greenhow's espionage in his own autobiography. Having been stung by criticism of the faulty intelligence he gave McClellan, Pinkerton embellished Greenhow's achievements to burnish his own image as the counterspy who had finally snared his prey.[13]

Yet a third account of Civil War espionage also perpetuated the Greenhow myth. Lafayette Baker, Pinkerton's rival, played no role in the Greenhow case, but in his self-serving memoir, he also subscribed to the myth that she routinely stole the minutes of Lincoln's cabinet meetings. Baker would hardly trumpet Greenhow's espionage achievements to acknowledge the importance of her arrest by Pinkerton. As Fishel notes, both Pinkerton and Baker emphasized that Greenhow had hoodwinked the Union before they arrived on the scene, and that "each man was telling his readers how bad things were until *he* took charge."[14] Moreover, Baker's tendency to stretch facts and spin tales from whole cloth marked his tenure as one of the Union's two counterespionage chiefs and earned him the unflattering sobriquet of the "most celebrated liar in American history."[15]

⊖ ⊖ ⊖

THE COUNTERSPY
AS TYRANT
LAFAYETTE BAKER

It's doubtful if Baker has in any one thing told the truth,
even by accident.

US HOUSE OF REPRESENTATIVES' *investigation of Lafayette Baker*
based on Baker's testimony regarding impeachment proceedings against
President Andrew Johnson, HR Report 7, 40th Congress

Lafayette Baker was responsible for the first in a series of dark periods in American counterespionage history when the pursuit of spies led to political persecution. Governments throughout history have used the threat of espionage and subversion as a thinly veiled pretext to persecute their citizens because of opposing political views, religious affiliation, or ethnic heritage. The United States has largely been immune to these authoritarian tendencies because of its constitutional guarantees of civil liberties. Yet despite this tradition, whenever Americans felt most threatened, from the Civil War to the Vietnam War, they slandered, investigated, arrested, and interned their fellow citizens on baseless charges of espionage and subversion. Apart from the abuse of civil liberties, these witch hunts have rarely unmasked a real spy jeopardizing America's national security.

Lafayette Baker's exploitation of Union paranoia in the Civil War set the unfortunate precedent. In the last two years of the conflict, Baker rounded up hundreds of suspects, trampled civil liberties, and missed genuine spies operating not only in the Union government but also in his own counterespionage service.

Baker was born in upstate New York in 1826 and spent his youth wandering across the country to the West Coast. He wound up in California during the Gold Rush of the 1850s and joined an army of vigilantes who tried to bring order to the lawless chaos of San Francisco. His vigilante experience would shape his later approach to law enforcement and counterespionage investigations.[1]

At the start of the Civil War Baker traveled to Washington to volunteer his services as a spy to General Winfield Scott, then the Union army's commander. Because the Union had no professional intelligence service, commanders routinely accepted such offers, and the elderly general tasked the young man to gather information about General Pierre Beauregard's forces in Manassas. Posing as an itinerant photographer, Baker went behind enemy lines but got caught twice. He was released and managed to collect the information that Scott wanted (or at least Baker claims this in his autobiography). Scott recommended Baker to Secretary of State William Seward, who then hired him on contract for $200 to sniff out Confederate spies and subversives in Maryland and Virginia.[2]

Baker, a power-hungry zealot for the Union cause, thrived in a climate where fear of Confederate subversion reigned. The Union capital of Washington was, after all, a Southern city at heart and was surrounded by Confederate sympathizers in Virginia and Maryland. Seward was particularly concerned about Southern influence in the capital, and so he established an informal "Treason Bureau" that relentlessly tracked Confederate subversives in and around the capital. The bureau arbitrarily detained suspects on the flimsiest evidence, ignored due process, and harshly interrogated suspects. Seward dispatched Baker on his first mission to root out subversives in southern Maryland, where the ambitious counterspy ingratiated himself with his ruthless boss by ravaging the countryside, burning buildings, and randomly rounding up hundreds of alleged plotters.

Seward was not alone in his aggressive hunt for subversives. Representative John Potter was concerned about "secession clerks," who were rebel sympathizers still remaining in Union service and had access to information of obvious interest to the enemy. The threat was a real one, and Potter launched a campaign to weed out these potential spies. Although he claimed "none shall be injured by mere malice or rumor," he charged about two hundred clerks with subversion, a harbinger of Senator Joe McCarthy's witch hunt against government officials in the early days of the Cold War.[3] Despite these mass arrests, key rebel clerks still evaded the net and spied for the Confederacy.

The most powerful supporter of a hard-line stance against spies and subversives was the president himself. Lincoln believed that the chief executive was not only entitled but also obligated to protect the republic by adopting measures in wartime that would ordinarily have been illegal. Early in the war he suspended the writ of habeas corpus whereby detainees could petition for relief from unlawful detention, a decision that gave Seward's Treason Bureau free rein to hold suspects without trial.

After Lincoln appointed Edwin Stanton as secretary of war in 1862, Baker was hired by the War Department as a special provost marshal. Stanton shared Seward's passion to root out subversives and provided Baker with secret funds to assemble a force to eradicate rebellion in the capital. Stanton's staunch antisubversive stance and Baker's thirst for political power proved to be an unhealthy union.

Baker decided to dub his new force the National Detective Police, to give the appearance that he exercised nationwide law enforcement authority even though he had absolutely no legal basis for the claim. Once Pinkerton's organization was disbanded, Baker headed the only Union counterespionage service. However, instead of a systematic search for spies, Baker simply detained hundreds of suspect Confederate sympathizers. The suspects were dragged from their homes in the dead of night, whisked away to prisons, interrogated, and locked up in bleak conditions for months. Many were browbeaten into confessions or confronted with phony witnesses to their crimes, who were usually Baker's own men posing as their accusers. Unlike others imprisoned by oppressive regimes, those arrested by Baker's men were not locked away for years in prison camps or summarily executed. Once they confessed to their crimes, whether real or imagined, they were only forced to swear an oath of allegiance to the Union and were then released.

Aside from his abuses of civil rights, Baker was extremely corrupt and prospered from a number of shady business deals during his tenure. Despite his self-righteous devotion to the Union cause, he managed to amass a nest egg ten times his salary while hunting for spies and subversives. As the historian Nathan Miller notes, "No man in the history of American intelligence would have a more unsavory reputation."[4]

At the same time, Baker deserves some begrudging credit for introducing innovative techniques into criminal and counterespionage investigations. He was the first to establish a criminal dossier system in the United States and the first to include photographs of criminals and suspects in police files. He is also credited with developing "disorientation" techniques and psychological manipulation in interrogating suspects (e.g., arresting and questioning in the early morning hours when subjects were most vulnerable, alternating between hostile and friendly questioning (the good cop / bad cop technique), and assigning his own agents as cellmates to elicit information.[5] However, some of his harsher methods, such as sleep deprivation, bordered on psychological torture.

The measure of counterespionage success is ultimately the catching of spies, and Baker failed miserably at the task. Although the sheer number of arrests for espionage and subversion netted some low-level informants, Baker failed to catch key spies operating under his nose in the War Department. The "secessionist clerks" were perhaps the most significant Confederate penetrations, especially those working for agencies that dealt with military, political, and economic secrets. Even though Representative Potter raised legitimate concerns about the threat, no one conducted systematic counterespionage investigations or even routine security checks to identify spies, especially in the War Department. As one example, John Lancaster, a War Department clerk, regularly screened messages that he was not authorized to read. Simple background checks would have revealed that his father and brother both served in the Confederate army. Instead, he served until late in Baker's tenure and was only caught by accident.[6]

A more damaging spy among the secessionist clerks may have been John Callan, who worked as a clerk both in the adjutant general's office and on the Senate Military Affairs Committee, which was headed by Henry Wilson. A routine check of Callan's background would have revealed that he was originally hired by the former senator from Mississippi, Jefferson Davis, who, of course, had become president of the Confederate States of

America. Callan's espionage for the South was never conclusively proven, but his appointment by Jefferson Davis should have been sufficient grounds for an intensive security review.[7]

More stunning than these cases was Baker's failure to unmask a major Confederate spy in the War Department who worked directly for him. Edward Norton was one of Baker's spy hunters and was fully aware of National Detective Police investigations that might threaten any real Southern operatives. Norton's unique position as the Confederate fox in the Union henhouse enabled him to warn one of the Confederacy's most active spymasters of Baker's attempts to capture him.[8]

THE CONFEDERACY'S REVEREND SPY

THOMAS CONRAD

In less than twenty-four hours, I could send a reliable dispatch from Washington to the Confederate capital.

THOMAS CONRAD, *Confederate Spy*

During the Civil War, women like Rose Greenhow spied unabashedly by exploiting Americans' sense of chivalry. Although their male counterparts did not enjoy these advantages, some worked in professions that aroused little suspicion and allowed them to steal secrets as handily as women did. Thomas Conrad, perhaps the most productive Confederate spy of the war, maneuvered easily behind Union lines without raising an eyebrow and was even accorded deference and respect while he spied on the enemy. Thomas Conrad was a Methodist preacher.

Conrad's story belongs to a long and somewhat paradoxical tradition in which espionage has mixed with religion and men of God have conspired with men of the world to influence the tide of history. No less a clerical eminence than Cardinal Richelieu created France's first spy service in the seventeenth century, aided by another priest, Father Joseph de Tremblay, one of Europe's most devious conspirators. Catholic priests spied against the Protestant Queen Elizabeth I, and clergymen spied during the French

Revolution. Priests and ministers hid behind their clerical collars to spy in the underground against Adolph Hitler during World War II. An American spy in the US Army during the Cold War, George Trofimoff, was recruited to the KGB by a boyhood friend who was a Russian Orthodox priest. As late as 2005, a Polish priest, Konrad Hejmo, was accused of spying against Pope John Paul II on behalf of the Soviet Bloc. Despite this rich history of clerical spying, clergymen like Thomas Conrad still invited little scrutiny from laymen who found it inconceivable that men of the cloth would engage in a secular activity as deceitful as espionage.

A Virginian by birth, Conrad studied theology at Dickinson College in Carlisle, Pennsylvania, a school with more Southern than Northern students. When war broke out, Conrad was headmaster of Georgetown College, a boy's school in Washington. Conrad was an outspoken secessionist and embarked on his espionage career for the Confederacy by persuading his students to send messages to rebel spies through an elaborate system of raising and lowering the shades in their dormitory rooms.[1] He was arrested by the Union authorities when he encouraged the school band to flagrantly play *Dixie* at its 1861 graduation, but he was released soon after with a warning, a common practice for handling sympathizers in the early days of the war.

Conrad left Washington and went south, where he was commissioned as a captain and appointed chaplain for General J. E. B. Stuart's cavalry in Virginia. Like most Civil War operatives, Conrad had no intelligence training, but Stuart recognized that the young preacher had natural instincts and an unassailable cover to gather information. Conrad was soon crossing Union lines posing as a federal chaplain, preaching sermons to soldiers while gathering information about troop and artillery strengths and battle plans.

Conrad was so effective that he was sent back to Washington to spy in the heart of enemy territory. He established his spy headquarters in a mansion conveniently located near the White House and War Department. Like other spies of the era, he developed his own primitive tradecraft to blend into enemy society and escape detection. He frequently used simple yet convincing disguises by merely changing the cut and length of his hair and moustache. He paid meticulous attention to seemingly trivial details that could have distinguished him as a Southerner to the discerning eye. Tobacco chewing was a popular habit at the time on both sides, but Northerners and Southerners chewed two distinctly different types of tobacco, and Conrad was careful to abandon his normal brand for the Northern version. Shoes and boots were also manufactured differently on both sides, and Conrad again was always sure to slip on Northern footwear before his forays into the capital.[2]

Conrad's spy ring in Washington had the best access of any Confederate network in the war. His agents were primarily the secessionist clerks buried in the heart of the Union War Department, little gray men who were secretly Southern sympathizers and shuffled papers that contained the Union's battle plans. Because of the incredibly lax security in the capital, Conrad also had unfettered access to the War Department Building, where he would sometimes even visit his agents. In one instance in the spring of 1862, he was alerted by a clerk about key intelligence and, by a prearranged plan, he walked into his spy's empty office at lunchtime, read the materials, and walked away undisturbed after memorizing the details.

Conrad's lunchtime raid on the War Department resulted in one of the most important espionage coups of his career. The Confederacy was aware of General George McClellan's plans to march along the Virginia peninsula between the York and James rivers to attack Richmond, but it needed information about the size of the Union commander's forces. As his agent had promised, Conrad found on the desk information about McClellan's order of battle and operational plans for the campaign. Meanwhile, Allan Pinkerton was feeding McClellan intelligence reports with grossly inflated Confederate troop numbers. The difference in each side's intelligence was evident in the outcome. Robert E. Lee and General Joseph Johnston repelled McClellan's forces back to the James River and protected the Southern capital.

Conrad almost achieved the most dramatic intelligence coup of the war a few months later. In August 1862 he learned that McClellan was rushing his forces from Washington to reinforce the beleaguered troops of General John Pope at the Second Battle of Bull Run. McClellan's hasty exit left the capital virtually defenseless to an attack by Stuart's nearby cavalry.

This critical information, however, was ultimately useless. Conrad's operation represented one of the more glaring examples of untimely delivery of intelligence because of slow communications. He tried to reach Stuart to convey the news about the unprotected capital but could not circumvent the Union troops that had been summoned to guard the city after McClellan's departure. Instead, Conrad was forced to report through tortuously slow channels to the Confederate Signal Service, which could not relay the information quickly enough. If Stuart had received Conrad's alert, the possibility exists that his cavalry could have raided the capital and even captured President Abraham Lincoln.

Conrad learned a bitter lesson from this experience and vowed it would not happen again. In November 1862 he learned from his War Department moles that McClellan would be replaced by General Ambrose Burnside, who would advance toward Richmond by way of Fredericksburg. Within a day Conrad personally delivered this intelligence to Lee, who reinforced Confederate troops deployed in Fredericksburg and ultimately crushed Burnside's army.[3]

Meanwhile, Lafayette Baker's operatives finally began to focus on real Confederate spies. But Conrad held a trump card. Edward Norton, one of his War Department penetrations, worked directly for Baker and was able to warn Conrad of any investigations of him or his agents. Conrad's mole demonstrates the importance of penetrations inside the enemy's counterespionage service. These penetrations provide information on the enemy's counterespionage tactics and investigations that allow the spy handler to run all his or her other spies securely. They also provide an early warning system that prevents the compromise and arrest of the spy handler and his agents.

Norton alerted Conrad about every phase of Baker's spy hunt and warned him that Baker was closing in. Conrad realized that his days in the capital were numbered and he had to escape soon. In an ingenious move, he advised Norton to identify him as one of the elusive spies Baker was hunting. Baker's men immediately raided Conrad's mansion, but the rebel spy, of course, had already fled. Norton, however, was still in place, his loyalty to the Union now beyond reproach because he had pinpointed Conrad as a rebel spy.

Conrad did not return to Washington until a year later. In June 1863 he learned from his War Department spies that the capital was yet again vulnerable as Union troops were redeployed away from the city to the Battle of Gettysburg. Once again, however, Conrad was unable to reach Confederate forces in time and missed his second chance to deliver intelligence that might have resulted in the capture of the Union capital.

Frustrated by his earlier experience, Conrad had played a significant role in establishing the "Doctor's Line," an organized system of couriers, often physicians ostensibly on house calls, who relayed intelligence to Richmond like runners passing batons in a marathon. The Confederates, however, had still not solved the second half of the problem, how to relay this information from its headquarters back out to field commanders. Even though the Confederacy had improved the speed of its intelligence communications, Conrad's warning still did not reach the troops who could have exploited the information. After Stuart received Conrad's news, he could only lament that he "would have charged down Pennsylvania Avenue, if it had been my last charge."[4]

Conrad's clever use of disguises enabled him to escape detection throughout the war, but ironically it also led to his arrest immediately after the war. On April 14, 1865, John Wilkes Booth assassinated President Lincoln at Ford's Theater in Washington, and Lafayette Baker launched an intensive manhunt for Booth and his fellow conspirators. Conrad, moving north to seek a postwar job, donned a moustache and hairdo that, unbeknownst to him, made him resemble Booth. He was snared by Baker's men, but his identity was quickly established. In a wry twist, he was brought to Baker, who had pursued the rebel spy for months. Baker simply ordered Conrad's release, and spy hunter and spy shook hands, a vivid symbol of the end of the espionage war between North and South.

Just before the end of the war, Conrad had been assigned to Confederate counterespionage in Richmond. But by then it was too late for the hapless rebel spy-catching effort to use his considerable talents. Although Pinkerton and Baker enjoyed some limited success catching spies against the Union, Confederate counterespionage had utterly failed to find a number of key Northern spies throughout the war.

UNION ESPIONAGE

The most productive espionage operation of the Civil War on either side.

EDWIN FISHEL, Secret War, *on Elizabeth Van Lew's espionage activities*

The glowing assessment of Elizabeth Van Lew's espionage activities by Edwin Fishel, a leading expert on Civil War espionage, is all the more striking because he largely dismissed most accounts of spying in the war as inaccurate, exaggerated, and melodramatic. Van Lew, however, stands out among her contemporaries as the spymaster of the most effective espionage operation of the war. Inside the Confederate capital of Richmond, she ran an extensive network of sources and couriers covertly sympathetic to the Union cause, including merchants, farmers, and slaves. This network provided Union military commanders with key intelligence as they prepared their decisive assault on the Confederate capital.

Van Lew, like the majority of Civil War spies, was motivated not by money but by ideological sympathy for her cause. She was passionately dedicated to the abolition of slavery and financed her espionage operation with her own funds to ensure a Union victory. She was born in 1818 to a wealthy merchant family in Richmond, and she never married and ostensibly lived the life of a Southern socialite. In her early years she was sent for schooling to Philadelphia, where moral reform groups actively supported the abolition of slavery. Her Northern education undoubtedly helped her develop the intense hatred of slavery that would alienate her from her Southern neighbors. After her father died years later, she freed his slaves, most of whom remained to work for her. She was as equally opposed to slavery as her Confederate counterpart Rose Greenhow supported it. Like Greenhow, she also exploited her social status to make possible her espionage activities.[1]

Van Lew's exploitation of her social status required effective role-playing. Although she belonged to a respected Richmond family, her loyalty to the Confederate cause was suspect. The city was well aware that she had freed her slaves and, in addition, she played an active role in ministering to the increasing number of captured Union soldiers held in Richmond's Libby Prison. She arranged for medical care for some prisoners, visited them in the local hospitals, and even risked lodging prison escapees in her Richmond mansion. Using her own funds, she arranged to provide prisoners with books, food, and money for bribes to secure better treatment from their jailers.

At the same time, her humanitarian efforts on behalf of Union soldiers masked her espionage work. The books and food brought in and out of Libby Prison also served as covert means of transmitting intelligence. Hollow spaces in book bindings and false bottoms in food platters were undetected by prison guards and contained firsthand information from the prisoners about the Confederate army that otherwise would have reached the Union more slowly in an era of tortoise-like communications.[2]

Van Lew's social status, as her biographer Elizabeth Varon notes, was "her most important asset" and enabled her to assist the Union both overtly and covertly.[3] To accomplish this, Van Lew had to maintain a delicate balance by convincing the Confederates of Richmond that her charitable deeds for Union soldiers were obliged by the Christian faith of a proper Southern lady and were in no way incompatible with her loyalty to the Confederate cause. Van Lew played the role effectively, but she constantly feared her underground activities would be discovered. These fears proved to be justified—Confederate officials in Richmond indeed were increasingly suspicious of her activities, and they even launched an investigation of her family in 1864.

This investigation, not surprisingly, revealed that Van Lew held pro-Union views but had done nothing to hurt the Confederate cause, so no further action was taken. In reaching this decision, Confederate officials took special note of her "wealth and position." Given Van Lew's status and gender, her role in espionage was unimaginable for the Confederates of Richmond: "Elitism and sexism disinclined Confederate authorities to believe a frail spinster lady capable of politically significant acts of disloyalty."[4]

Van Lew's social status was not the only protection for her espionage activities. She also developed primitive yet extremely effective clandestine tradecraft methods to protect her network and ensure the secure communication of her information. Her ingenuity in developing her own tradecraft is all the more remarkable because she received no espionage training and little guidance from any Union intelligence officers. As one example, because she was a prominent socialite and already under suspicion, she sometimes dressed in tattered clothes and acted slightly eccentric on the streets of Richmond to disguise herself as she contacted her spies throughout the city.[5]

Van Lew's tradecraft methods also relied on a layered system of redundant security measures so that compromise of any single measure would still not enable the enemy to read her communications. She developed her own code and, unlike the careless Rose Greenhow, she enciphered all her messages that contained intelligence information. She never shared the code with anyone, and her cipher key, which she concealed in the back of her watch, was only discovered after her death in 1900. For an added layer of security, she wrote messages with secret ink between the lines of innocuous cover letters, which, if intercepted and read, were intended to bore postal censors. Even after all these precautions, she still divided the messages into sections and dispatched them along different courier routes, and these couriers often carried the information concealed in their clothing, in the soles of their shoes, or in egg baskets.[6]

Van Lew also ensured the timeliness as well as the security of her communications. Similar to the Confederates' Doctors' Line, she established a relay system of five way stations and exploited Southern prejudice by using as couriers slaves, who were considered second-class citizens and thus attracted no attention while conveying rebel secrets to the Union.[7]

Few records remain to detail the intelligence that Van Lew and the Richmond Underground provided. After the war, she feared recriminations from

Richmond natives and asked the US Department of War to return all her intelligence messages. The department agreed and she promptly destroyed them all.[8] And, unlike many of her Civil War spying counterparts, she never wrote her memoirs and carried her secrets to the grave. There is no evidence of any intelligence from her that turned the tide in a single battle. Ultimately, her intelligence was valuable in the aggregate, keeping Union forces apprised of general Confederate troop strengths and deployments and of the details about Richmond's defenses, which were all of critical importance as the Union prepared its final assault on the Southern capital.

Although Van Lew's messages were destroyed, Union leaders after the war acknowledged the value of her espionage activity. Colonel George Sharpe, Grant's intelligence chief, claimed that "for a long time she represented all that was left of the power of the United States government in Richmond."[9] Grant himself ordered a guard around her home after Union forces occupied Richmond and, after he became president, he appointed her postmaster general of the city.

Van Lew spied for the Union because of her passionate opposition to slavery. Like many other spies on both sides, she received no compensation and she was impoverished by the end of the war from funding her own espionage network. She was also shunned until her death by Richmond natives because of her pro-Union activities and was eventually forgotten and abandoned by the federal government for which she had spied. She died penniless, supported only by her former slaves and the former Union soldiers she had tended in Libby Prison.

Among Van Lew's former slaves was one of the best-placed spies of the Civil War. Van Lew had freed and sent one of her former slaves, Mary Bowser, to be educated in the North.[10] After her return, Bowser agreed to Van Lew's proposal to work in the home of Confederate president Jefferson Davis. Any intelligence service would relish a spy inside the home of the enemy's leader, especially a spy whose lowly status would attract not an iota of scrutiny. Intelligence services hunt for spies among the ranks of high-level policymakers and military commanders, but equally valuable are the little gray men—and, in this case, women—who labor as maids, gardeners, and drivers. They are often treated as invisible, mere fixtures like furniture, yet precisely because of their low-level positions they pick up golden nuggets of intelligence as their employers let their secrets slip in unguarded moments.

Bowser, among other chores in the Jefferson household, worked as a serving maid, where she could eavesdrop on guests at the president's dinner table, which included the Confederate government's decision makers and military leaders. Although Bowser was dismissed as a mere untutored slave, another Union spy reported that she had a photographic memory and could report every word of a conversation she had overheard or a document she had read.[11] As P. K. Rose notes in his incisive study of the espionage activities of slaves in the Civil War, "Because of the culture of slavery in the South, Negroes involved in menial activities could move about without suspicion. Also, officials and officers tended to ignore their presence as personal servants when discussing war-related matters."[12]

Van Lew was not the only Union spymaster to use slaves for intelligence activities. Slaves were among Pinkerton's best collectors and couriers of espionage information. And one of his most effective collectors was John Scobell, a freed slave who had been educated by his Scottish owner. Like other Civil War spies, Scobell was an adept role player and posed in a variety of menial jobs ranging from deckhand to cook, and he often teamed up with agents like Timothy Webster to aid their missions. His most important cover, of course, was the color of his skin, which allowed him to pass through Union lines, observe, eavesdrop, and carry information back to Union lines without suspicion.

Another freed slave, Mary Touvestre, worked in the Norfolk house of a Southern engineer engaged in refitting the *Merrimac,* the Confederacy's powerful ironclad warship. She filched the engineer's plans for the ship and escaped north to hand them over to the Union War Department, which further convinced military planners to accelerate work on their own version of an ironclad, the *Monitor.*[13]

Slave cover was so effective for Union intelligence that at least one white spy used it. The Union spy Emma Edmonds's use of cover and disguise was perhaps the most diverse of the Civil War, crossing both gender and racial lines to penetrate the Confederacy. Edmonds actually used "cover" to join the Union army. Realizing that she could not enlist as a woman, she disguised herself as a young man and, after four unsuccessful attempts to enlist, was inducted as a male nurse. Both sides needed soldiers quickly, so induction examinations were cursory or nonexistent. A medical examiner merely accepted Edmonds's word that she was in good health.[14]

Still impersonating a man, Edmonds responded to a call from General George McClellan for volunteers to spy behind rebel lines. For her first mission she dyed her skin with silver nitrate, donned a minstrel wig, and posed in double disguise as a man and an African American. Playing the role of a slave called "Cuff," she was put to work on rebel ramparts and in rebel kitchens. After collecting information on troop numbers, fortifications, and morale, she reported personally to McClellan. On her next mission, Edmonds, still posing as a man to her Union superiors, pretended to be a woman, this time a pudgy Irish immigrant named Bridget O'Shea who peddled pots and pans among Confederate troops.

To collect intelligence for General Phillip Sheridan in the Shenandoah campaign, Edmonds reverted to slave disguise again, working as a female laundress in a rebel camp. During this mission, she discovered Confederate war plans by accident one day in an officer's coat she was cleaning. Later, she supported General Ambrose Burnside's campaign in Kentucky by infiltrating Louisville society as a young man named Charles Mayberry, a Northerner with supposed Southern sympathies.

In a tragicomic twist, Edmonds contracted malaria and, fearing her true gender would be revealed in a Union hospital, she deserted. Almost twenty years after the Civil War's end, Congress voted her an honorable discharge. This spy of many disguises was the only female member of the Grand Army of the Republic, an organization of Union soldiers begun after the war.

In spite of the ingenious disguises and tradecraft used by Edmonds and other Civil War spies, intelligence collection and counterespionage still remained haphazard, primitive, and uncoordinated by the end of the war. On the counterespionage front, Pinkerton and Baker had both applied modern investigative and intelligence techniques to the pursuit of spies, although their practices were often sounder in theory than in practice. Although Pinkerton and Baker had established fledgling counterspy organizations, the existence of two competing units portended the interagency rivalries that would plague American efforts to catch spies until World War II.

EMMA EDMONDS disguised herself as a man to enlist in the Second Michigan Infantry. She later undertook espionage missions for the Union behind Confederate lines. *University of Michigan*

Both of the Union counterspy services simply dissolved by the war's end as Americans focused on the reconstruction of their shattered country, largely undisturbed by threats from abroad. The focus was understandable—more than 20 percent of American male youth had been killed or wounded in the four bloody years of the conflict and $15 billion had been spent on the war at a time when a laborer earned $1 a day.

The spies and spy hunters of the Civil War, like their Revolutionary War counterparts, also returned home to rebuild their lives in calmer pursuits, and the experience they gained was lost. Pinkerton went on to establish America's leading detective agency, and Thomas Conrad returned to the world of academe, where he served as president of two colleges. Elizabeth Van Lew was appointed postmaster general of Richmond by a grateful President Grant. Emma Edmonds wrote her autobiography, *Nurse and Spy of the Union Army,* married, and settled down as a housewife and mother in the Midwest. Edmonds was among more than two dozen Civil War spies and spy hunters who penned their memoirs. These accounts were, unfortunately, so laced with melodrama and fiction that they hardly served as a body of professional knowledge for the generations to come.

More than a century after its birth, the United States had still not faced an espionage threat from an enemy whose people spoke a foreign language or shared a different cultural heritage. Thus it was no surprise that, again, the United States was totally unprepared to discover spies in its midst on the eve of the twentieth century.

PART **3**

ESPIONAGE DURING THE WORLD WARS, 1914–45

ESPIONAGE BEFORE
WORLD WAR I

*Weary of war and burdened with debt, the American people
eagerly turned to filling out the nation's frontiers and
exploiting its rich resources.*

NATHAN MILLER, *Spying for America*

A half century passed before the United States was again embroiled in a
conflict on the scale of the Civil War. During this time the nation turned
inward to heal the wounds of the Civil War and accelerate the growth of its
economy. Americans constructed railways linking the country from coast
to coast, discovered huge deposits of oil, illuminated their cities with
Thomas Edison's electric light, and communicated across the vast expanse
of the country with Alexander Graham Bell's telephone.

One area that did not expand was the military. The prospering nation faced
no threats from within or without and remained reluctant to support a large
standing army in peacetime. The military, however, did take the first steps
toward an intelligence collection ability. In 1882 the US Navy established the
Office of Naval Intelligence, and the army followed a few years later by
establishing the Military Intelligence Division. Though both these units
were small and inexperienced, they represented the nation's first institutionalized intelligence services and were a significant improvement over the
amateur organizations that had been cobbled together during past conflicts.

The intelligence services were tested for the first time in the Spanish-American War, the nation's first major conflict since the Civil War. As the nineteenth century drew to a close, Cuba began to rebel against the oppression of its Spanish masters, and the tabloid press in America stirred up public opinion over Spanish atrocities against the island's citizens. In February 1898 an explosion aboard the USS *Maine* in Havana Harbor killed 266 naval personnel. Although sabotage was never proven, the American press blamed Spain and was soon pushing the nation toward war. Unlike the conflicts of the late twentieth century, the Spanish-American War was immensely popular with Americans, many of whom viewed it as a just cause in the fight for liberty against the European imperialism they had come to loathe.

The United States won the war after a few short months, and America's fledgling intelligence services contributed to the victory. Counterespionage, however, was another matter. The United States had still not established a counterespionage agency following the Civil War, and the government's only investigative capability rested with the US Secret Service, which focused almost exclusively on counterfeiting. The Secret Service was given the mission of combating Spanish espionage, which fortunately proved to be grossly inept.

After the United States declared war, Spanish diplomats in Washington returned home, but Ramon Carranza, Spain's naval attaché, went to Canada to organize a spy network against the American enemy. Carranza was not an intelligence professional and never noticed the US Secret Service agent, known to history only as "Tracer," who tracked him into Canada.[1] Compounding the mistake, Carranza met a recruited agent in a Toronto hotel room as the Secret Service eavesdropped on the conspiratorial pair from an adjoining room. The spy, a retired naval petty officer tasked with gathering information on coastal defenses, was arrested while mailing a letter in Washington to his Spanish handlers.

After the arrest a Secret Service agent entered Carranza's rented house in Montreal as a prospective tenant and blatantly stole a letter that the careless Spaniard had left on his desk. This letter included sufficient detail about his spy tasks and was given to the Canadian authorities, which expelled Carranza and ended Spain's hapless foray into espionage against the United States.[2]

America's quick victory and Spain's luckless espionage attempts provoked little support for a national counterespionage agency after the conflict. The Secret Service's spy-catching mission was abruptly ended, and its agents were again limited only to investigations related to Treasury matters. On the eve of America's entry into a world war, the country still had no federal agency tasked with the responsibility to combat espionage.

The spark that ignited World War I was lit on June 28, 1914, by a radical Bosnian student named Gavrilo Princip. Princip stepped out from a crowd lined along a cobble-stoned Sarajevo street to watch the passing motorcade of Archduke Franz Ferdinand of Austria. He pulled out a pistol and killed the Austrian nobleman and his wife and blew the lid off a simmering cauldron of militarist nationalism that had plagued Europe for centuries. The Austro-Hungarian Empire confronted Serbia, and soon the European powers lined up on their respective sides of the fight. Germany sided with its German-speaking ally, Austria; Russia backed its Slavic brother, Serbia; France joined its partner, Russia; and, once Germany had marched through Belgium and violated its neutrality, Great Britain joined the fray against Kaiser Wilhelm II. The United States remained neutral.

As in the Revolutionary War and the Civil War, American public opinion was divided about the European conflict. Many viewed the Germans as aggressors and supported the Allies, some were pro-Germany, and others favored neutrality. A new demographic phenomenon also influenced American public opinion. As the nation prospered and ethnic strife erupted in Europe, immigrants from the continent poured into the United States in droves. By 1900 one-third of the American populace was foreign born or had foreign parents.

These millions of new immigrants from Ireland, Greece, Germany, Italy, and Eastern Europe significantly shaped public opinion toward the war in Europe. Pockets of sympathy for the kaiser existed among German Americans in America's largest cities, and Irish Americans supported Germany out of hatred for Great Britain. Other immigrants, like the nation's first settlers, had endured the arduous voyage across the Atlantic to escape European intrigues and wanted no part of the war now that they were safe in America.

Nevertheless, America could not maintain its neutrality for long. The nation had developed a lucrative economic relationship with the Allied powers, which desperately needed the arms and food that America produced and sold them at great profit. The Germans, conversely, fumed over America's policy of selling arms to their enemies while professing neutrality.

In response to this policy Germany pursued a dual strategy of keeping the Americans out of the war while cutting off their supplies to the Allies. Germany's initial protests to the United States about the shipments fell on deaf ears, so, left with no other options, its U-boats began sinking ships crossing the Atlantic with military cargo bound for the Allies. On May 7, 1915, German torpedoes took the lives of almost 1,200 noncombatants aboard the ocean liner *Lusitania,* and the incident shifted the tide of American public opinion. Although the Germans agreed to pay an indemnity, the sinking of the *Lusitania* stretched American neutrality to its limit. President Woodrow Wilson, who was struggling to maintain this neutrality, was outraged. Although he refused to abandon neutrality, he ordered the Secret Service to begin monitoring German activities on American soil. Its discoveries would drive the United States further along the path to war.

PRELUDE TO WAR

GERMANY'S FIRST SPY NETWORK

*Lost on Saturday. On 3:30 Harlem elevated train at
50th St. Station, Brown Leather Bag, Containing Documents.
Deliver to G. H. Hoffman, 5 E. 47th St., Against $20 Reward.*

ADVERTISEMENT IN *THE NEW YORK EVENING TELEGRAM,* JULY 27, 1915,
placed by a German diplomat who left espionage documents on a New York train.
Quoted by Rafalko, *Counterintelligence Reader*

Immediately after the outbreak of war in 1914, the German ambassador in Washington, Count Johann von Bernstorff, was summoned to Berlin and ordered to establish an espionage and sabotage network inside the United States. Bernstorff was troubled by his new task, because he realized that spying and sabotage on American soil could undermine the policy of Kaiser Wilhelm II by hastening rather than preventing America's entry into the war. Besides, German intelligence was unable to provide him with any qualified officers to help in the task because most of them were actively spying against their enemies in Europe. Bernstorff could only rely on his three embassy attachés—Captain Franz von Papen, naval attaché Karl Boy-Ed, and commercial attaché Heinrich Albert—all of whom were as unskilled in espionage and sabotage as he was.

Von Papen, the chief of the operation, was a blustery thirty-five-year-old cavalry officer who got his embassy post through his wife's connections. After the war, von Papen used these same connections to become German chancellor and, when he was shunted aside in 1932, he persuaded the president of the Weimar Republic, Field Marshall Paul von Hindenburg, to replace him with Adolph Hitler.[1] Karl Boy-Ed was half German and half Turkish and was an experienced naval attaché, if not a professional intelligence officer. The last of the trio, Albert, was the paymaster for German diplomatic and espionage operations and would commit the costly tradecraft error that revealed their espionage plans to the US government.

The three Germans made little attempt to recruit spies in the US government who could provide them with secrets about American intentions. They recruited no one who could serve as an agent of influence to persuade the US government to remain neutral in the European conflict. The von Papen ring's failure to penetrate the US government is all the more bewildering because American participation in the war could tip the scales irrevocably against Germany. Knowledge of the United States' policy intentions, especially regarding its continued neutrality, was essential for German war strategy. How far could Germany go in sinking American ships without pushing the United States into the war? How prepared was the United States to wage war against Germany? What incentives were the Allies using to induce America to join the fight? All these were vital questions for the kaiser's government, but Germany was so obsessed with stopping the arms flow that it made little attempt to find spies in US policy circles with the answers.

Instead, von Papen's ring focused almost solely on sabotage and merely recruited low-level spies and saboteurs among German sailors and immigrants who were sympathetic to the homeland and Irish American longshoremen who hated the British. These spies observed and reported on factories, docks, and other strategic targets—all useful for sabotage but unenlightening on key intelligence issues.

Von Papen's operations were stymied in the end by a silly mistake. Albert, the spy network's paymaster, left his New York City office on July 15, 1915, and headed toward the Sixth Avenue subway with a bulging briefcase in hand. Because an enraged President Woodrow Wilson had ordered surveil-

NAVAL ATTACHÉ CAPT. KARL BOY-ED was part of an amateurish spy ring of German diplomats. *Library of Congress*

CAPT. FRANZ VON PAPEN departing America for Germany after the exposure of the spy ring. *Library of Congress*

lance of German diplomats after the *Lusitania* incident, the stocky German diplomat was tailed by a US Secret Service agent. Albert dozed off in the sweltering July heat and awoke with a start as the train jerked to a stop at the 50th Street Station. He rushed out of the car, leaving the briefcase behind. Realizing his mistake, he jumped back on the train, but the bag was already gone.

The Secret Service agent had quickly snatched the bag and slipped out of the train. Albert chased the agent, who jumped on a trolley and eluded him. The documents in Albert's bag outlined German subversion plans for America. The US government was wary of admitting that its agent had filched a briefcase belonging to a diplomat, so it leaked the documents to the *New York World* for publication. Once the story hit the press, Albert was hounded for interviews and even issued a statement claiming that the documents had been misinterpreted by news hungry journalists, who began to ridicule him as "the minister without portfolio."[2] Von Papen and Boy-Ed were recalled to Germany, and the revelation of their conspiracy further inflamed American public opinion against Germany.

A few months before Albert's blunder, the Germans had already dispatched another agent to the United States, Captain Franz Rintelen von Kleist, of the Admiralty staff, who claimed that he was replacing the bumbling von Papen and would operate independently of the ambassador. Like von Papen's ring, Rintelen also focused on sabotage to stop the flow of munitions from America. Ambitious and fiercely loyal to the kaiser, Rintelen devised an aggressive plan to incite labor strikes, firebomb ships in American ports, and stir up revolution in Mexico. Among his plans, he set up a bomb factory in the engine room of a German ship and recruited a chemist born in Germany who fabricated firebombs concealed in hollow cigar tubes. Although Rintelen recruited a ring of saboteurs, he pursued few targets with access to policy-level information.

The Germans missed a golden opportunity. Rintelen had lived in the United States in his youth, spoke unaccented American English, and was well acquainted with New York's financial circles. He was handsome, dashing, and socially adept, clearly an intelligence officer with potential to spot and cultivate targets with access. He mixed in high society along the eastern seaboard and was a member of the prestigious New York Yacht Club (the only other German members of the exclusive club were the kaiser and his brother). And just as he found saboteurs among German Americans and Irish Americans, he could have also targeted government officials who might have succumbed to recruitment either as providers of secret information on US policy or agents of influence. But the German government, fixated on stopping the arms flow from America, remained obsessed with sabotage.[3]

Rintelen successfully sabotaged some ships, but eventually the US authorities began to suspect him. In August 1915 he was recalled for consultations to Germany and traveled back through Great Britain on a Swiss passport using an alias. The British had obtained a German codebook and learned of Rintelen's travel by deciphering a message that included his alias. He was arrested by the British as soon as his ship pulled into port, but he arrogantly insisted that he was not German. His British interrogators then caught him off guard and trapped him.

Rintelen conversed with his interrogators in his perfect English until one of them suddenly barked an order in German. Rintelen snapped to attention and clicked his heels. Immediately realizing his mistake, he admitted his identity. The British extradited him to the United States, where he was tried and convicted for conspiracy to instigate labor strikes, the only spy ever sentenced under this provision of the Sherman Anti-Trust Act. He sat out the war in an Atlanta prison. Years later, like the American spies of the Civil War, he wrote his spy memoir, melodramatically titled *The Dark Invader*. Like those Civil War autobiographies, Rintelen's account was self-serving and riddled with his own fantasies.[4]

The Germans missed their best chance to gather intelligence on American intentions by wasting Rintelen's talents and access and focusing him on sabotage. After his arrest, the Germans continued sabotage activities on American soil and in the process subverted their own policy goals by angering the American public and hastening the United States' entry into the war. One particularly dramatic act of sabotage that galvanized the American public was the destruction of a pier on Black Tom Island in New York Harbor on July 30, 1916. Black Tom was a storage and shipping terminal for thousands of tons of explosives and munitions destined for shipment to the Allies. On that hot summer night in New York, the pier "suddenly caught fire and exploded with a force that scarred the Statue of Liberty with shrapnel, shattered windows in Times Square, rocked the Brooklyn Bridge and woke sleepers as far away as Maryland."[5]

US investigators initially concluded that this explosion was an accident, but the press quickly spread the story that Black Tom was the evil handiwork of German saboteurs, which in fact was proven to be true. The Black Tom explosion was the latest in a series of incidents—the *Lusitania* sinking, U-boat attacks against merchant ships, and the exposure of German spy and sabotage rings—that inflamed public opinion and inched the United States closer to war. Still, President Wilson was as committed to neutrality as the Germans were to halting arms shipments to the Allies. However, in early 1917, less than a year after Black Tom, the Germans dashed the last hope of preventing American entry into the European war.

The British intercepted and deciphered a shocking message from German foreign secretary Arthur Zimmerman to his ambassador in Mexico. In this message Zimmerman informed his ambassador of Germany's proposal for an alliance with Mexico whereby America's southern neighbor would receive the territories of Texas, Arizona, and New Mexico after a German victory in exchange for its support of the kaiser. The British, hoping to shake America out of its neutrality, passed this infamous "Zimmerman telegram" to the US government. Wilson was livid at Germany's deceit and leaked the message to the press, which raised anti-German sentiment to the boiling point.

The last shred of hope was Germany's expressed willingness to negotiate a peace, although the kaiser's diplomats insisted on territorial claims in Europe that were unpalatable to the Allies. The Germans also bluntly threatened unrestricted submarine warfare if talks remained at an impasse. They did—and, on April 6, 1917, America declared war on Germany.

US Counterespionage and World War I

The whole sordid Black Tom–Kingsland episode has served one good purpose. . . . It has shown the need in this country of an efficient counterespionage system in time of peace as well as war.

WASHINGTON EVENING STAR editorial, 1939.
Quoted by Witcover, *Sabotage at Black Tom*

German sabotage had not only pushed America into war but had also awakened the government to the dangers of foreign spies. After a century and a half without a professional counterespionage agency, the United States was at last ready to establish one on the eve of World War I, but its efforts were plagued from the onset by turf battles between agencies vying for the task.[1]

When war broke out in Europe, a mishmash of government agencies shared counterespionage duties. The Department of State was responsible for monitoring foreign intelligence activities in the United States, but it had no investigative capability and had to borrow detectives from the Secret Service and the Justice Department's Bureau of Investigation.[2] The Bureau of Investigation had been formed by Attorney General Charles Bonaparte in 1908 and would become the forerunner of the Federal Bureau of Investigation. Moreover, State was traditionally uncomfortable with any intelligence or investigative role that could taint its primary mission of diplomacy.

In 1915 Treasury Secretary William McAdoo helped President Woodrow Wilson focus on the threat of foreign espionage and tried to convince him that the Treasury's Secret Service could best track German activities in the United States. McAdoo had a clear advantage over his counterparts in the cabinet because he had managed Wilson's presidential campaign and had married the president's daughter a year earlier.

Meanwhile, Attorney General Thomas Gregory was eager for the Department of Justice's Bureau of Investigation to assume counterespionage responsibilities. Gregory argued that the bureau's investigations must be limited to possible violations of the law and thus asked his attorneys to draft legislative proposals to give him the legal authority he believed his agents needed. These proposals died on the vine. The media condemned Gregory for seeking arbitrary police powers; and Congress, which was wary of domestic spying, took no action.

The attorney general was still not deterred and fought with McAdoo and the Treasury Department for the next two years over control of counterespionage. He expanded the Bureau of Investigation to three hundred agents to surpass the personnel numbers of his Secret Service rivals. In 1916 he also obtained a congressional amendment to the Justice Department's appropriations bill that allowed the bureau to conduct investigations on behalf of the State Department. The battle lines between Justice and Treasury had been drawn.

Because of the interagency bickering, Secretary of State Robert Lansing pleaded with Wilson to intervene and resolve the issue. But Wilson ignored intelligence matters and simply dismissed Lansing's concern about the counterespionage turf war. Without any authorization or any presidential intervention in the internecine squabble, the Bureau of Investigation and Secret Service continued to pursue the same threats and wasted valuable time protesting each other's abuses of authority.

McAdoo tried to leverage his close relationship with Wilson to urge the formation of a centralized intelligence bureau either under Treasury's or State's direction—a subtle power play, because State had no interest in mixing diplomacy with clandestine operations. To bolster his case McAdoo accused the Justice Department of abusing civil rights by using vigilantes from the civilian American Protective League (APL) as a supplemental law enforcement arm. Wilson took no action on McAdoo's proposal but reacted strongly to McAdoo's complaint about the Justice Department's support of the APL.[3]

The APL epitomized the dangers of efforts to pursue spies and saboteurs unsupported by law and precisely defined authorities. The APL was a makeshift vigilante organization formed in February 1917 that volunteered manpower to the Justice Department and military counterintelligence to root out subversives and draft dodgers. Although Justice explicitly warned the APL that it had no legal authority, overzealous members assumed that they had been deputized and arrested citizens without cause. In one collaborative operation with Justice's Bureau of Investigation, APL vigilantes in New York and New Jersey rounded up about 50,000 men on alleged charges of draft dodging. Wilson challenged the attorney general about these excesses. Gregory defended his civilian volunteers but agreed to change their identification badges lest they be confused with government investigators. The preoccupied president moved off to other matters of state.

President Wilson, however, still remained concerned about German spies and convinced Congress to pass the Espionage Act on June 15, 1917, the country's first comprehensive law since the Continental Congress had established the death penalty for spying in 1776. However, Congress stopped short of resolving the turf war between the Secret Service and Bureau of Investigation. The law gave Justice authority to prosecute persons for violations of the Espionage Act but also authorized the president to use the Secret Service for national security investigations when a state of emergency was declared. Without precisely defined authorities, both agencies simply continued to hunt for spies.

Some voices called for military control of counterespionage, but this idea was squelched because of America's historical concern about military involvement in the domestic arena. The military, in fact, had already played a role in hunting spies. The army's Military Intelligence Division (MID) also relied on the APL to assist in monitoring subversion and espionage around military bases. Although the army's counterespionage role was restricted to military facilities and personnel, MID ventured beyond these limits into the civilian realm. In one case, MID recruited two African Americans to infiltrate ghettos to gauge the morale of the black population toward the war, an operation clearly beyond its military counterespionage charter.[4] After World War I MID's counterintelligence branch was disbanded because of criticism of its role in domestic spying and its collaboration with the vigilante APL.

Attorney General Gregory strongly opposed military control of counterespionage and tried to allay the mass hysteria about foreign spies under every bed by claiming that German espionage in America had been eliminated. In a sarcastic note to a Justice Department colleague in April 1918, Gregory dismissed fears about widespread espionage: "There is quite a deal of hysteria in the country about German spies. If you will kindly box up and send me from one to a dozen I will pay you very handsomely for your trouble. We are looking for them constantly, but it is a little difficult to shoot them until they have been found."[5]

Gregory proved to be right. The departure of failed intelligence officers like Rintelen, Von Papen, Boy-Ed, and Albert ended any significant German espionage in America. No major German spy was discovered for the rest of the war. As the war wound down and Gregory's assessment proved correct, the Secret Service's legal authority in a "state of emergency" no longer held much force. The Justice Department's Bureau of Investigation remained the only agency authorized and capable of pursuing spies. In spite of the turf wars, presidential neglect of the issue, and congressional reluctance to clarify jurisdictions, the responsibility for finding spies ultimately rested by default with the Department of Justice, the agency responsible for enforcement of the nation's laws and safeguarding civil liberties. Yet ironically, in the first years after World War I, the department abused rather than safeguarded these liberties in its zealous pursuit of spies and saboteurs.

SPY HYSTERIA BETWEEN THE WORLD WARS

Palmer, do not let this country see red!

PRESIDENT WOODROW WILSON *to his attorney general, Mitchell Palmer,*
at a cabinet meeting in April 1920.
Quoted by Morison, *Oxford History of the American People*

During World War I, the US government combated subversion at home by launching an ambitious propaganda campaign to alert its citizens about the dangers of foreign spies. The warning of British poet Rudyard Kipling—"The Hun is at the gate!"—became the watchword of the day. Various states went beyond the federal government's propaganda campaign to enact legislation banning German books and teaching the German language. Although the majority of German American citizens supported the war against the kaiser, some Americans viewed them with suspicion, if not downright hostility. Prejudice against German Americans set an unfortunate precedent that has continued until the present. During the next war, Japanese were interned in camps; in the early days of the Cold War, anyone remotely suspected of pro-Soviet communist leanings was persecuted; and soon after the tragic terrorist attacks on September 11, 2001, more than 700 violent incidents against Americans of Middle Eastern descent occurred.[1]

The hysterical fear of German Americans ended after the kaiser's defeat, but suspicion of foreigners was still fueled by the inflation, unemployment, and labor unrest that afflicted the nation after World War I. Immigrants willing to work for meager wages that were high by standards in their native countries became scapegoats for the economic woes of American-born laborers. A small minority of new immigrants had also fallen under the spell of the anarchism and communism that were spreading throughout Europe.

In the midst of World War I Russia had undergone a tumultuous revolution that was to set the course of twentieth-century history. Emboldened by their victory, the new communist rulers noisily insisted their movement was international in scope and would inevitably spread, by violence and subversion if necessary, beyond Russia to Europe and even to the shores of America. Meanwhile, anarchists had spread their influence in the American labor movement.

The economic downturn in America provided fertile ground for communists and anarchists. Their more radical brethren advocated the violent overthrow of the government and fomented unrest through riots and labor strikes. In 1919 letter bombs were mailed to thirty-six prominent American industrialists and political leaders, though only one reached its target and caused slight injuries.

The new attorney general, Mitchell Palmer, exploited America's edgy mood by inflaming spy mania throughout the country. A Pennsylvania Quaker, Palmer had his eye on the White House and decided to boost his presidential hopes by cracking down on the "Red menace" of Soviet communism. Palmer himself had been the victim of an anarchist assassination attempt. In the twilight hours of June 2, 1919, a thunderous blast shattered his elegant home on Washington's fashionable Embassy Row. The bungling terrorist failed to assassinate Palmer but accidentally blew himself up when he stumbled at the doorway.[2]

Palmer exploited this bombing to launch his crusade against radicals of all stripes. He immediately established a General Intelligence Division within the Justice Department's Bureau of Investigation specifically to root out radicals and named as its head an ambitious young lawyer named J. Edgar Hoover. Other agencies like the military's Office of Naval Intelligence and the army's Military Intelligence Division joined the crusade in hopes of reversing the cutbacks in their budgets and personnel after World War I.

All the agencies bumped into each other in their feverish rush to penetrate labor unions, the Socialist Party, the leftist Industrial Workers of the World, and even the American Jewish Congress, among others.[3]

At the dawn of the new decade, on January 2, 1920, Hoover's undercover agents arranged mass meetings of the radical groups they had infiltrated across the nation, and the Bureau of Investigation rounded up thousands of alleged subversives as they convened in thirty-three American cities. These "Palmer Raids" were conducted without warrants or any form of due process. Citizens without any radical connections were illegally held in detention, and in some cases were even denied food. Almost all were soon released, and only a few were deported as undesirable aliens. Palmer, who initially had been hailed as a hero, was condemned once the truth emerged about the raids. In a final act of desperation he sounded a nationwide alarm about an impending plot to overthrow the government on May 1, 1920. But May Day ended with a yawn, and so did Palmer's presidential hopes.

Palmer's campaign failed to unmask any spies or massive conspiracies against the government, and his lawless methods discredited counterespionage and made it synonymous with political persecution. American suspicions of arbitrary government actions against alleged spies and subversives dashed any hope of establishing a central counterespionage agency. As a result the United States would remain blind to the penetration of its government by the Soviet Union two decades later.

GERMAN ESPIONAGE IN WORLD WAR II

*We have at least one of our operatives at every strategic point
in the United States; in every armament factory, in every
shipyard in America we have a spy, several in key positions.
The US cannot plan a warship, design an airplane, or develop
a device we do not know about at once.*

IGNATZ GRIEBL, *head of a German spy ring in the United States.*
Quoted by Farago, *Game of the Foxes*

The decade of the 1920s began with Mitchell Palmer's massive manhunt against radicals, but fears of Bolshevism and the Red Menace were quickly forgotten during the Roaring Twenties, an era marked by prosperity, decadent materialism, jazz, and the bootlegging of illegally smuggled liquor. America had turned inward and isolationist again, and foreign threats seemed distant and harmless.

The Bureau of Investigation also shifted its attention from spy hunting to fighting the rising tide of gangsterism that was spawned by the Volstead Act, which prohibited the manufacture, sale, and importing of alcohol. Because of Palmer's excesses, counterespionage activities were severely curtailed in the bureau and the military agencies. In 1924 President Calvin Coolidge appointed his Amherst College classmate Harlan Fiske Stone as attorney general. Stone, who was later to become chief justice of the Supreme Court, named J. Edgar Hoover to head the Bureau of Investigation, which would be renamed the Federal Bureau of Investigation in 1935. Although Hoover orchestrated the Palmer raids, he escaped responsibility because he claimed he was only implementing Palmer's orders. The days of hunting Reds were over, but so, unfortunately, were any efforts to catch real spies.

Intelligence collection, which still remained uncoordinated by the end of World War I, was also significantly diminished. The army's Military Intelligence Division shriveled up to a mere 90 personnel from its peak of 1,441 at the end of the war, and its budget was reduced tenfold.[1] Spying was still associated in the United States with European intrigue, and was seen as conspiratorial, insidious, and inconsistent with American values. This distaste for espionage was epitomized by Secretary of State Henry Stimson's decision to cease funding for the cryptographic activities of Herbert Yardley's "Black Chamber," which enabled the United States to read the secret diplomatic traffic of other countries. As Stimson remarked later about his decision, "Gentlemen do not read each other's mail."[2]

Other nations experienced none of these moral qualms about collecting intelligence for their national defense. In the aftermath of World War I, the collapse of the global economy sparked a rising tide of militarist nationalism that set the stage for another world war. Espionage was on the rise around the world as nations jockeyed for power. As a result of America's pivotal role in World War I, the nation became a prime target. In the 1930s the United States would experience the most intensive spying against the country since its birth.

By the 1930s the smoldering resentment of the nations defeated in World War I spawned a new generation of tyrants bent on global domination. Adolph Hitler became German chancellor in 1933 by exploiting his nation's bitterness over perceived postwar humiliation by the Allies. Italy's new dictator, Benito Mussolini, defied the toothless League of Nations by occupying Ethiopia. And Japan's increasingly powerful militarists hungrily eyed China as their first step toward the domination of Asia.

Long before World War II, Germany and Japan anticipated that, despite American isolationism, their forces might fight a war one day against the United States. To prepare for that day, both countries began to establish spy networks inside the United States in the early 1930s. The Germans and Japanese focused their espionage activities on American industrial might and military preparedness. As in World War I, the Germans still made little attempt to acquire political intelligence on US plans and intentions, an incredible oversight considering their intelligence failure in misreading America's entry into World War I.

German espionage against the United States had still not improved between the wars. Suspicion of German Americans had largely dissipated after World War I, and, although "ninety percent of German Americans were hostile to Nazi interference . . . in the United States," German intelligence failed to find among the remaining 10 percent any major spies who might have had access to US plans and intentions.[3] The Germans also suffered from the same bureaucratic turf battles that plagued America's fledgling espionage efforts. The Abwehr, German military intelligence, led by Admiral Wilhelm Canaris, was the country's primary intelligence arm, but a host of other agencies in the Nazi bureaucracy also competed in the espionage arena. The army, navy, and air force all ran independent spy operations, as did the Nazi Party's Security Service, the Sicherheitsdienst under Heinrich Himmler. Even the New York office of German State Railways tried to run spy operations in America.

Most German intelligence activities in the United States concentrated on assessing America's war-fighting readiness, but the Germans also sought to steal technical secrets that could advance their own combat capabilities. Before World War II Germany was often able to obtain technology without resorting to espionage. American industrialists, who were naive about Nazi expansionism and supportive of Hitler as a bulwark against Soviet communism, simply sold information that would be of use to the German defense industry. The chief researcher for Standard Oil gave the Germans his company's synthetic rubber formula, which later enhanced the Nazi army's motorized warfare in Europe. The Sperry Gyroscope Company sold directional gyroscopes, and Bendix Aviation marketed its advanced airplane instruments to the Luftwaffe.[4]

The naïveté of American industry was understandable in the context of America's domestic troubles at the time. The United States was more preoccupied with recovery from the Great Depression in the 1930s than the plans of foreign dictators for world domination. The Depression had spawned a new generation of violent gangsters, and Hoover's Federal Bureau of Investigation was engaged in chasing hoodlums like Al Capone, John Dillinger, and Pretty Boy Floyd. The FBI, however, was still the agency responsible for thwarting foreign espionage, and it gradually increased its monitoring of Germans and Japanese in the United States. Fortunately, German intelligence agents often proved to be even more bumbling than their World War I counterparts.

The incompetence of German espionage in the United States before World War II is best illustrated by the case of Gustav Rumrich.[5] He was born in 1911 in Chicago, where his father worked at the Austrian Consulate and was thus a US citizen by law. After his father's reassignment, Rumrich grew up in Europe but returned to the United States and enlisted in the army. An arrogant spendthrift, he went AWOL, spent six months in the brig, returned to active duty, and went AWOL once again. He drifted from job to job in New York City, failing at all, even in one stint as a dishwasher. Desperate, he came up with the brainstorm of spying for the Nazis.

Rumrich volunteered by sending a letter to a retired German spymaster from World War I, Colonel Walther Nicolai, and he asked the Germans to signal their acceptance of his offer by placing an ad in the *New York Times*. In April 1936 the ad appeared, and Rumrich began his bizarre career as a Nazi spy in America. The nascent espionage relationship was often carried on through the US mail, with Rumrich receiving two $20 bills in an envelope for his first tidbits of information on a US Army regiment in Panama.

For almost two years Rumrich supplied his Nazi spymasters with a wide range of information about the American military. He wandered the docks of New York City and elicited tidbits of information from sailors and stevedores about ship movements, cargoes, and warship construction.[6] However, driven by his need for money, he often devised harebrained schemes to respond to Nazi intelligence requirements. When his handler expressed an urgent Nazi need for US Army mobilization plans, he concocted a ridiculous scheme to lure an army colonel to a hotel room, knock him unconscious, and swipe the plans. German intelligence headquarters nixed this scheme, but surprisingly it raised no concerns about its agent's mental stability.

In 1938 Rumrich's handlers tasked him to obtain thirty-five blank American passports for use by German agents to be infiltrated into Russia. He had absolutely no access to the State Department and received no guidance from his Nazi employers regarding the task. Tempted by the offer of $1,000 for the blanks, Rumrich summoned "his inexhaustible reserves of stupidity" to obtain them.[7] In an incredibly ridiculous scam, he simply called the local passport office in New York, claimed that he was the secretary of state, and ordered the blanks to be brought to an assistant at a hotel in Manhattan.

When Rumrich called the hotel to inquire about the delivery and learned that the blanks had not arrived, he called Western Union to hire a messenger to retrieve the package when it arrived and return it to the telegraph office, where he would then pick it up. To Rumrich's delight, the next morning he contacted Western Union and was told that his package had arrived. As soon as he had the package in hand, he was arrested. After the State Department clerk had received Rumrich's suspicious request, he alerted the authorities, who had quickly tracked down the hapless spy.

Because Rumrich was motivated solely by greed, he felt little loyalty to the German cause, and so he quickly incriminated other Nazi spies and saboteurs. In exchange for his cooperation he was sentenced to a mere two years in prison.[8] Among the spies he named was Dr. Ignatz Griebl, a prominent obstetrician who had emigrated from Germany and become a leader in the pro-Nazi German American Bund. Griebl also ran an effective espionage network, which had focused on US military technology. His spies were widely dispersed in the defense industry and had stolen blueprints for new navy destroyers, army bombers, and communications equipment.[9]

Once Griebl was confronted by the FBI, he too chose to turn on his Nazi brethren and revealed details about German spying.[10] However, the lead FBI agent on the case bungled the investigation. According to the official FBI website, the lead agent, Leon Turrou, interviewed those who had been named by Rumrich and warned them that they would need to testify before a grand jury, which prompted most of them, including the ringleader Griebl, to flee the country. As a result, only Rumrich and two others were sentenced to prison.[11] Although most of the Nazi spies escaped prosecution, Rumrich's blunders had still closed down the network and had stopped the leak of American secrets to Germany.

The exposure of a massive espionage ring suddenly turned into a public relations debacle for the FBI. President Roosevelt and FBI director J. Edgar Hoover came under considerable pressure to address the problem of Nazi infiltration. A congressional committee on Axis subversion headed by Martin Dies was loudly trumpeting the dangers of German and Japanese espionage. Rumrich's bumbling spy efforts highlighted to the American public Nazi subversion in the United States, just as Albert's lost briefcase had done before World War I (see chapter 13).

Popular sentiment about espionage intensified. Newspapers and magazines spread alerts about ubiquitous Axis agents, and posters with caricatures of bespectacled, buck-toothed Japanese and sneering, mustachioed Germans warned citizens of foreign threats lurking behind every American door. A row of spy films dealt with ordinary citizens who became embroiled in international conspiracies controlled by sinister Nazis. America's deeply rooted fears of alien subversion were reflected in the widespread panic sparked by an October 1938 radio broadcast about a Martian invasion of Earth. Although some listeners believed that the broadcast conveyed news of a real attack, it was merely an adaptation of H. G. Wells's science fiction novel *War of the Worlds.*

In response to these growing fears about foreign spies, Roosevelt issued a secret directive on June 26, 1939, that ceded counterespionage responsibilities to the FBI, the army's Military Intelligence Division, and the Office of Naval Intelligence.[12] The FBI was now the primary agency tasked with domestic espionage because the military's mission was strictly limited to counterespionage involving its personnel and facilities. A few months later, Germany invaded Poland. Within days, Roosevelt issued a public presidential directive formalizing the FBI's authority.[13] One hundred and sixty-three years after John Jay's Committee on Detecting and Defeating Conspiracies, the president of the United States finally institutionalized and centralized America's counterespionage efforts.

The FBI—now armed with authority, a significant budget, and more personnel—vigorously pursued Axis spies. In this pursuit its agents discovered one of the few major German espionage successes before the war.

⊖ ⊖ ⊖

THE SPY IN US INDUSTRY

THE NORDEN BOMBSIGHT

*America has been good to me. But I can never forget the Fatherland.
And I want Germany to have this wonderful invention, for
she may need it in the future.*

Nazi spy, HERMANN LANG, *to a fellow Nazi.*
Quoted by Wighton and Peis, *Hitler's Spies and Saboteurs*

The Nazis were well aware that air power would be crucial to their plans to dominate Europe. Although Germany possessed some of the most brilliant scientific minds on the planet, the Nazis were too impatient to wait for the fruits of their research to improve the capabilities of their air force. Nazi intelligence was tasked to steal American aviation technology in order to accelerate the development of German air capabilities. Aviation secrets would become as critical to the warring powers in the 1930s as atomic bomb secrets would be in the 1940s.

In World War I aircraft were primarily used for reconnaissance purposes, though some attempts were made at aerial bombardment. Simple physics complicated dropping bombs from the sky. The higher an airplane flew to drop a bomb, the more chance it would miss. The lower the plane flew, the more vulnerable it was to enemy ground fire. Precision bombing at high altitudes seemed impossible unless a scientific solution could be found.

A Dutch émigré to the United States solved this problem. Carl Norden, who was born in the East Indies of Dutch parents, worked as a mechanical engineer in Europe before emigrating to the United States, where he was hired by the Sperry Company to design gyroscopes for the US Navy. In the process Norden applied the technology to invent a precision bombsight and founded his own company to manufacture the instrument in mass quantity for the US military.

Using a gyroscope, Norden devised a stable platform for the bombsight that would be unaffected by the changing position of a moving airplane. The sight held the target in its crosshairs in a fixed position relative to the Earth, which enabled a bombardier to determine the exact second to release his payload. Aeronautical engineers at Norden claimed a bomb "could be dropped into a pickle barrel from twenty-five thousand feet."[1] Although this may have been an exaggeration, during a test run in 1939, B-17 bombers repeatedly dropped six 300-pound bombs squarely on target from a height of 12,000 to 15,000 feet.[2]

The Norden bombsight provided such a decisive advantage in air combat that the US government shrouded the entire project in secrecy.[3] Any shipments of machinery or parts for the bombsight were transported in trucks covered with canvas. The bombsight itself was covered until it was aboard an aircraft for a mission and was locked in a vault the rest of the time. Anyone involved in handling the instrument was required to sign an acknowledgment that he had read and was familiar with the Espionage Act of 1917. Pilots flew with strict instructions to destroy the bombsight if they had to abandon their aircraft, including firing pistol rounds into the scope and jettisoning it overboard. Before the development of the atomic bomb in the Manhattan Project, the Norden bombsight was one of America's most closely guarded military secrets.

These strict security measures, unfortunately, did not include intensive screening of those with access to the secret bombsight. When Norden founded his company, he hired a number of immigrants like himself who were skilled in mechanical and aeronautical engineering. Many were of German extraction, but American fears about "the Hun at the gate" had dissipated in the two decades after World War I. Among the German-born engineers Norden hired was Hermann Lang, a stocky, dark-haired immigrant who worked as a draftsman in the bombsight production plant in

Manhattan. Lang was a simple working man and lived a simple life in a modest home with his wife and daughter on Long Island. His quiet and reserved diligence on the job won him a promotion to assembly line inspector at Norden. Lang had no craving for money, no personal problems, and no resentment against his employer or adopted country.[4] Lang was simply a German patriot. And so he became a German spy.

He was the quintessential little "gray man" who becomes an extraordinarily effective spy precisely because he attracts no attention. Off duty, Lang sometimes mingled in haunts frequented by other German Americans that were prime hunting grounds for Nazi intelligence. In one of these haunts Lang met a low-level Abwehr informant and passed him some drawings regarding the Norden bombsight. One of Lang's duties as an inspector was to secure all the blueprints for the bombsight in a safe at the end of each workday. Instead, he took them home and, after his family went to bed, traced page after page onto sheets of paper. He was deeply, almost childishly, attached to his native country and believed it might need the secret device someday for its defense.

The chief of the Abwehr's Aviation Section, Major Nikolaus Ritter, was so intrigued by Lang's drawings that he traveled to New York in October 1937 to meet his new spy. Ritter had lived in the United States for ten years operating a textile plant and spoke perfect English. Ritter was pleasantly surprised when Lang laid out a tall stack of more drawings based on the bombsight blueprints. He offered to pay Lang for the information, but the engineer recoiled. "If you give me money, I would throw it away," Lang shot back. "It would be dirty money."[5] Although Lang's motivation may have initially been purely ideological, he claimed later that the Germans paid him 10,000 marks for the bombsight secrets.[6]

Ritter arranged for Nazi couriers to smuggle the bulky blueprints out of the United States in rolled up umbrellas.[7] Once the umbrellas arrived in Germany, Ritter took all of Lang's drawings directly to Canaris, who congratulated

THE NORDEN BOMBSIGHT.
US Air Force

the major for the intelligence coup. "The present high-level bombsight of the Luftwaffe is useless," Canaris told Ritter. "That is why we're building so many dive bombers, . . . because they are the only planes with which we have been able to be certain we could hit a target. This will revolutionize our whole bombing strategy."[8]

The impact of Lang's espionage could have been tremendous. According to the intelligence historian David Kahn, the bombsight was "Ritter's greatest spy success" and could have provided the Nazis with a "remarkable advantage over other European air forces."[9] The Germans, however, lacked the ability to mass-produce the bombsight. Lang traveled ostensibly on vacation to Germany to brief Nazi specialists on production of the bombsight, but the Germans were never able to fully exploit the fruits of their espionage by producing the instrument in mass quantities.

The Nazis were also unable to devise countermeasures against this accurate bombsight. In 1943 and 1944 the Third Reich was subjected to relentless pounding by almost 10,000 tons of American bombs that wreaked devastation on Germany industry, first obliterating Luftwaffe planes and aircraft factories, and then key industrial targets like oil facilities, steel plants, and transportation systems.

Still, the Norden bombsight could have been one of the most serious American espionage losses in history. The spy operation also reflected the dichotomy of America's melting pot of nationalities. One industrious immigrant had invented a device to defend his adopted country, and another had stolen it and passed it to a foreign enemy. In return for his secrets Lang was invited by the Nazis to resettle in Germany and assist in production of the bombsight. Yet for all his professed love for the Fatherland, he declined the offer, a decision he would later regret.

THE DOUBLE AGENT

WILLIAM SEBOLD

Gestapo official: "We can use men like you in America."
William Sebold: "But I am an American citizen."

Conversation between WILLIAM SEBOLD *and a Gestapo official.*
Quoted by Sayers and Kahn, *Sabotage*

Hermann Lang was the premier spy in a network of more than thirty sources reporting to Ritter from the United States. Ritter was pressured by his Abwehr superiors to establish better communications with the ring for more expeditious delivery of information. The Gestapo offered him a promising candidate in William Sebold, a German American who was visiting his family's homeland in the Ruhr Valley.[1]

William Sebold was born Wilhelm Debowski in Germany, where he served as a machine gunner in the army during World War I. After military service, he traveled to the United States as a sailor in the early 1920s and jumped ship in Galveston, Texas. He changed his name to Sebold, got married, and found a job as a mechanic in the Consolidated Aircraft Company in San Diego. In 1939 Sebold returned to Germany to visit his family, a decision that altered the course of Germany's prewar espionage in America.

A German American working at a US aircraft plant was clearly of interest to the Gestapo, who summoned him for an interview. Since he was now an American citizen, Sebold ignored the summons, but the Gestapo would hardly be deterred. After surveilling Sebold throughout his visit, Gestapo officers confronted him and demanded his cooperation. Sebold demurred until the Gestapo reminded him of his brief imprisonment in Germany years before on a smuggling charge, a trivial matter he had not listed on his application for US citizenship. If Sebold refused to cooperate, the Gestapo warned him, they would ensure the information reached the Americans. For good measure, the Gestapo had also stolen Sebold's passport, thus preventing his travel back to the United States.[2] His only other option was to be thrown into a Nazi concentration camp. As the Gestapo blackmailed him, Sebold heard loudspeakers on the street blaring out news about the Nazi invasion of Poland on September 1, 1939. Desperate, Sebold agreed to cooperate.

The Gestapo sent Sebold to the Abwehr where he was interviewed by Ritter. The Abwehr spymaster realized he should perform some security checks on Sebold, but the Gestapo had already interviewed the émigré and Ritter was sorely in need of a communicator. The war had started with the invasion of Poland and Ritter wanted to deliver intelligence from his American spies in the defense industry as rapidly as possible. Ritter advised Sebold he would be trained in communications for a few months and then dispatched to the United States. Sebold agreed to the task but told Ritter that, to avoid arousing any suspicions over his lengthier stay in Germany, he had to visit the US Consulate in Cologne to wire money to his wife.

After his training at a Nazi spy school, Sebold entered the United States in late January 1940 under the alias William Sawyer and set himself up as an engineering consultant in an office on Forty-Second Street in Manhattan. His front company, Diesel Research, was soon frequented by a row of Nazi spies with intelligence on the US defense industry. Sebold bought equipment to build a radio transmitter at his home in Centerport, Long Island, so he could forward the information immediately to Berlin. The Abwehr was so pleased to receive the timely intelligence that Sebold would eventually be used by more and more Nazi agents in the United States as the primary conduit to Berlin.

Among the agents Sebold met was Hermann Lang. Sebold suggested that Lang could provide invaluable information to Germany about the Norden bombsight. Lang looked at him quizzically. "Well, you work in the Norden works, don't you?" Sebold asked. Lang blurted out "Steal the Norden sight? Steal it—what do you mean? Why, man, I have already given the bombsight to Germany. . . . I'm a true follower of Der Führer."[3] Lang was proud to admit the achievement to his fellow German spy but he had committed a grave error. Sebold was a double agent working for the FBI.

Sebold had used the visit to the US consulate as a ruse to reveal the Abwehr operation to American officials. He agreed to play along with the Nazis and follow the FBI's direction. The FBI, in fact, had assisted him in establishing his office in New York and an FBI agent, not Sebold, operated his radio and communicated with the Abwehr. Every Nazi agent, including Lang, who visited Sebold's Manhattan office was recorded by FBI microphones and filmed through a one-way mirror by FBI cameras. From December 1940 to June 1941, eighty-one meetings between Sebold and Nazi agents were recorded by cameras and audio devices.[4] The FBI even fed tidbits of minimally useful information to the Abwehr to enhance Sebold's cover and improve his standing with his supposed German masters.

Double agents are an extremely effective counterespionage tool because they can accomplish a broad range of objectives. The double agent can identify his handlers and, at times, other agents. The double agent receives intelligence requirements, questions that can pinpoint specific interests of the enemy and targets that may require additional security or development of countermeasures. The counterespionage service can also analyze these requirements to identify other agents who might be trying to obtain answers to the same questions. The service can also use the double agent to feed false information to deceive the enemy. The double agent can also provide information about enemy modus operandi and communications that can assist in identifying, arresting, and convicting genuine agents of the foreign power.

Sebold accomplished all these objectives and more. As the principal communications link between Berlin and the its spy ring, Sebold knew the identities of over thirty Nazi spies. He also passed a dazzling array of Nazi requirements to the FBI, questions about American biological warfare, anti-aircraft munitions, gas masks, and ship movements. He was also the first to alert the FBI to Nazi progress in using microphotography to miniaturize information in size in order to prevent detection and facilitate secure transport. Sebold provided the FBI with the wristwatch he wore into the United States inside of which he had five microdots with instructions and codes for Nazi spies in America.[5]

Intelligence services can defend against double agents with proper tradecraft. At a bare minimum, newly recruited spies should be screened, their backgrounds checked, their information constantly assessed and corroborated to determine if they are telling the truth, spinning tales of their own or feeding information supplied by the opposition. The Nazis took none of these basic measures with Sebold since Ritter sacrificed basic security checks in his haste to improve communications from his spies in the United States.

Ritter's failure to investigate Sebold is all the more striking since Sebold was blackmailed. American and other Western intelligence services have abandoned blackmail as a recruitment tactic since the unwilling spy is cooperating under duress and will try to give as little information as possible or deceive his blackmailers. Because Sebold had been coerced into spying, the Nazis should have monitored him even more carefully before entrusting him with the vitally important job of espionage communications. The Germans had enough informants in the United States to perform at least some rudimentary checks on Sebold's comment about or attitudes toward the Nazi regime, and their suspicions should certainly have been raised by his request to return to the US Consulate, no matter how plausible his explanation may have seemed.

Even if the Germans found nothing suspicious about Sebold, basic security sense dictates that the identities of agents should be exposed to as few members of a network as possible, especially to one whose cooperation was coerced. Nazi intelligence violated this basic rule as well and compounded tradecraft errors even further by exposing Sebold to the entire network, a practice that should be avoided even with fully trusted agents. Ritter apparently was unable to find anyone else to serve as a communicator for his US ring, even though he could have presumably trained one or more of his many informants in America to perform the sensitive task. However, the information that Sebold was conveying to Berlin, which was carefully filtered by the FBI, was well received and thus the Germans decided on production and speed over fundamental tradecraft procedures.

The Nazis paid a heavy price for the lapse. At the end of July 1941, as the United States' entry into the war became imminent, the FBI swooped in on every member of the network in a single night, including Lang, the Norden bombsight spy.

On September 2, fourteen members of the ring stood trial; nineteen others had already pled guilty. The horrified Nazi intelligence chiefs and their arrested spies finally learned the source of the compromise. Sebold himself appeared in court as a surprise witness for the prosecution, and his testimony sealed the fate of the ring. As one FBI agent put it, "it was like shooting fish in a barrel."[6] The thirty-three Nazi agents were convicted a week after the attack on Pearl Harbor and sentenced to more than three hundred years in prison.

The Sebold case illustrates the dangers of using coercion and blackmail to recruit spies. As a result of the Gestapo's pressure against one loyal naturalized American citizen, the Germans went blind and deaf at the very moment they needed their eyes and ears in America the most. William Sebold was the first double agent run by the FBI and he dealt the Nazis a counterespionage blow in the United States from which they never recovered.[7] Their last futile efforts at espionage and sabotage inside the United States during the war would be testimony to the abysmal state of German intelligence activities in America.

GERMAN INTELLIGENCE FAILURES IN WORLD WAR II

This is utter madness.

The reaction by ADMIRAL WILHELM CANARIS, *chief of German Military Intelligence,*
upon hearing the details of Operation Pastorius.
Quoted by Wighton and Peis, *Hitler's Spies and Saboteurs*

He was odd in a goofy sort of way, not mean or harmful. . . .
You couldn't put your finger on it, but he was different.

Description of WILLIAM COLEPAUGH, *a Nazi spy, given by Willing in* "William Colepaugh"

Adolph Hitler was furious over the disintegration of the Abwehr's spy ring and immediately ordered an all-out sabotage effort inside America. Although Der Führer was surrounded by lickspittles who usually nodded in agreement with his most bizarre schemes, Admiral Wilhelm Canaris argued against the suggestion, insisting that planning sabotage first required solid intelligence, something the Nazis had now lost in America. Hitler, however, suspected Canaris's allegiance and stubbornly dismissed his arguments.[1]

Conversely, the slavishly loyal Nazi Party responded to Hitler's command. Walther Kappe, a dedicated Nazi who had spent twelve years in America as the propaganda chief of the pro-Hitler German American Bund, devised a plan and assembled a team of saboteurs. Kappe was a trusted member of the party because he had become one of its early members back in the 1920s.[2] At the same time, although he had become an Abwehr officer, he had little operational experience. He chose eleven men who were equally unschooled for the job and rushed them through a crash course on sabotage. Their only qualifications for the mission were that they were all German Americans, had lived in the United States, and spoke American English.

Kappe wryly dubbed his plan Operation Pastorius, after the leader of the first group of German immigrants in America. The amateur spies would be ferried in two teams to the East Coast of the United States by German submarines, one team disembarking at Amagansett, Long Island, and the other just south of Jacksonville, Florida. Both teams were supplied with bundles of dollars, forged documents, and concealed explosives. Once they had landed, the ten would disperse and begin preparing their attacks. Among their targets were aluminum plants, hydroelectric power stations, New York City bridges, and a railroad terminal in Newark. George Dasch, a former left-wing agitator who had spent twenty years in the United States and worked there primarily as a waiter, was appointed leader of one team; and Edward Kerling, a devoted Nazi and early supporter of Hitler who had lived in America for eleven years, headed the second one.

Operation Pastorius got off to a rocky start. Two of the candidates were drummed out of training. En route to the launch point on the French coast, the team stopped in Paris, and another member wriggled out of the mission by claiming that he had contracted venereal disease. Team members quarreled, one lost his alias identification documents on a train, and another discovered that their superiors had mistakenly furnished them with American dollars that were no longer in circulation.[3]

On the other side of the Atlantic, the operation fared no better. The Long Island team reached shore in June 1942 but immediately ran into a young coast guard officer, John Cullen, who was patrolling the beach. Dasch and his team members outnumbered the officer and intimidated him into letting the team go on its way. Cullen immediately reported the suspicious encounter to his superiors. By the next morning a coast guard team had investigated the shoreline and discovered caches of explosives that the team had buried. The local coast guard informed the FBI.

The FBI was aided in its search by the saboteurs themselves. Dasch and another saboteur, Peter Burger, went off together to New York City. No sooner had they arrived than Dasch informed Burger that he had no intention of blowing up a single target and planned to betray Operation Pastorius to the FBI. Burger had spent seventeen months in a Gestapo prison because he had been on the losing side of internal Nazi Party infighting and still harbored a grudge. He confessed to Dasch that he, too, had never intended to sabotage any targets.[4]

Dasch traveled to Washington and provided the FBI with details that matched the coast guard's information. The FBI agents now realized that they had discovered the mysterious foreign saboteurs who had landed on Long Island. Dasch passed enough detail to the FBI to identify all his fellow conspirators, who were all nabbed within two weeks after they landed on American soil.

On June 28, 1942, the FBI announced the arrests. Hitler threw one of his usual temper tantrums and tried to blame Canaris, but the Abwehr chief politely reminded his Führer that the Nazi Party had organized the debacle. The entire team of saboteurs was tried in a secret US military tribunal and found guilty. Defense attorneys appealed to the Supreme Court about the legality of a military tribunal, but the justices upheld the decision. Six of the saboteurs were sentenced to death and were executed in the electric chair in August. Burger was given life imprisonment and Dasch was sentenced to thirty years, but both were released and deported to Germany in 1948.[5]

In spite of this fiasco, the stubborn Führer refused to abandon espionage and sabotage in the United States. In November 1944 the Nazis dispatched two more spies to American shores to collect information on aircraft, shipbuilding, and rockets. The two spies, William Colepaugh and Erich Gimpel, were rowed in from a German submarine to the coast of Maine on a frigid New England night.[6] Gimpel was a German citizen who spoke English and had been recruited by the Nazis in Peru in 1935 to spy on cargo shipments to the Allies. After Pearl Harbor he returned to Germany and worked as an Abwehr courier before assignment to the Nazis' spy school.

Colepaugh was born into a middle-class family in Connecticut. His father owned a plumbing repair business, and his mother was of German heritage. Like Gustav Rumrich, Colepaugh was a ne'er-do-well. He flunked out of the Massachusetts Institute of Technology and was discharged from the navy as a disciplinary problem. He had a romantic attraction to Nazi militarism and made his way to Germany as a deckhand after his brief naval career came to a halt. Once again, the Germans failed to investigate his checkered past because they considered knowledge of English and German heritage sufficient qualifications for spying in the United States.

This ill-conceived operation was doomed from the start. Colepaugh and Gimpel came ashore near Bar Harbor, Maine, and trudged along remote country roads lugging bulky suitcases and dressed in trench coats totally unsuited for New England's harsh winter. Unbeknownst to the two spies, the British had torpedoed their submarine after they disembarked and had alerted the FBI that the ship could have been on a clandestine mission along the New England coast.

Colepaugh and Gimpel still managed to clear the area and catch a train to New York. Colepaugh spent his first few days in the city drinking and partying around town, behavior incompatible with the low profile of a spy. Suddenly, following in Dasch's footsteps, Colepaugh contacted a friend in Queens and confessed that he was on a Nazi spy mission. A few days later Colepaugh turned himself in to the FBI. Gimpel had already grown concerned about his partner's behavior and had abandoned their lodgings, but, with Colepaugh now cooperating with the FBI, he was caught a week later.

Both were tried in a closed military court. Although Colepaugh testified that he intended to compromise the mission from the onset, the jury believed he had a "belated change of heart."[7] Colepaugh and Gimpel were sentenced to death, but the pair received a reprieve when President Roosevelt died and the execution was delayed. President Truman later commuted their sentences to life, and both were released after the war. Colepaugh retired to a quiet life in Pennsylvania, and Gimpel returned to his homeland and wrote the story of his short and undistinguished espionage career.

Colepaugh occupied an obscure but unique place in American espionage history: He was the only native-born American to defect to Nazi Germany and sneak back into the country as a spy.

The failed operation rang the death knell for German espionage in America during World War II. The Sebold, Pastorius, and Colepaugh operations all epitomized serious flaws in German espionage that were rooted in Nazi philosophy. The Nazis' arrogant belief in their own superiority blinded them to the possibility of common human frailties among those blessed with German blood. The betrayal of the Fatherland by anyone born with superior German blood was inconceivable, no matter how many years he lived in a foreign land and absorbed foreign values. Hitler himself proceeded with the ill-fated Operation Pastorius against the advice of his military intelligence chief, convinced that professed loyalty to Nazi Germany outweighed experience in intelligence operations.

Because of this blindness, Nazi intelligence failed to perform even basic security checks of spies and saboteurs who were either born in Germany or of German heritage but who had lived for years in the United States. Because of this oversight, William Sebold, George Dasch, and William Colepaugh, all for different reasons, betrayed their Nazi spy handlers.

Just as in World War I, the Germans made little effort before World War II to penetrate the US government and acquire political intelligence that would have been crucial to gauging American isolationism and determining the plans and intentions of the Roosevelt administration about entering the war. Of course, even if German spies had obtained those secrets, the chief intelligence consumer, Hitler, would have undoubtedly ignored it. The supreme example of Nazi arrogance, Hitler preferred his preconceived notions to hard facts. The more he fumed over intelligence that did not fit these preconceived notions, the less he received accurate information from his cowering aides. As one Nazi intelligence analyst told a colleague, "When the Führer has made a decision, we must no longer disturb his intuition."[8] Hitler was more interested in derogatory information about his nemesis, Franklin D. Roosevelt, than secret American policy deliberations.[9] Hitler was obsessed with proving that Roosevelt had Jewish blood and eagerly pored over the most bizarre reporting about "the Jew Rosenfeld," as the German tyrant dubbed him.

Nazi intelligence failed not only in America but also throughout Europe. The majority of the spies whom Germany infiltrated into Great Britain were caught, and the British turned most of them into double agents in the well-orchestrated "Double Cross" operation that ultimately deceived Nazi intelligence about the site of the Allied landing on D-Day. "Germany lost the intelligence war," as David Kahn notes. "At every one of the strategic turning points of World War II, her intelligence failed. It underestimated Russia, it blacked out before the North African invasion, awaited the Sicily landing in the Balkans, and fell for thinking the Normandy landing a feint."[10]

Despite the Nazis' bungling, they did receive critical intelligence from an American spy that indicated the United States would enter the European war. This intelligence was sourced to Franklin Roosevelt himself, and, aside from its value to the Germans, it could have influenced the outcome of a US presidential election.

THE SPY IN THE
STATE DEPARTMENT

TYLER KENT

I believed myself to have been presented with a moral dilemma.

TYLER KENT, *a US diplomat and spy, September 1982*

Tyler Kent was a State Department officer assigned to one of America's most important embassies in one of its most sensitive jobs at a critical point before World War II. More than seventy years have passed since Kent was arrested for espionage. Although his case faded into obscurity after World War II, some historians still dispute whether he was even a spy. Others believe he spied for both the Soviets and the Germans, and still others claim he was an unwitting dupe in a British plot to lure the United States into war against the Axis powers.

Kent came from a long line of Virginia's landed gentry but was born in Manchuria in 1911 and was raised in various foreign countries where his father served as an American diplomat. Kent seemed to be an ideal candidate to follow family tradition in the diplomatic service. He studied at Princeton University, the University of Madrid, and the Sorbonne in Paris, and he mastered six languages on his world travels. However, he failed the oral examination for the Foreign Service, but his father's connections enabled him to join it as a communications clerk in 1934.[1]

Kent was first assigned to Moscow, where he later claimed that he developed an intense hatred of Soviet communism. At the same time, some observers, including KGB defector Oleg Gordievsky, claim that Kent had a Russian mistress and was recruited by the Soviet intelligence services to provide codebooks and classified documents.[2] Kent certainly exhibited some of the traits fitting a spy's profile. He was described by college classmates as a "brilliant linguist but a loner."[3] Given his aristocratic roots, Kent also deeply resented the inferior treatment he received at the embassy because he was a code clerk and not a full-fledged diplomat.

Embassy officers like Kent were easy targets for the Soviet intelligence services. Security was notoriously slipshod, and Moscow was a stark posting that offered few diversions for foreigners. US diplomats spent their off-duty hours drinking and partying, often with Russian women who were controlled by Soviet intelligence. Although he may have been a loner, Kent was an active partygoer and womanizer and also lived beyond his means.

After his Moscow tour, Kent was dispatched to London in 1939. By the time he left the USSR, the idealistic Kent had fallen under the spell of Nazi propaganda and firmly believed that the Jews were the cause of the looming conflict in Europe. As an embassy code clerk, he was able to read all correspondence between London and Washington on the growing Nazi threat to the continent.

Kent was appalled by some of the messages he read. He was privy to secret communications between President Franklin Roosevelt and Winston Churchill relayed through the embassy, a highly unusual correspondence because Churchill was the lord of the Admiralty at the time and not yet the prime minister. Although the vast majority of the American people favored neutrality, Roosevelt and Churchill were conducting a dialogue regarding possible US assistance to the British in the future.

Kent, who was both a virulent isolationist and a Nazi sympathizer, was outraged as he read the correspondence. Roosevelt, in his view, was secretly scheming with Churchill to drive the United States into a war that was opposed by the American public. The young communicator decided to copy all the correspondence and provide it to isolationist US legislators so Roosevelt's plotting could be exposed. But suddenly another opportunity arose.

In 1940 Kent met Anna Volkova, a Russian émigré who was as passionately anti-Semitic as he was. Volkova consorted with a group of pro-Nazi

Englishmen called the Right Club whose members frequented the Russian Tea Room, her father's London restaurant. When the club was formed in 1939, its leader, Archibald Ramsay, claimed that "Hitler is a splendid fellow with whom we should be proud to be friends."[4] Kent met Ramsay through Volkova and showed his new fascist friends the proof of Roosevelt's perfidy in his correspondence with Churchill.[5]

Kent later admitted that he showed the documents to his new friends and that Volkova borrowed some of them, which Kent assumed she was reviewing in further depth with Ramsay.[6] Volkova, however, was actually providing the documents to Duco del Monte, the Italian naval attaché in London, for onward passage to the Nazis.

The Kent–Volkova operation lasted only a few months. Both were arrested by the British police in May 1940, just seven months after Kent's arrival in London. The operation was most likely foiled because of both British penetration of the Axis and Kent's shoddy tradecraft. Britain's cryptographic service intercepted Nazi traffic indicating that the German ambassador in Italy was receiving messages from the US Embassy in London, including the Roosevelt–Churchill correspondence. The British domestic spy agency, MI-5, focused on the Italian presence in London, and its investigation led to the naval attaché, Volkova and, finally, Kent. The clumsy Kent then confirmed MI-5's suspicions. He was overwhelmed by processing hundreds of photographed documents and foolishly brought some of his film to a commercial photography store. Once the film was developed, the proprietor realized something was amiss and alerted MI-5.

According to a more conspiratorial version, MI-5 infiltrated the Right Club and learned that Kent had shown Volkova the Roosevelt–Churchill exchanges. The British then manipulated Volkova through their infiltrators into convincing Kent that the information should be passed to the Germans. These machinations would have allegedly served two British policy goals. Exposure of the operation would provide a pretext to round up Right Club fascists and, more important, embarrass and discredit the US ambassador to London, Joseph Kennedy (the father of the future president), who opposed America's entry into the war because he believed that the British were incapable of resisting Germany.[7]

Although the British may have truly wished to dispense with their homegrown fascists and Kennedy, this theory is challenged by other facts.

Kent also passed Volkova documents that strengthened Germany's strategic position in the war. The embassy messages contained information on British troop strength, strategy, and deployments around France. Testimony from captured German military officers after the war revealed that the Nazis had learned from Kent's documents that Britain lacked the men and equipment to launch an offensive in the winter months of 1940, which allowed the German army to prepare for its drive in the spring into France and the Netherlands.[8]

After Kent's arrest, the two governments arrived at an unprecedented resolution of the espionage case, undoubtedly because of the explosive nature of the Roosevelt–Churchill exchange. In a highly unusual move, the State Department stripped Kent of his diplomatic immunity and the British charged him with violations of the Official Secrets Act. A search of his apartment turned up more than 1,500 messages that he had squirreled away in clear violation of basic security regulations; and he had also given away State Department codes to the Germans, a betrayal that went beyond his political protest over the Roosevelt–Churchill dialogue.[9]

Because Kent was accused of violating Britain's Official Secrets Act, his trial was held in secret, a legal protocol that allowed the British to conceal from the public on both sides of the Atlantic the politically explosive messages that he had stolen. At the time of his arrest, Roosevelt was running for reelection against Wendell Wilkie. In the isolationist climate before Pearl Harbor, any hint of presidential cooperation with the British to pave the way for American entry into the war might have cost Roosevelt the election. On the British side, Churchill had been elected prime minister just ten days before Kent's arrest, but the new leader may have begun his term with some political embarrassment if revelations had surfaced of a secret dialogue with the US president behind the back of his predecessor, Neville Chamberlain.

Both Kent and Volkova were found guilty. She was sentenced to ten years in prison, and Kent was sentenced to seven years, but he was released at the end of the war after serving only five years. The United States did not prosecute Kent for espionage when he returned home—a decision, or perhaps oversight, that fueled speculation that he may not have spied at all.

Kent himself revived his case by suing the State Department for firing him without cause. He lost the suit but persisted in maintaining his innocence and attacking Roosevelt's conspiracy. In a speech as late as 1982, when he was seventy-one years old, he still reveled in his anti-Semitism and alleged that America's conquest of the Nazis had led to the conversion of a great part of the planet to communism. He insisted that he had only passed documents to his British friends out of loyalty to a higher cause, the US Constitution. In his last years, he descended into a self-absorbed fantasy world of conspiracy theories, including an allegation that the Holocaust never occurred and was fabricated by Zionists. He died in a Texas trailer park in 1988, leaving behind unanswered questions to a little-known but potentially controversial mystery of World War II.[10]

The Roosevelt–Churchill correspondence was made public in 1971 and revealed no evidence to support Kent's allegations of a conspiracy between the two leaders to push the United States into the war. In the isolationist climate of 1940, public revelation of the Roosevelt–Churchill dialogue could have had a far greater impact. If Kent had surfaced the dialogue publicly, would Roosevelt have been reelected in 1940? Would Churchill have become prime minister? Would America have entered the war with a different president? Although these are all now moot questions, Kent surely possessed perhaps the most explosive information of any spy in the crucial years just before America entered the war.

Still, revelations of the Roosevelt–Churchill exchange would probably not have altered the Japanese surprise attack at Pearl Harbor. Like the Germans, the Japanese actively spied on an unsuspecting America to prepare for their surprise attack on Pearl Harbor; but aside from a few notable successes, they did not fare much better than their Nazi ally.

Japanese Espionage
in World War II

*Unlike some other nations, the Japanese regard spying as
an honourable and patriotic duty.*

RICHARD DEACON, *Kempeitai*

Long before the shooting started in World War II, the Japanese government prepared for war by allocating the equivalent of $4 million for intelligence in 1934, when the United States had not dedicated a penny.[1] This government funding enabled Japanese intelligence operatives to fulfill their "honorable and patriotic duty" by planting networks of spies inside the United States for the remainder of the decade.

Some of these Japanese funds were devoted to funding fishing boats along the California coast to monitor American ship movements. Japanese companies in the United States also ferreted out defense-related information while conducting legitimate business. Even Shinto shrines were spying platforms, where monks tied miniature cameras to the talons of carrier pigeons and sent the feathered spies flying over military bases.[2] Before the attack on Pearl Harbor, Japanese intelligence had produced a 200-page guidebook on the US Navy, including clandestine photographs, maps, and locations of airfields and naval bases.[3]

Like Germany, Japan could also seek intelligence sources among its émigré population in the American melting pot. However, like German Americans, the vast majority of Americans of Japanese descent were loyal to the United States, and many would serve proudly in the armed forces during the war. Although hints of possible espionage by Japanese Americans appeared in messages between Tokyo and its consulates in the United States, no evidence has surfaced of any Japanese American in the US government spying against America before or during the war.

The use of Japanese Americans also had some obvious drawbacks. German Americans and German nationals speaking excellent English could pass as Caucasians of any nationality with false documentation, a racial advantage not enjoyed by Asian Americans. Once war was declared against Japan, the average citizen looked askance at any Asian in America, even if he or she was not Japanese. The pool of any potential spies further diminished when President Franklin D. Roosevelt ordered the internment of Japanese Americans a few months after the attack on Pearl Harbor.

In the 1930s, however, Americans harbored few suspicions about the Japanese. One group that actively spied without attracting attention was made up of Japanese naval intelligence officers studying English in the United States, a legitimate cover to live on the West Coast and seek out recruits in bars and clubs frequented by American sailors. Two of these officers handled the only noteworthy Americans spying for the Japanese before the war, both of whom were former US Navy personnel.

Former military or government officials are ripe targets for foreign intelligence services. They no longer undergo periodic security reinvestigations; nor are they subject to restrictions on travel or contact with foreigners. They may also work in postretirement jobs outside the government that allow easier access for foreign intelligence officers to establish and maintain contact with them for espionage purposes. Some may be unemployed and vulnerable to financial incentives offered by foreign agents. Most important, though these former officials may lose direct access to secrets, they often sustain relationships with friends and colleagues still in service and can elicit valuable information from them.

Harry Thompson, a twenty-eight-year-old farmhand from Maryland, fit this profile to a tee.[4] Thompson joined the navy and left after his first hitch with yeoman rank. Unable to find work, he drifted along the San

Pedro, California, waterfront until he was recruited by Toshio Miyazaki, a naval intelligence officer under cover as a language student at Stanford University, to spy for Japan in return for money. Thompson's motivation was pure greed, and he was the forerunner of a legion of active duty and retired enlisted military personnel who would offer to spy for money during the Cold War. He not only had easy access to talkative former colleagues but also bought a navy uniform and brazenly went aboard ships to pump seamen for information on gunnery and maneuvers in the Pacific. On one occasion he impersonated an active duty officer on inspection duty to steal information for his Japanese handler.

Sloppy tradecraft ended Thompson's career as a spy. He shared a cheap apartment in Long Beach with William Turntine, a jobless native of Saint Louis who had traveled west to seek work. Thompson, eager to expand his spy business, was drunk one night and hinted to Turntine that he could make good money by assisting him in his work for the Japanese. "The world owes you a living, don't it?" he badgered Turntine. "Okay, if your own country don't give it to you, another country will."[5]

His suspicions aroused, Turntine later stole a letter from Thompson's coat pocket from a "Mr. Tanni," Miyazaki's alias. Aside from Thompson's indiscreet revelation to his roommate, Miyazaki had blundered by sending a letter to his spy through the US postal system that contained espionage requirements and references to Thompson's spy salary. Turntine, frantic now that he realized what his roommate was doing, alerted the Office of Naval Intelligence.[6]

The Office of Naval Intelligence notified the FBI, which then set up surveillance on Thompson. Miyazaki's letter had been postmarked Palo Alto, so the agents decided on a hunch that the Japanese spy handler may have been among the English language students at Stanford. The FBI asked the university for handwriting samples of the students and easily identified Miyazaki from them. The identification was corroborated when, in another tradecraft lapse, Miyazaki was spotted by FBI surveillance meeting Thompson at his Long Beach home.

Thompson's sister was interviewed and told FBI agents that her brother had been working for the Japanese Embassy in Washington since early 1933. FBI agents also found the draft of a letter Thompson had written to Miyazaki in which, ironically, he advised that "I respectfully request that this letter be treated as my resignation from the service of your country."[7] The resignation came too late as the trap closed on Thompson. He was arrested and sentenced to fifteen years' imprisonment for the sale of US Navy secrets to a Japanese agent. If he had spied five years later, after war was declared, he would have been executed for espionage in wartime.

Thompson received a $500 payment from Miyazaki and a salary of $200 a month for his spying. In all, he received about $5,000 from the Japanese, or less than $7 a week for each week of his federal prison sentence.[8] The damage he did was as minimal as his payments because the US Navy was not at war and had time to develop countermeasures for the lost secrets. If anything, his case sensitized the public to Japanese espionage.

Two weeks after Thompson's sentencing, the American public would be further shocked by revelations about the arrest of yet another naval spy, but this time it was a former officer. John Semer Farnsworth seemed to be an unlikely prospect for a spy.[9] He was born in Cincinnati, and he finished first in his class in high school and excelled at the Naval Academy at Annapolis, where the 1915 yearbook noted that "had he lived long ago, he would have been famous for his desperate deeds and hairbreadth escapes."[10] After serving on US Navy destroyers during World War I, he returned home to study aeronautical engineering at the Massachusetts Institute of Technology and was then promoted to lieutenant commander.

Farnsworth also married a wealthy socialite. Dapper and handsome, he moved well in high society but soon enjoyed a lavish lifestyle that was even beyond his in-laws' considerable means. Heavily in debt, he violated nonfraternization regulations by borrowing money from an enlisted man. He refused to repay the debt and tried to intimidate the lender into denying that the loan was ever made. When he was thirty-four years old, in 1927, he was court-martialed and drummed out of the navy with a dishonorable discharge. He was unable to find work for years and eventually decided to peddle his aviation skills to foreign governments. He made the rounds of various embassies, including Russia, China, Peru, and Japan. Only the Japanese responded to his offer, but they were interested not in aeronautical advice but in naval secrets.

Farnsworth was an aggressive collector for his Japanese spymasters. In 1934 and 1935 he cut a wide swath through the Navy Department in

Washington and the Naval Academy at Annapolis to obtain codebooks, diagrams, and ship blueprints. On one occasion he stole a manual from under the nose of a former colleague while meeting in his Navy Department office. Distribution of this manual, *The Service of Information and Security,* was limited to a handful of high-ranking naval officers, and specialists later said that this theft may have required an entire reshaping of US fleet strategy.[11]

Farnsworth's former colleague, another lieutenant commander, was frantic when he noticed that the manual was missing but was immensely relieved when Farnsworth told him that he had only "borrowed" it because he simply wanted to keep his finger on the navy's pulse in his eternal hope of reinstatement. Such are the bonds of military camaraderie. Again, another American had refused to believe the unimaginable and never reported the incident. Farnsworth returned the book the next day, after copying it for his Japanese employers.

Farnsworth's aggressive hunt for naval secrets ultimately compromised him. As he made the rounds of his former naval colleagues, he made a grave mistake on one occasion, when he pressed the wife of another lieutenant commander for information about a new destroyer. The wife was suspicious about his heavy-handed, insistent request for an answer. Although he had easily elicited information from his fellow naval officers, a woman ultimately sounded the alarm. The Office of Naval Intelligence was notified of the navy wife's suspicions and was soon collaborating with the FBI to investigate Farnsworth.

Farnsworth also facilitated the FBI's investigation with other blunders. He was surveilled several times visiting the Japanese Embassy in Washington, a grievous tradecraft mistake that linked the spy directly with his handlers. Always the big spender, he also committed the cardinal error of flaunting his wealth by flashing crisp $100 bills around bars while under observation by federal agents. An investigation of bank records also showed that he had no explainable source of income. Meanwhile, FBI agents checked the bank records of Japanese naval attachés and found one, Lieutenant Commander Josiyuki Itimiya, with sizable deposits from the Japanese Embassy far in excess of his meager military pay. A bit more digging revealed that Itimiya often withdrew cash in crisp $100 bills like those that Farnsworth used to pay his bar tabs. Finally, an FBI review of telephone records revealed several calls by Farnsworth to Itimiya's apartment.

Farnsworth exhibited many of the flaws of those who would follow him in betraying their country during the Cold War. Visiting the embassy of the country for which you are spying and calling your spy handler on open telephones lines are classic security blunders in the espionage business, but many Americans would commit these same errors in the future. The revelation of unexplained wealth, however, is often the first evidence of possible cooperation with a foreign power, and Farnsworth's freewheeling spending provided the initial hard evidence of his espionage.

After the Thompson arrest, the Japanese suspended contact with Farnsworth and recalled his case officer to Tokyo, the usual procedure as an intelligence service pauses to assess the impact of a compromise. It was, however, too late for Farnsworth.

The day of Harry Thompson's sentencing, FBI surveillants noticed that Farnsworth was visibly shaken as he read the headlines at a newsstand. He immediately rushed to a bar and got drunk. Hung over the next morning, he went to a news service and offered a story on Japanese espionage activities in the United States. He claimed that he had been pretending to spy for the Japanese and had supplied them with false information as a clever ruse to divine their plans toward the United States. Avaricious to the core, he even dared to ask for $20,000 in exchange for the sensational story that he hoped would save him from a jail term. The news service refused to take the bait and went straight to the Office of Naval Intelligence. The FBI arrested Farnsworth a few hours later and charged him with providing Japanese naval attachés with documents unlawfully obtained from the Department of the Navy.

A dilemma emerged for the US government that would recur in other spy cases in years to come. The government was uncomfortable about a trial that would publicly reveal the naval secrets that Farnsworth had betrayed. Fortunately, Farnsworth agreed to plead nolo contendere, in effect a guilty plea whereby the defendant does not contest the charges. Farnsworth later tried to reverse his plea to innocent, but the judge refused his appeal, thus saving the government from discussing classified information in open court. On February 26, 1937, Farnsworth was sentenced from four to twelve years in prison, a light punishment because

Japan was not yet at war with the United States, and he remained in prison for eleven years of the sentence. Like Thompson, Farnsworth would have been executed if he had spied a few years later.

Farnsworth received about $20,000 from the Japanese for his four years of espionage. He had provided information about two naval destroyers, the *Saratoga* and the *Ranger;* a comprehensive navy handbook; and the firing patterns of weapons on every US Navy vessel.[12] If the United States had been at war with Japan at the time, his espionage would have eroded US naval capabilities against the enemy and undoubtedly would have cost the lives of American seamen. Fortunately, he was exposed in time for the navy to take countermeasures.

The Farnsworth and Thompson cases prompted intensive FBI monitoring of Japanese activities in America. In August 1941, just a few months before Pearl Harbor, the FBI and immigration authorities raided a Japanese bank in Los Angeles and surveilled Japanese diplomats in California, operations that netted more than 100 Japanese with false passports.[13] By the time the war came to an end, Japanese intelligence was pathetically relying on Swedish journalists to obtain intelligence on the United States.[14] As a result, Japan experienced one of history's most colossal intelligence failures—none of its spies evidently had an inkling of American plans to drop the most lethal weapon in the history of humankind on its citizens.

Even if the Japanese had recruited a well-placed spy in the US government, his career might not have lasted long because of a formidable American counterespionage weapon. During World War I Herbert Yardley, a State Department clerk, joined the army and established its "Black Chamber," the nation's first cryptographic unit. Yardley's success at breaking enemy codes was unprecedented, and it continued after the war at the State Department, where he provided American negotiators at the 1921 naval disarmament conference with the bargaining positions of the other nations at the table.

In 1929 a shocked secretary of state, Henry Stimson, found Yardley's work unethical and cut funding for the project, claiming that "gentlemen do not read each other's mail." Fortunately, the project was kept alive in the army signals service under William Friedman, one of Yardley's protégés. In August 1940, after eighteen months of intensive research, Friedman's code breakers cracked Japanese diplomatic and naval codes. They had already broken the Nazi codes with the help of Polish allies, who had stolen the "Enigma," Germany's electromechanical encryption machine. The Japanese, wary of the German invention, had devised their own state-of-the-art cryptographic machine, code-named "Purple" by Friedman's code breakers.

The Japanese considered their code impregnable and disbelieved the possibility of anyone breaking it. The decryption operation, code-named "Magic," yielded timely information about the Axis's military capabilities and plans. Decrypted messages from Tokyo indicated that the Japanese would not surrender even if the Allies launched an all-out land invasion of the country, intelligence that played a role in President Harry Truman's decision to drop the atomic bomb on the country.

Because the Japanese spy networks were run out of the Foreign Office and the country's embassies, the diplomatic traffic read by "Magic" also revealed complete details about spy operations. If there had been any highly placed spy in the US government, "Magic" would have undoubtedly pinpointed him. American cryptographers were also to play a major counterespionage role after World War II in uncovering the most formidable spy network in US history.

PART

THE GOLDEN AGE OF SOVIET ESPIONAGE— THE 1930S AND 1940S

The Origins of Cold War Espionage

They come not single spies but in battalions.

WILLIAM SHAKESPEARE, *Hamlet*

We should never send a spy to the Soviet Union. There is no weapon at once so disarming and effective in a relationship with the Communists as sheer honesty.

US ambassador William C. Bullitt's message to Secretary of State Cordell Hull, April 20, 1936. Quoted by Bohlen, *Witness to History.*

Although Ambassador Bullitt's comments quoted above may seem misguided in hindsight, they accurately reflect American naïveté about the Soviet Union in the 1930s. At the time Bullitt sent his message, the Soviet intelligence services were riddling the US government and defense industry with the most pervasive espionage network in American history. Five years later, Bullitt, sobered after his Moscow experience, changed his opinion and wrote President Franklin D. Roosevelt that the "communists in the United States are just as dangerous enemies as ever, and should not be allowed to crawl into our productive mechanism in order later to wreck it when they get new orders from somewhere abroad."[1] But by then his warning was too late.

An ideal confluence of circumstances contributed to the Golden Age of Soviet espionage against America in the 1930s and 1940s.[2] Communism had broadened its appeal to Americans impoverished during the Great Depression. The CPUSA, founded at the end of World War I, was hardly a mainstream movement in the 1920s. During the Depression, however, its membership tripled to more than 100,000 new converts who were disillusioned with capitalism and had been lured by the promise of the Great Soviet Experiment.

Impoverished Americans marveled at newsreels of Soviets constructing huge power plants and churning out tons of steel in gargantuan mills throughout the USSR. And along with this feverish industrialization, Joseph Stalin's resistance to the rising tide of fascism appealed to Americans who were increasingly alarmed by events in Europe. Communism had become respectable in America and was embraced by a wide swath of society, from labor unions and farmers to Ivy League intellectuals and antifascists. Roosevelt's New Deal policy of federal intervention to cure the nation's ailing economy seemed compatible with communist ideology and attracted Soviet sympathizers to work in his administration.

Extensive sympathy for communism, the presence of a large CPUSA infrastructure, and a wartime alliance between the USSR and United States were not the only factors that facilitated Soviet espionage in America. As a generally trusting and open people, Americans were easy prey for Russian operatives, who came from a nation where conspiracy was an intrinsic part of everyday life. Spying on one's neighbors, colleagues, and even family was as ingrained in the Russian soul as privacy rights and free speech are in America.

A twentieth-century visitor to a Soviet apartment would first be greeted by his or her host with a cautionary finger on the lips to keep silent. The host would then spin the dial on his rotary phone a half turn and insert a stubby pencil in one of the holes, a primitive tactic that allegedly neutralized bugging devices in the phone. Such rituals were commonplace during the Soviet era, when an average citizen could be reported by his or her neighbor for an idle comment perceived as antiregime and end up another victim of dissident purges. Even spying on one's family was glorified as patriotic. For instance, a thirteen-year-old boy, Pavlik Morozov, was hailed in the USSR as a martyr when he was murdered after snitching on his own father's anti-Soviet activity to the authorities. Although this story is apocryphal, Morozov was lionized in Soviet propaganda as a model for the youth of the country.

The new Soviet government brought this espionage tradition to the United States by dispatching its first intelligence officer there in 1921.[3] Three years later, in the United States, the Soviets opened Amtorg, a company designed to facilitate bilateral trade that was primarily a front for stealing industrial secrets. Soviet espionage, however, only began to flourish after diplomatic relations were established between the United States and the USSR in 1933, which enabled the OGPU, the civilian intelligence arm, and the GRU, military intelligence, to infiltrate their officers into the United States as diplomats.[4] The CPUSA was also ordered by Moscow to establish an underground espionage network to collaborate with Soviet officers. After Pearl Harbor, the CPUSA publicly supported a united front against the fascist enemy, and this common cause enabled Soviet intelligence operatives to broaden their contacts and burrow even more deeply into the US government and American industry.

The CPUSA underground and Soviet intelligence services achieved the most thorough penetration of the United States in its history. Every key agency of the executive branch was peppered with Soviet moles: the State, Treasury, Justice, and War departments, and a host of other wartime and New Deal relief agencies. The new Office of Strategic Services, the first central intelligence service in American history, was infiltrated with Soviet spies. In the legislative branch, staff members of Senate committees and one US representative, Samuel Dickstein of New York, were among the agents in the Soviets' network. Even the White House fell prey when a presidential adviser spied for America's supposed ally. The Soviets also spread their tentacles into the American defense industry and even penetrated the nation's most closely guarded wartime secret, the development of the atomic bomb in the Manhattan Project.

This Soviet espionage network in the United States had depth as well as breadth and reached into the senior levels of the US government. One Soviet spy, Harry Dexter White, became assistant secretary of the Treasury. At the State Department, Alger Hiss worked as an adviser to Secretary of State Edward Stettinius and was later a US delegate to the Yalta Conference in 1945, where the postwar map of Europe and the United

Nations were charted. Lauchlin Currie, initially White's colleague at the Treasury, entered the inner circle of the Roosevelt administration as a White House economic adviser. Duncan Lee, the personal aide of Office of Strategic Services chief William Donovan, spied against his own intelligence service for the Soviets. These well-placed spies were joined by a legion of lower-level informants who flooded Moscow with secrets. At one point the Soviet intelligence services were amassing so many documents from their spies that they could barely supply them with microfilm to photograph all the secrets.[5]

The sheer scope of the Soviets' network was an intelligence service's dream—and not only because of the volume of reporting but also because of the ability to corroborate information from the wealth of sources. Spies are imperfect, often seriously flawed human beings who can confuse information or forget details. Spies can be simple peddlers, fabricating information just to make money, or, more ominously, they can be double agents feeding information designed to deceive the enemy. With layers of sources in each key US agency, the Soviets had the luxury of cross-checking information and determining the accuracy and reliability of their individual spies. Stalin's intelligence chief, Lavrentiy Beria, was so stunned by the information that his spies had stolen about America's atomic bomb that he insisted on confirming it through other sources before telling Stalin. And the Soviet intelligence services were able to provide this confirmation because they had so many individual sources inside the Manhattan Project.

Soviet espionage in the 1930s and 1940s may have also been the most cost-effective spy operation in history. American spies from the time of Benedict Arnold to the present have betrayed their country for money, but the Soviet spies of the World War II era, driven by an ideological commitment to a communist future, were unique in their almost universal rejection of payment. Most of these Soviet agents not only refused money but, if they were CPUSA members, they also paid their party dues religiously "for the privilege of spying for the Soviet Union."[6]

The ideological motivation of this generation of spies did pose some problems for the Soviets. Intelligence services prefer to pay their spies to ensure financial dependence and thereby exert greater control. The USSR's unpaid and ideologically committed spies in America, however, resisted any such control. These spies were first bred in Marxist discussion groups that evolved into underground networks, but they never abandoned their coffee klatch mindset or practiced basic security. Discussion group leaders became "principal agents," which is spy jargon for an agent who for security purposes serves as the main conduit between the intelligence service and other spies. These principal agents believed that they knew their American environment better than the Soviet foreigners, and used the CPUSA's significant influence with Moscow to resist any control and ignore guidance from their handlers.

In most of the Soviet spy rings, all the members knew the identities of the others and openly discussed their spying for the Soviets with each other—a cardinal error in basic spy tradecraft. Because of these open associations, if a single spy was compromised, it could easily lead to the arrest of an entire network. Some of the spies also displayed admirable initiative without consulting their Soviet masters but disregarded security rules in doing so. Thus when Alger Hiss, an agent of the GRU, tried to recruit Noel Field, his State Department colleague, Field readily admitted to him that he was already working for the NKVD (then the name of the Soviet security service).[7]

In 1943 an exasperated Moscow Center finally cracked down and ordered its officers in the United States to improve operational security. Soviet intelligence officers advised their principal agents and couriers that they would now meet directly with individual spies rather than handling them through CPUSA intermediaries. Some of the spy ringleaders were livid and resisted. The order aroused such hostility in one courier, Elizabeth Bentley, that she took measures in 1945 that would begin to unravel Soviet spy networks in America (see chapter 25). Ironically, Moscow's attempt to improve the shaky security of its American spy apparatus would ultimately destroy it.

Until 1945, however, the Soviets still operated with impunity despite the shoddy tradecraft of their spies. Soviet spies did not slip through the cracks; they simply escaped through the gaping chasm of inadequate American counterespionage. The FBI was preoccupied with combating the more imminent threats of German and Japanese espionage and with fighting the domestic crime sparked by the harsh economic conditions of the Depression.

The FBI, however, did not totally neglect the Soviet threat. In 1936 an increasingly concerned President Roosevelt asked FBI director J. Edgar

J. EDGAR HOOVER in 1924. *Library of Congress*

Hoover for a "broad picture" of subversion in America, and in response the FBI began to penetrate both the CPUSA and fascist organizations. But the FBI's focus was on subversion, not espionage. Hoover was more obsessed with the threat that communism could spread its influence in America than with the Soviet theft of state secrets. FBI agents busily infiltrated communist cells to learn their members' identities and gathered information on prominent CPUSA leaders whose activities were largely overt.

This focus on subversion led the FBI to neglect basic counterespionage operations. One of the most effective ways to catch spies is with your own spies, who have penetrated the rival intelligence service and thus can reveal the enemy's spying activities. The FBI, however, passed up opportunities to pursue Soviet officials who could have served as such moles. The establishment of diplomatic relations between the United States and USSR cut both ways in the spy game. The opening of the USSR's embassy in Washington enabled the Soviet intelligence services to place officers under diplomatic cover but also provided potential recruitment targets for US counterespionage. The FBI, however, failed to take the offensive to recruit sources from among these Soviet intelligence officers.

As one example, Walter Krivitsky, a Soviet intelligence officer, fled to the United States and appeared in 1939 before a congressional committee on subversion to reveal a wealth of information about the USSR's intelligence activities. Besides their obvious intelligence value, defectors like Krivitsky can also pinpoint vulnerabilities among colleagues who might be disaffected—but again the FBI never exploited him for such leads. In another example, the FBI received an anonymous letter in 1943 whose author was undoubtedly an official at the Soviet embassy. The letter named the Soviet intelligence chief at the embassy and several of his colleagues and referred to a "networks of agents."[8] The FBI fielded surveillance on the Soviet officials named in the letter, but yet again it made little attempt to recruit them as sources.

The timing for the recruitment of Soviet intelligence officers to spy on the USSR was particularly ripe in the late 1930s and 1940s. Stalin's purges had escalated, and the Red Army and the Soviet intelligence services were under intense scrutiny for possible disaffection with his regime. A summons to return to Moscow or a curtailment of an overseas tour could have been a harbinger of imprisonment in a Siberian camp or even execution. News of Stalin's show trials had already reached the West by the late 1930s, and this drove disillusioned members from the CPUSA. Stalin's purges presented an excellent pretext for the FBI to sidle up to Soviet intelligence operatives concerned about their fate and offer them safe harbor—in return, of course, for information about Soviet espionage in the United States.

In fairness to the FBI, no other pertinent agency of the US government paid much attention to Soviet activities, especially after the USSR became a wartime ally. President Roosevelt himself was wary about alienating the USSR, and thus a rejected recruitment approach to a Soviet official that was followed by diplomatic protests from Moscow may have incurred the president's wrath against the FBI. The Office of Strategic Services was focused on espionage against the Axis powers, and its chief, "Wild Bill" Donovan, believed that the establishment of an intelligence-sharing relationship with the nation's new Soviet ally would be beneficial, but Hoover quashed the proposal. Other senior US government officials, including the president himself, would dismiss warnings even when confronted with glaring proof of Soviet spying.

Americans were generally incredulous that their Soviet ally would have the temerity to infiltrate its spies into the US government and that prominent US government officials would be so disloyal as to collaborate with them. Eventually, however, evidence of widespread Soviet espionage surfaced through defectors from the cause—but even then many naive Americans refused to accept the fact that US government officials who had been entrusted with the nation's secrets were engaging in espionage. Yet the extent of Soviet espionage in the 1930s and 1940s was finally confirmed beyond doubt—though not through the FBI's monitoring of communist subversion but by defectors and a squad of American cryptographers who toiled in obscurity during and after World War II.

America's
Counterespionage
Weapon

Venona

I stood in the vestibule of the enemy's house,
having entered by stealth.

ROBERT LAMPHERE, *FBI liaison to the Venona Project,*
in his book The FBI–KGB War

The story of American counterespionage in the years immediately after
World War II is the story of the Venona Project.[1] Ironically, Joseph Stalin
himself was responsible for a project that led to the discovery of the most
extensive spy network in American history.

Stalin's decision to sign a nonaggression pact with Adolph Hitler in 1939
not only drove American communists from the Communist Party but also
jolted the US government. As a result, the FBI intensified its hunt for communists, and the army, which was responsible for signals intelligence, also
took action. In a move that was to have a monumental impact on Soviet
espionage, the US Army started collecting enciphered message traffic from
Soviet diplomatic and trade missions in the United States. Long before the
days of satellite communications, foreign missions used the commercial
telephone lines of the host country to communicate their correspondence
to their capitals. Like other embassies, the USSR's diplomatic missions

encrypted these communications, and the unreadable Soviet messages simply stacked up on army desks for the next few years.

Hitler violated the pact and invaded Russia in 1941, the Japanese attacked Pearl Harbor in December of that same year, and the United States and USSR became wartime allies. The messages continued to pile up until rumblings of independent peace overtures by Stalin to Hitler prompted the army to attempt decryption of the traffic.[2] A team of cryptographers labored in strict secrecy during the next two years on a seemingly impossible task in Arlington Hall, a girls' school in suburban Virginia that had been converted into an army facility.

The Soviets used a simple yet unbreakable encryption system of "one-time pads." The system involved substituting random sets of numbers on the pads for the letters of the text. The sender and recipient had identical copies of the pad, and each used his copy to encrypt and decrypt messages. Although the army could intercept the encrypted messages, the random nature of the numbers made decryption impossible. At the same time the contribution of American cryptography to national security had progressed considerably since Elbridge Gerry, Samuel West, and Elisha Porter deciphered the letter proving Benjamin Church's espionage in 1775. Meredith Gardner, a brilliant linguist, had already worked on the successful breaking of Japanese codes in the "Magic" project, and he was among the cryptographers assigned to tackle Venona, the code name for the Russian codebreaking task.

The hours were long and the work unglamorous for Gardner and his colleagues as they labored to discern patterns among the incomprehensible jumble of numbers that could enable them to crack the code. A decisive breakthrough occurred in 1944, when Venona cryptographers discovered a gross mistake by the Soviets. Even the simplest mistake can be costly in espionage. A single error can compromise an entire operation, and there is no more glaring illustration of this in espionage history than the Soviet misstep with their encryption system in the early 1940s.

Ironically, the sheer volume of intelligence activity was responsible for the mistake. The Soviets were collecting so much information that demand for one-time pads outpaced production. In 1942, someone in the NKVD simply made copies of pads and sent them out for reuse to overseas installations. The blunder negated the basic "one time" principle in the system.[3]

The Venona team learned of the mistake by distinguishing patterns that showed separate messages had been enciphered using the same pad. Even with this breakthrough, the army code breakers were only able to decode portions of messages.

Gardner and his colleagues began a slow and painstaking reconstruction of Soviet codes, and by the summer of 1946 Venona research had revealed that the traffic not only concerned diplomatic and trade issues but also Soviet intelligence activities. Gardner made a startling discovery on December 20, 1946, ironically the twenty-ninth anniversary of the Soviet intelligence services. Officers of the MGB (Ministry of State Security, then the name of the Soviet security service) celebrated this anniversary around the world clinking vodka glasses in toasts, unaware that the Americans were tugging on the first threads that would unravel the greatest spy network in the history of the Soviet intelligence services. Gardner decoded a 1944 message that included the names of scientists working on the development of an atomic bomb, the first indication that Soviet intelligence had penetrated the US government's most guarded secret of World War II.[4]

Gardner had uncovered a nugget in a counterespionage gold mine. From 1947 to 1952 his Venona team deciphered messages sent between Moscow and its US installations during the period 1942–44. The messages decrypted by Venona revealed a massive Soviet espionage conspiracy that included 349 covert agents (180 identified by name), which undoubtedly did not represent the entire network because the decrypts represented only a fraction of Soviet correspondence.[5] Among these agents were high-ranking government officials who had already been exposed by defectors and whose cases had been politicized by both liberals and conservatives in the debate over communist influence in America. Venona also uncovered more nuggets about Soviet penetration of the Manhattan Project that would lead to the most controversial espionage trial of the century.

The deciphered messages offered considerable insight into Soviet tradecraft. The Soviets employed two parallel espionage structures to collect intelligence. The "legal" operation was run by Soviet diplomats under cover in official installations in the United States. A parallel "illegal" system was operated by Soviet intelligence officers who lived and worked in foreign countries with no ostensible affiliation with official Soviet establishments so they could escape detection by local security services. These "illegals" had no diplomatic immunity and were thus vulnerable to arrest and imprisonment if caught spying, but the benign operating environment in the unsuspecting United States encouraged the Soviets to flood illegals into the country.

The FBI was advised about the Venona messages, and Special Agent Robert Lamphere was assigned as liaison to the project in October 1948 to determine the identities of the many code-named spies in the messages. His job was as frustrating as it was rewarding. Because of the sensitivity of the project, information derived from Venona, no matter how damning, could not be used in open court, and FBI counterspies had to search for other evidence to convict the traitors unmasked in the deciphered messages.

The Venona Project was initially shrouded in such secrecy that the CIA was not advised about it until late 1952, undoubtedly because the intercepted messages revealed that its forerunner, the wartime Office of Strategic Services, had been extensively penetrated by the Soviets.[6] The CIA was not the only one kept in the dark; debate still continues today about Truman's knowledge of the project.[7] In 1995, forty years after the end of World War II, Director of Central Intelligence John Deutch declassified the Venona Project and released forty-nine messages. During the next year almost 2,900 messages were released to the public.

Before the release, however, the KGB had been better informed about Venona than the US president and the American public. Presidential adviser Lauchlin Currie had stumbled onto information about American attempts to break Soviet codes and tipped the CPUSA as early as 1944, and Kim Philby, a Soviet spy in British intelligence, was given access to Venona material during his tour as intelligence liaison from 1949 to 1951. Even more damaging was the presence of a Soviet mole, William Weisband, inside the project itself.

Weisband was born in 1908 in Odessa to Russian parents who emigrated with their three sons to the United States in 1924. After studying at American University in Washington, Weisband reportedly made a trip to Russia and was recruited in 1934 by the Soviet intelligence services at the young age of twenty-six. Although his motives for committing espionage still remain unclear, Soviet intelligence correspondence that has surfaced in recent years has revealed that he supported communism but was also paid for his labors.

Weisband had no natural access to American secrets and was used initially as an agent handler and courier for technical sources. He illustrated the perseverance of the Soviet intelligence services in maintaining contact with their low-level sources and support agents in the event that, by luck or design, their circumstances changed and they suddenly obtained jobs with access to intelligence. Weisband began his spy career as a young courier but would land a position where, in the words of the historians John Haynes and Harvey Klehr, he "did incalculable damage to American interests and likely changed the course of the early Cold War." [8]

Drafted into the wartime US Army in 1942, Weisband was commissioned as a lieutenant the following year, and he served in North Africa and Italy with the Army Signals Security Agency. Because of his native Russian, after his discharge from the army, he was hired by this agency in 1945 and assigned to its facility at Arlington Hall. "With the exception of atomic espionage," as Haynes and Klehr note, "one could hardly imagine a post of greater interest to Soviet intelligence." [9] The Soviets were about to learn about the increasing discovery of their spies through the Venona Project.

Gardner would later recall that Weisband used to look over his shoulder and watch him decrypt the list of atomic scientists in the fateful NKGB message of December 1944 (the name for the Soviet security service was changed from the NKVD to NKGB, the Russian acronym for the People's Commissariat for State Security, in 1943). Although the NKGB learned the secret of Venona years before the CIA did, Weisband did not deliver the explosive news to them until 1948. [10] For security reasons, the NKGB had suspended contact with its most valuable spies, including Weisband, after defectors from the Soviet cause began to expose the vast extent of Soviet espionage in America.

Once the Soviets learned of the compromise of their ciphers, they implemented measures to prevent further American code breaking. An agitated Weisband reported to the NKGB that his colleagues were experiencing new difficulties in reading Soviet correspondence and suspected a spy in their midst. Fearing he would be unmasked, Weisband asked his NKGB handlers for asylum, which they eventually granted, but he never chose that path.

Ironically, the Venona secret that he betrayed ultimately led to his exposure. Decryption of Soviet messages eventually led to a number of sources betraying technical information to the Soviets, including Jones York, an aeronautical engineer in the Northrop Corporation. When questioned by the FBI in the late 1940s, York confessed that he had passed classified information on aircraft specifications, and he identified one of his handlers as "Bill Villesbend" (Weisband had made a tradecraft error by once divulging his real surname to York, who garbled it to the FBI).[11] Weisband had now come to the attention of American counterespionage not as a suspect spy in the Venona Project but as a courier and agent handler.

Weisband was questioned by the FBI both in 1950 and 1953, and he steadfastly denied any espionage and absolutely refused to cooperate further. He and his wife, a fellow employee at the National Security Agency (the reorganized successor to the Army Signal Security Agency), were both fired for disloyalty. He was also summoned to appear before a grand jury regarding his possible Communist Party activity. Instead of appearing and taking the Fifth Amendment, he simply ignored the subpoena. As a result, he was convicted for contempt and sentenced to a year in prison. He was never prosecuted for espionage. York's identification was considered insufficient evidence, and once again the existence of the Venona Project was deemed too sensitive to be revealed in court.

Although Weisband still remains a relatively unknown figure in the pantheon of Soviet spies of the era, his compromise of the Venona Project inflicted significant damage well beyond the realm of counterespionage. The cryptographers at Arlington Hall had also succeeded in deciphering Soviet military along with intelligence correspondence. The Soviets, armed with this knowledge, switched to new systems and destroyed the United States' ability to monitor the Red Army in the early days of the Cold War. As Haynes and Klehr indicate, an emboldened Stalin moved massive amounts of arms and military equipment to North Korea and approved the regime's invasion of the south in June 1950. American code breakers, then deaf to these maneuvers, could provide no warning of the surprise attack of South Korea to policymakers who may have been able to exercise options to prevent a conflict that resulted in the deaths of 35,000 American soldiers.[12]

Weisband spent a year in prison for passing secrets that ultimately played a role in causing these American deaths. After his imprisonment he spent the rest of his life in obscurity and died of a massive heart attack in May 1967 while driving his car.[13] He was taking his family on a Mother's

Day outing to the Smithsonian Institution, an American traitor ironically engaged in a typically American activity.

Despite the valuable information Weisband stole for the Soviets, they could do little about the messages already in American hands except warn their agents. The Venona Project, however, was not the first indication of Soviet espionage against the United States. Defectors from the communist cause had already sounded alarms about spy rings and, just weeks after the end of World War II, these revelations of Soviet treachery would sow the first seeds of the Cold War.

THE GOLDEN AGE EXPOSED

IGOR GOUZENKO

We can't do business with Stalin. He has broken every one
of the promises made at Yalta.

PRESIDENT FRANKLIN D. ROOSEVELT, *March 1945.*
Quoted by Freidel, *Franklin D. Roosevelt*

Roosevelt's prescient comment, uttered only weeks before his death in April 1945, proved to be an understatement when the first revelations of Soviet espionage against the West surfaced. A month after the United States dropped the atomic bomb on Japan, Igor Gouzenko, a GRU code clerk at the USSR Embassy in Ottawa, dropped his own bombshell. On September 5, 1945, he walked out of the embassy for the last time and requested asylum from the Canadian government. In return he offered information of stunning proportions on Soviet espionage in Canada and other Western countries.[1]

For intelligence professionals, defectors are manna from heaven. Intelligence officers spend long hours spotting and cultivating potential targets in hopes of persuading them to become spies, but a defector appears unannounced with a trove of secrets, talks willingly, and, to some degree, is easily controllable because he or she wants a new life from and is dependent on his or her hosts.

Gouzenko would be the first of many Soviet defectors who would later abandon the USSR during the Cold War. After a year on his first assignment in a relatively plush foreign capital, Gouzenko was shocked when his boss advised him that Moscow was recalling him home. Soviets abroad still harbored vivid memories about the fates of their colleagues who had been recalled to Moscow during the Stalinist purges. Gouzenko resided in an apartment outside the Soviet compound, a practice frowned on for code clerks, who would be under less scrutiny by the NKGB and thus were more vulnerable to capitalist temptations. A suspicious senior GRU officer on an inspection tour in Ottawa learned about Gouzenko's living arrangements and had him ordered home for a review of the situation. Gouzenko was enjoying life in Ottawa with his wife and son and had another child on the way. Faced with an uncertain future back home, Gouzenko jumped ship.[2]

The gift of a defector can also be a Trojan horse, a stratagem by the opposition to feed false information or smoke out identities and the modus operandi of the enemy's intelligence service. Aside from initial skepticism about Gouzenko, the Canadians were reluctant to disrupt relations with their wartime ally over the tall stories of a disgruntled code clerk eager to settle in the West. Gouzenko knew that his story alone would be insufficient to win Canadian sympathy, so he squirreled away more than one hundred documents detailing espionage activities and passed them to the Canadians.

Despite Gouzenko's documentary proof, Canadian prime minister William Mackenzie King was still afraid to offend Stalin by harboring a treasonous Russian. But the scope of Soviet espionage in the documents was too overwhelming to ignore, so Gouzenko was granted asylum. The shock waves of Gouzenko's evidence of Soviet espionage reverberated beyond Canada to the United States, Great Britain, and Australia. Although Gouzenko had worked for the GRU, his knowledge of Soviet espionage also extended to the NKGB. In Canada alone, the information he supplied resulted in the prosecution of twenty-one of its citizens for espionage.

Gouzenko's information would also have a profound impact on the United States. Other Soviets had defected before Gouzenko, but their allegations were undocumented and were dismissed during the wartime alliance with the USSR. Gouzenko, however, had backed his claims with irrefutable documentary proof and provided details of specific operations with significant national defense implications. Among his revelations, he revealed that Alan Nunn May, a British scientist in Montreal, was a Soviet spy who had joined the Communist Party while studying at Cambridge. Nunn May had been involved in atomic bomb research, and the Americans crossed their fingers in hopes that he was an isolated case of Soviet penetration of the Manhattan Project. Unfortunately, a year later the decrypted Venona message with the names of Manhattan Project scientists in Los Alamos would dash those hopes.

Gouzenko also told the Canadians of a Soviet agent who was an "assistant to the assistant secretary of state under Stettinius." When the FBI later debriefed him, Gouzenko described the spy as "an assistant to Stettinius."[3] This difference was crucial because the latter profile considerably narrowed down the slate of possible suspects. The information pointed to Alger Hiss, who was not only an assistant to Secretary of State Edward Stettinius but also played a key role in developing the blueprint for the United Nations.

Gouzenko's defection was also a crushing blow to the Soviets, but they were able to mitigate the damage because of Kim Philby, their mole inside British intelligence. The Canadians kept the British and the Americans informed about Gouzenko's revelations. Philby learned details of these debriefings and dutifully passed the information to Moscow. Philby illustrated the importance of a penetration inside enemy counterespionage. He was in an excellent position not only to protect himself but also to warn the Soviets of the exposure of other agents.

Having been warned by Philby, the Soviet intelligence services scrambled to alert their agents and suspend contact with them. Stalin's NKGB chief, Lavrentiy Beria, who was angry not only at Gouzenko's GRU bosses but also at his own men, issued a harsh assessment to his overseas residencies about Gouzenko's defection: "The most elementary principles of security were ignored, complacency and self-satisfaction went unchecked. All this was the result of a decline in political vigilance and sense of responsibility for work entrusted by the Party and the government. G's defection has caused great damage to our country and has, in particular, very greatly complicated our work in the American countries."[4]

While the Soviets healed their wounds, J. Edgar Hoover was exploiting the Gouzenko affair to bolster support for the FBI's spy hunting efforts. Although Roosevelt was concerned about communist subversion and enlisted Hoover's FBI to combat it, even he was incredulous about the extent of Soviet espionage and dismissed earlier reports of spies in his administration's inner circle. After Roosevelt's death, Hoover believed that President Truman was just plain soft on communism. The Gouzenko case gave Hoover the ammunition he needed to prove the president wrong. And within two months of Gouzenko's defection, Hoover would receive another gift, this time from a defector at the heart of the Soviet espionage network in America.

THE "RED SPY QUEEN"

ELIZABETH BENTLEY

Heaven has no rage like love to hatred turned, No hell a fury like a woman scorned.

WILLIAM CONGREVE, *The Mourning Bride*

In November 1945 Elizabeth Bentley, a woman scorned not by a lover but by her Soviet spymasters, walked into the New York office of the FBI and told a startling story that was to shake the foundation of Soviet espionage in the United States.[1] Bentley presented the FBI with a wealth of detail about the espionage of CPUSA members, many of whom were already suspected of spying for the Soviets. By the end of the month, the information Bentley had supplied about the vast extent of Soviet espionage in the United States filled an FBI dossier of 115 pages. Still, the agents were surprised. Bentley hardly fit the image of a spy either by looks or background. She was frumpy and drably dressed in a simple flowered print dress and felt hat of the era. Her background was even more incompatible with the shadowy world of espionage. Born in 1908 to a New England merchant family, her roots dated back to the Mayflower, and one of her distant relatives, Roger Sherman, was a signatory of the Declaration of Independence. In an age when few women went on to higher education, she had also graduated from prestigious Vassar College.

As a student of Romance languages, after college Bentley went to Italy to perfect her language skills, a move that would have a profound impact on her future. Her Puritan ethic an ocean away, she enjoyed the bohemian life of an American abroad, but she was also revolted by the fascism in Musso-lini's Italy. Her social conscience was further kindled when she returned home to New York. In the midst of the Depression, jobs for linguists were few, so she worked for the city's emergency relief bureau, where she was sickened by the poverty around her.[2]

Bentley was ripe for recruitment by the CPUSA. As she later claimed in her autobiography, she was "haunted by the problem of our maladjusted economic system."[3] She typified the Ivy League intellectuals of the time, who flirted with communism because of its utopian ideals of equality and social justice. While studying nights at Columbia University in 1935, she was convinced by a friend to join the party. As her biographer, Lauren Kes-sler, suggests, she was lured to communism not only because she deplored fascism and social injustice but also because she had an urgent need to reb-el against her White Anglo-Saxon Protestant roots.[4] And her rebellion became complete when she went one step further and agreed to join the communist underground.

She was an ideal candidate for espionage precisely because no one would ever suspect her. Educated in the best schools, bred in a respectable New England family, Bentley appeared American to the core. Unlike the many CPUSA underground members of Slavic descent, she could maneuver in American society without attracting an iota of suspicion. Moreover, she was single and without family responsibilities and thus could devote all her energies to spying. Her only drawback was her membership in the party, but she readily followed the underground's orders to sever all overt ties to the CPUSA.

Her cover now improved, Bentley was assigned to Jacob Golos as her spy handler. Golos was born in Russia and grew up as an ardent Bolshevik. After the Revolution of 1917, he worked briefly for the secret police and was then trained in espionage by the Soviet intelligence services in Mos-cow. He was one of the early founders of the CPUSA, and he was dis-patched by his Soviet handlers to New York, where, as cover for his espionage activity, he ran the World Tourists travel agency, a Soviet front company.

Bentley worked her way from the ground up in the spy business. Golos initially used her simply as a courier to ferry documents from agents in Canada and as a "mail drop," an intermediary to receive communications between the underground and its spies. Bentley performed these low-level spy chores well, and her relationship with Golos flourished to the point where the spy handler and spy became lovers. The lonely world of espionage had brought together a fifty-year-old Russian immigrant and a far younger Vassar graduate.

ELIZABETH BENTLEY, the "Red Spy Queen," who later turned on her Soviet masters and gave a wealth of evidence to the FBI. *Library of Congress*

The relationship between spy and handler is a complex one. The spy depends on the handler to fill the need that drove him or her to espionage—whether money, ego gratification, or revenge—and the handler in turn depends on the spy for secrets. The sense of shared secret purpose and the heightened emotions from risk and danger of exposure often forge close bonds. In the case of a man and a woman, those bonds may develop into a romance, in which emotions may affect the objectivity of their professional relationship, sometimes with dire consequences. The complex relationship between Bentley and Golos would eventually symbolize the dangers of mixing romance with espionage.

Bentley's love for Golos heightened the emotions that already motivated her work, and he soon embodied her ideological commitment to spy for Soviet communism. She had no one with whom to share her secrets, not even her CPUSA comrades, whom she was forced to ignore because of her underground activity, so Golos became her friend, her lover, and her emotional anchor. Bentley herself later admitted that she "craved companionship desperately" and that Golos filled her need.[5] He also helped rationalize any doubts about her espionage commitment. When Bentley, like other American communists, became disillusioned by Stalin's surprising pact with Hitler, Golos convinced her that the alliance was merely a tactical move designed to ensure the survival of the USSR. Once her trusted lover allayed her fears, Bentley continued to spy.

Golos began to entrust Bentley with more responsibility. Under increased scrutiny by the FBI, Golos gave her control of a productive spy ring run by Nathan Silvermaster, a Russian-born economist who held a number of mid-level jobs in federal agencies. Silvermaster's network provided secrets on a broad spectrum of topics of interest to the Soviets, including war production figures, plans for postwar Germany, and political reports from the Office of Strategic Services about countries around the globe.[6]

Golos began to show the strains of running spy rings and hiding his activities from an increasingly watchful FBI, which grew suspicious of his flimsy tourist agency cover. In 1939 he was arrested for violating foreign agent registration laws, but he was released in a plea bargain in which he received probation and a light fine.[7] At the same time, in the paranoid era of Stalinist purges, some officials in Moscow believed that he had been turned against the Soviets by the FBI. In ill health and under siege by both friend and foe, Golos suddenly died of a heart attack on Thanksgiving Day 1943.

Bentley was devastated by Golos's death but vowed to soldier on to honor her lover's memory. In death as in life, Golos remained the driving force behind Bentley's spying. With her lover gone, she assumed control of his networks, but the KGB viewed Golos's death as an opportunity to improve the security of their operations and exert direct control over its spies.[8]

Moscow had grown particularly concerned about the security of Golos's network after his arrest by the FBI, and it tried to wrest control of its spies from him, primarily so it could reverse the slipshod tradecraft that jeopardized the network. The members of the Silvermaster Group all knew each other, a cardinal sin of operational tradecraft. They and their wives socialized with each other, and some of the wives even typed their husband's secret information. Golos himself exercised poor security and could have been directly linked through his association with Silvermaster to two well-placed agents, Harry Dexter White and Lauchlin Currie. Because he had attracted the attention of the FBI, Golos had to avoid contact with the network and let Bentley run it rather than cave to Soviet pressure to assume direct control. He was influential in the CPUSA and had a close relationship with the party chairman, Earl Browder, who in turn was well connected in Moscow. Browder fended off Soviet attempts to control the networks.[9]

With Golos now gone, however, the Soviets met with Bentley and pressed again for direct control of the Silvermaster network. Her case officer, known to her only as "Bill," was Itzhak Akhmerov, who had studied English at Columbia University in 1934 and had returned to America in 1941 as the chief of Soviet illegals in the United States. Akhmerov's attempts to persuade Bentley were met with stony resistance. Bentley later noted in her memoirs that "Bill" struck her as a "young whipper-snapper" with "menace in his voice," so she ignored him and enlisted Browder's support to retain control over the network.[10]

Browder initially sided with Bentley but, in the summer of 1944, NKGB headquarters finally forced him to turn over the network to its officers. Browder sheepishly advised Bentley, "Don't be naive. You know that, when the cards are down, I have to take my orders from them."[11] Browder gave her control of another network, the Perlo group, but she was soon stripped of that because of her sloppy tradecraft in using the telephone to call agents and meeting them at her apartment.[12] Bentley grew increasingly distressed as she lost the sole passion in her life, running Golos's spy networks.

The Soviets faced a dilemma. Bentley knew the identities of the entire networks and was rapidly becoming disgruntled because she could no longer handle them. Akhmerov tried to shower Bentley with money and gifts, which only insulted her noble ideological motives. "What kind of racket is this," she snapped back at him, "where they pay you to do your duty?"[13] To mollify Bentley, Anatoliy Gorsky, the NKGB chief in Washington, met her to announce proudly that she had been awarded the Order of the Red Star, a prize that also entitled her to ride streetcars for free in the USSR. This feeble, almost comic, attempt to placate Bentley backfired. She later complained in her memoirs that she felt Gorsky was buying her off.[14]

The Soviets had underestimated the emotional toll of severing Bentley's contact with the spy networks. In her view, they had destroyed her reason for living. Even after her defection, she claimed that her spying days were "the best years of my life, . . . security, a sense of doing something constructive, . . . the warmth of comradeship, the close bond of experiences shared."[15]

She grew increasingly alienated as she perceived that the Soviets were demeaning Golos's principles and his life's work. Lonely and without real friends, she would at points alternately flirt with her Soviet contacts or rage at them. Akhmerov even suggested to Moscow that the KGB find her a husband to fill her emotional void.[16]

By the summer of 1945, Bentley's nerves were frayed. She was gripped by paranoia and began to suspect that the FBI and NKGB were both pursuing her. She showed up drunk at a September meeting with Gorsky and harangued him, calling Russians "gangsters" and even threatening to go to the FBI. Gorsky ended the meeting and suggested to Moscow Center that Bentley be assassinated, an extreme solution that was rejected.[17]

Although Moscow dismissed Gorsky's radical suggestion, the NKGB shared his concerns about Bentley's instability and its potential impact on Soviet spy networks. These concerns proved to be justified. About a month after her meeting with Gorsky, Bentley approached the FBI with her sensational story.

The FBI debriefed Bentley extensively in the fall of 1945. She revealed the identities of more than eighty Soviet agents, twenty-seven of whom worked in the US government.[18] Unlike Igor Gouzenko, however, Bentley brought no documentary evidence to confirm her account of Soviet espionage.

The FBI tried to replicate its success in the prewar case of William Sebold by doubling Bentley back against the Soviets, but by then they were too suspicious of her erratic behavior to take the bait. After a meeting with Bentley at a New York restaurant in November 1945, Gorsky spotted surveillance as soon as he left. Gorsky's now-heightened suspicions about Bentley were confirmed the day after the meeting. Upon arriving at his office, he received a message from Moscow advising him that Bentley was cooperating with the FBI.

Once again, the NKGB's early warning system worked. Kim Philby was advised about Bentley's defection by his American cousins, and he in turn quickly told his Soviet masters. The FBI never stood a chance in doubling Bentley back against the Soviets.

Philby's news about Bentley ultimately saved almost the entire network from arrest. Because she had provided no documentary evidence to back up her story, the FBI was forced to obtain other evidence of incriminating activity. Thanks to Philby, the NKGB suspended contact with the agents

Bentley had named, and the FBI was unable to discover a shred of evidence of their spying. Once these spies were eventually confronted, they either denied knowing Bentley or simply explained their acquaintance with her in more benign terms.

Only two of the agents identified by Bentley were prosecuted and convicted, both on minor charges far less serious than espionage.[19] Soviet messages decrypted by the Venona Project eventually confirmed Bentley's allegations, but the information would remain too sensitive for use in court. Long before Venona was declassified, Bentley died of abdominal cancer in 1963.

Bentley's contribution to exposing Soviet espionage in the United States was never recognized during her lifetime. She was targeted in libel suits because of her revelations, and liberal critics persistently vilified her as an alcoholic who fantasized the spy stories to garner attention and fill the void in her lonely life. As one example, Archibald MacLeish, the famed poet and librarian of Congress, penned these verses in a scathing attack on Bentley: "God help the country where informers thrive, / Where slander flourishes and lies contrive."[20]

Although her lack of documentary evidence and the early alert to the NKGB provided by Philby may have saved the Soviets' vast network from prosecution, Elizabeth Bentley had ultimately dealt a mortal blow to their espionage activities in the United States. Soviet spies were neutralized by the revelations and ceased passing secrets, and experienced NKGB intelligence officers unmasked by her revelations were recalled home, further undermining Soviet ability to collect sorely needed information. The CPUSA was no longer viewed as a political party but as an underground subversive organization, and the American government and public were finally awakened to the dangers of Soviet espionage. As John Earl Haynes and Harvey Klehr, leading historians of the era, noted, "The single most disastrous event in the history of Soviet intelligence in America was Elizabeth Bentley's decision to turn herself into the FBI in 1945 and tell all she knew."[21]

For a brief time Bentley became a media celebrity when she was summoned to testify before the House Un-American Activities Committee in 1948. Dubbed the "Red Spy Queen" by the media, she was the first American to reveal to the public the vast extent of Soviet penetration of the US defense and national security establishment. She did not take the stage alone, however. She was joined by another American defector from the communist cause whose earlier warnings about the Soviets were ignored by the highest levels of the US government.

SPY VERSUS SPY

WHITTAKER CHAMBERS AND ALGER HISS

The [Alger Hiss] case had all the elements of a fine drama, accusations of treason, unusual evidence, the launching of a presidential career, and enough inconsistencies and ambiguities to leave the issue of guilt or innocence in doubt for decades.

JOHN EHRMAN, "The Alger Hiss Case"

Elizabeth Bentley's information revived the FBI's interest in earlier warnings of Soviet espionage from Whittaker Chambers, a former communist who left the party after he became disillusioned by the Stalinist purges. Chambers's warnings about spies in the government had been ignored over the years, but they were taken more seriously after Bentley's defection because her story echoed much of his information. Chambers was summoned to appear at the hearings of the House Un-American Activities Committee (HUAC) with Bentley and named Alger Hiss as a Soviet spy, which launched a case that would highlight the debate over communism in America for decades to come.

Chambers left the CPUSA in 1938, the year Bentley joined it. He was one of the rare native-born Americans in the CPUSA when he joined the party in 1925. Like Bentley, he was a student at Columbia University and his

American roots made him an attractive prospect for work in the CPUSA underground. After a stint as an editor for the *New Masses,* a CPUSA journal, Chambers cut his overt ties to the party and worked as a courier for the Ware Group, a spy ring of more radical New Deal officials run by Harold Ware of the Department of Agriculture.

Among the New Dealers in the Ware Group was Alger Hiss, then an official of the Agricultural Adjustment Administration, an agency created under President Franklin D. Roosevelt's New Deal to balance supply and demand for agricultural commodities. As Allen Weinstein noted, Chambers and Hiss were born "three years, 200 miles and two worlds apart."[1] Chambers grew up in a broken middle-class home where his father was an alcoholic, and he dropped out of college to live a bohemian existence. He was a talented writer and linguist and published an acclaimed translation of *Bambi* from the original German, the novel that inspired the famed Disney film. He grew increasingly alienated from mainstream American society during the Depression and gravitated toward communism like many other intellectuals of the era.

Hiss, conversely, was destined for success from childhood. He was born into a patrician family in Baltimore, but his early youth was clouded by his father's suicide. Hiss was later a brilliant student at Johns Hopkins University and Harvard Law School, where he studied under Felix Frankfurter, who later recommended him for a clerkship under Supreme Court justice Oliver Wendell Holmes. After Harvard, Hiss practiced law in Boston and New York until Roosevelt's election. Attracted by New Deal social reforms, Hiss entered government and worked in various agencies before joining the State Department in 1936.

During his college years, Hiss dabbled in leftist politics. The Depression ripened his socialist beliefs, and in the early 1930s, he joined the Ware Group. Like the Silvermaster and Perlo networks, Ware's circle started as a Marxist discussion group but soon evolved into a spy ring. For the CPUSA and its Soviet masters, these networks were excellent seeding mechanisms where one member could advance another into government jobs with increasing responsibility and access to intelligence. Hiss was a seed that flowered brilliantly. As he ascended in the State Department's ranks, he became a key intelligence producer for the ring and microfilmed classified documents to pass to Chambers, who would then courier them to the Soviets.[2]

WHITTAKER CHAMBERS, a former Communist Party USA member and spy, became famous when he denounced State Department official Alger Hiss as a Soviet mole. *Library of Congress*

ALGER HISS was eventually convicted of perjury rather than espionage, but the declassified VENONA decrypts and documents from the Soviet archives eventually proved without a doubt that Hiss had been a spy. *Library of Congress*

By the late 1930s Chambers's commitment to communism had been shaken by news of Stalin's purges. Chambers left the party in 1938 and urged fellow communists to follow his example. He pleaded with Harry Dexter White and Hiss to abandon communism and was shocked that Hiss and his wife were unfazed by Stalin's show trials.[3] Fearing reprisals from the Soviets, Chambers went into hiding. He got word to the NKVD that he would expose its spying if he or his family were threatened, but he also feared that he would be arrested for espionage if he went to the FBI. Besides, he thought, the FBI would dismiss his warnings about Soviet espionage given the antifascist climate of the day.

Stalin's pact with Hitler changed Chambers's mind. With the looming possibility of the United States being at war with both Germany and the USSR, Chambers arranged a meeting with Assistant Secretary of State Adolph Berle at which he revealed the identities of thirteen spies, including Hiss and Currie. The information Berle received from Chambers was passed to the White House, apparently to the president himself.[4] Chambers claimed in his autobiography that the president was indeed notified and told Berle to "go jump in a lake."[5] A separate source, the popular news columnist Walter Winchell, claimed that he learned of the allegations and told the president but was similarly dismissed. According to Winchell, Roosevelt angrily told him "I don't want to hear another thing about it; . . . it isn't true."[6] Discouraged by the president's reaction, Chambers abandoned his attempts to sound the alarm and focused on his new job as a writer for *Time* magazine.

Berle never passed the allegations to the FBI, which eventually learned about Chambers and interviewed him in 1942. Chambers's information prompted no action, because the FBI was preoccupied with thwarting Nazi and Japanese espionage in the midst of the war and by then the Soviets were allies. In 1945, however, information from Bentley and Gouzenko seemed to dovetail with Chambers's alerts. Gouzenko had warned of a Soviet spy close to the secretary of state, and Bentley and Chambers had both named Hiss as a spy. In addition, French intelligence had already passed a tip to the FBI in 1939 that both Hiss and his brother Donald were Soviet moles in the State Department.[7] Information about Hiss's spying had now been conveyed to the United States by multiple sources.

Meanwhile, Hiss's career had soared at the State Department. He had become director of State's Office of Special Political Affairs and was then named secretary-general of the United Nations founding conference in San Francisco. His rising career was halted when rumors about his spying for the Soviets escalated and he was forced to resign in 1946. Still, he had powerful backers who remained skeptical about the rumors; and one of them, John Foster Dulles, arranged for his appointment as head of the prestigious Carnegie Endowment for International Peace.

Hiss's fall from grace began at the HUAC hearings in August 1948, where the Golden Age of Soviet espionage was laid bare to the American public. Testimony by Bentley and Chambers shocked the nation, especially when Chambers publicly named Hiss as a Soviet spy. The HUAC hearings also sparked a raging political debate on the eve of presidential elections. President Roosevelt's party had occupied the White House for sixteen years, and Republicans hoped to regain it by exploiting HUAC revelations as proof of Democratic complacency about the communist threat. The most vocal HUAC member, young California representative Richard Nixon, captured the limelight at the hearings and launched a political career over the Hiss affair that would ultimately lead him to the presidency.

Democrats dismissed Republican harangues as election year posturing. Truman himself was skeptical about Hiss's spying and angrily accused his opponents of whipping up hysteria about the Red menace. Democrats attacked the credibility of Bentley and Chambers and pointed to their previous CPUSA membership and contradictions in their testimonies as proof that their stories were fabricated.

The accused people finally had their day in court. A parade of those named as spies, including Hiss, appeared at HUAC to respond to the allegations by the two defectors. Hiss flatly denied any involvement in espionage. Chambers was protected by congressional immunity for his testimony against Hiss at the HUAC hearing, but he abandoned that immunity when he repeated the charges in a press interview. Hiss sued Chambers for slander, but the trial in May 1949 ended with a hung jury and the judge's declaration of a mistrial.

A second trial began in November the same year. In the intervening months the Cold War had intensified—NATO had been formed as a bulwark against the Soviet Bloc, and the USSR had successfully tested its own atomic bomb. Chambers's allegation about Soviet espionage now seemed entirely plausible. Faced with this new turn of events, Hiss's defense lawyers savagely attacked Chambers's credibility by claiming that he had had homosexual affairs, emphasizing his past spying for the CPUSA, and insinuating that his allegations had been a political ploy to defeat the Democrats in the presidential race, which Harry Truman had just won by a razor-thin margin.

Despite the attack on Chambers, Hiss was damned in the end by documentary proof of his espionage, some of it in his own handwriting and typed on his own typewriter. Unlike Bentley, Chambers kept documentary evidence of Soviet espionage as insurance against any threat of reprisal for his abandonment of the party. Chambers produced four pages of State Department information in Hiss's handwriting and sixty-five pages of typewritten State Department secrets. A forensic expert testified that the documents had been typed on Hiss's typewriter, which was yet another illustration of the slipshod security of CPUSA agents. To supplement these documents, Chambers revealed the "Pumpkin Papers," microfilmed documents that included Hiss's initials, which Chambers had hidden in a hollowed-out pumpkin at his Maryland farm.

Hiss's patrician composure on the stand began to crack as he fumbled to explain away the documents and the mountain of details that Chambers provided about their espionage relationship. The tide had shifted against him. Prominent leaders in the executive branch, including presidents Roosevelt and Truman, had found it inconceivable that a trusted senior State Department official who had been integral to planning the post–World War II landscape could be a spy; but this time the evidence was overwhelming. After a day's deliberations, the jury found Hiss guilty of perjury in January 1950. He was sentenced to five years in prison.

Hiss was released from prison in 1954 and launched a campaign to prove his innocence that persisted until his death in 1996. The Hiss case became a bellwether of American attitudes toward communism for the next four decades. Debate on Hiss's guilt or innocence centered more on prevailing political trends than on objective assessment of the facts of the case. Depending on one's political views, Hiss was either an innocent victim of right-wing "Red baiting" tactics or a symbol of liberal complicity in the Soviet conspiracy against America.

In the early 1950s the Hiss case fueled Senator Joseph McCarthy's anticommunist hysteria by providing implicit proof of the senator's claim that more than 200 spies worked at the State Department. Besides, the USSR's overthrow of a democratically elected government in Czechoslovakia and its successful atomic bomb test, along with Mao Zedong's ascension to power in China, all inflamed anticommunism in the United States and shifted sentiment against Hiss. In the 1960s and 1970s, however, the pendulum swung the other way: McCarthy had been disgraced; Hoover was discredited for excesses in pursuing domestic subversion; and Vietnam and Watergate had tarnished the reputation of Hiss's nemesis, Richard Nixon, and sparked widespread suspicion of the federal government.

Amid all this debate over his case, Hiss had still supplied no new facts to prove his innocence. In the secretive National Security Agency, however, the truth had been known for years. The Venona Project continued in strict secrecy long after the end of World War II inside America's cryptographic agency. In August 1969, almost two decades after Hiss was convicted, Venona cryptographers deciphered a Soviet message about a meeting between NKGB illegal Itzhak Akhmerov and an agent code-named ALES. In the message Akhmerov reports that ALES proudly boasted to him that he received a Soviet medal for his work at the Yalta Conference in 1945.[8] The message included sufficient detail about ALES to pinpoint Hiss and, as John Ehrman notes, was "the single most convincing piece of evidence . . . to emerge since 1950."[9]

The ALES message was released in the declassification of the Venona Project in 1995 and 1996. Although some diehards persisted in maintaining Hiss's innocence, other evidence of his guilt provided overwhelming proof that he had been a Soviet spy. In the mid-1990s, Allen Weinstein and Alexander Vassiliev were granted access to Stalinist-era Soviet intelligence files, and their research, which culminated in *The Haunted Wood,* turned up more information of Hiss's espionage. A Soviet defector, Vasili Mitrokhin, who smuggled out voluminous KGB archives to back his claims, also fingered Hiss as a spy.

The ALES message is critical not only because it identifies Hiss but also because it provides some insight into his importance to the Soviets. The Yalta Conference was the last summit of the three great powers— America, Great Britain, and Russia—before the end of World War II, and it charted a course that led to the postwar world order. Roosevelt, who was to die of a cerebral hemorrhage a few months after Yalta, was already ill and has since been blamed for relinquishing control of Eastern Europe to the Soviets at the conference.

Roosevelt's primary objective at Yalta was to ensure Soviet participation in the new United Nations, and spies like Hiss undoubtedly informed the Soviets of the importance of the issue for the president. Armed with this foreknowledge of Roosevelt's bargaining position, Stalin was well prepared to insist on his own concessions, some of which had lasting consequences during the Cold War. As one example, Roosevelt's agreement to Stalin's insistence on veto power for permanent members of the United Nations Security Council like the USSR would have diplomatic ramifications on a number of issues for the next four decades.

Hiss was hardly responsible for the USSR's occupation of Eastern Europe and all its implications during the Cold War. Roosevelt's health, naïveté about Stalin's intentions, and preoccupation with the war in Japan all were among the complex issues that influenced Yalta's outcomes. But the foundations of large geopolitical events are built from several small stones, and Hiss's spying was surely one of them.

Alger Hiss may have become a bellwether of America's political attitudes toward communism, but he was only one among a legion of well-placed Soviet spies. And some of his fellow conspirators were even better positioned in the innermost circles of the US government.

The Spy in the Treasury

Harry Dexter White

*Under Stalinist leadership the lineaments of the archetypal
communist had entirely changed. The resolute and romantic
organizer of street war had been put away into a museum.
Into his place had stepped the iron bureaucrat—the well-dressed,
soft-spoken, capable executive who sat in the boardroom or on
the government committee. This man with a briefcase led a secret
life of his own.*

NATHANIEL WEYL, *an underground member of the*
Communist Party of the United States of America.
Quoted by Rees, *Harry Dexter White*

The strains of recovering from the Depression and fighting a world war had
already begun to affect Roosevelt's health in his third term. His vice president during that term, the progressive Democrat Henry Wallace, was
already contemplating his own cabinet choices if Roosevelt died in office.
Wallace, however, clashed with conservative Democrats, and Roosevelt
replaced him with Harry Truman on the ticket for his fourth term. This
choice was a stroke of luck for American national security, because Wallace
later said that he would have named Laurence Duggan secretary of state
and Harry Dexter White secretary of the Treasury.[1]

Duggan and White were both Soviet spies. After Duggan was recruited in 1936, he passed classified documents to the Soviets for the next eight years as he rose to chief of the State Department's Latin American Division and became a foreign affairs adviser to Wallace. His Soviet case officer described Duggan as a Communist sympathizer and "100 percent American patriot," a seeming contradiction that plagued him through his espionage career.[2] Duggan remained a starry-eyed Marxist idealist but a reluctant spy, because he was troubled by Stalin's purges, by constant fear of exposure, and the increasing concerns of State Department security officers about his loyalty. These security concerns led to his resignation from State in 1944. In 1948 he was questioned by the FBI regarding Chambers's allegations against Hiss. Nine days later, he fell to his death from the sixteenth floor of his office building.[3]

Wallace's other choice for a cabinet post, however, proved far more valuable to the Soviet Union than Duggan. Harry Dexter White was the most highly placed Soviet spy in FDR's administration. White—one of Treasury Secretary Henry Morgenthau's closest advisers—rose to the position of assistant secretary of the Treasury and was instrumental in establishing the World Bank and International Monetary Fund. His meteoric rise at Treasury mirrored Alger Hiss's ascension at State. White was born in Boston in 1892 to Lithuanian émigré parents who had anglicized their name, and his early years portended a successful future. After serving in the army in France during World War I, he studied at Stanford University and received a PhD in economics at Harvard University. After a brief stint as an economics professor at Lawrence College in Wisconsin, he was among the liberal intellectuals drawn by Roosevelt's New Deal to work in the administration.

White entered the Treasury Department in 1934 as an analyst on banking and monetary policy. Parallel to his government work, sometime in 1935, he was introduced into the Ware Group (see chapter 26) and started to pass Treasury Department documents to the Soviets through Whittaker Chambers. White's motivation was ideological and stemmed from his specific concerns about US economic policies. He gradually came to believe that New Deal economic reforms were insufficient and that the type of centralized control over trade and foreign exchange practiced in the USSR was essential to heal the world economy. And he had also been fascinated with

Russia since college and at one point had considered pursuing a fellowship to study in Moscow.[4]

White never joined the CPUSA and was thus less subject to control by his handlers than the spies who pledged allegiance to the party. In attempts to exert more control, the Soviets contrived to find ways to remunerate White and other ideologically motivated agents without insulting them. In White's case, however, the evidence suggests that the Soviets' lack of full control had little impact on his prolific intelligence production and exercise of covert influence within the Roosevelt administration.

In 1938 White was appointed director of monetary research for the Treasury Department. His career was progressing rapidly when his underground activity suddenly hit a roadblock. Chambers told White that he was leaving the CPUSA and urged his agent to stop spying. White, who was described by one Soviet intelligence chief in the United States as "a very nervous and cowardly person," was petrified.[5] He cut contact with the Soviets for a few years while most of the other agents known to Chambers were eventually transferred from the GRU to NKVD control.

While White was out of contact with the Soviets, Stalin continued his purges and signed a pact with Hitler. White was clearly unaffected by these developments because he readily agreed to cooperate when the NKVD recontacted him in 1941 and enlisted him in the Silvermaster group. By now he was a key assistant to Treasury Secretary Henry Morgenthau, so he was in an excellent position not only to pass secrets but also to influence US policy.

White's Soviet case officer, Vitaliy Pavlov, provided him with a list of Soviet points to use in influencing US policy toward Japan.[6] The Red Army was unequipped to wage war on the USSR's Asian front because its officer ranks had been decimated by Stalin's purges and it had suffered Germany's surprise attack in June 1941. To buy time to rebuild the military and focus attention elsewhere, the Soviets instructed White to push points that included harsh demands, such as the withdrawal of Japanese forces from China and Manchuria, which were designed to antagonize Japan, prevent any attempt to pursue a rapprochement, and spark war against the United States instead of the Soviets.

White dutifully included all these Soviet-directed points in a memorandum to Morgenthau, which was then submitted to Roosevelt and Secretary of State Cordell Hull. The president approved the harsh points, and Hull delivered the ultimatum to the Japanese at the end of November, which undoubtedly strengthened the hand of war hawks in the Japanese military. Less than two weeks later, the Japanese attacked Pearl Harbor.

White and the Soviets were hardly responsible for the Pearl Harbor attack. Roosevelt and his advisers were already exasperated with Japan's saber rattling and would have been unable to avert war with a nation where militancy increasingly predominated. But White's memorandum illustrated his ability to covertly advance Soviet foreign policy goals and also obtain intelligence from Roosevelt's inner circle of advisers.

White would continue to promote the Soviet foreign policy agenda as an agent of influence throughout the war. In 1942 he was the prime author of the Morgenthau Plan for postwar Germany, which was designed to crush any chance of resurgent German militarism by transforming the country into a hodgepodge of agricultural provinces. This plan conformed with the Soviets' goal to reduce Germany to a third-rate power. Roosevelt and Churchill eventually rejected the plan, which demonstrated that White's ability to manipulate policy was limited.

Aside from formulating the Morgenthau Plan, in July 1944 White was the key player at the Bretton Woods Conference, where the International Monetary Fund and World Bank were established. And after he was named assistant secretary of the Treasury, he was tapped as the department's representative to the United Nations founding conference in May 1945. With Alger Hiss as the acting secretary-general of the conference, the Soviets would have two well-placed agents at a meeting destined to shape the new world order. White and Hiss kept the Soviets fully informed of the United States' negotiating strategy at the UN conference. White also assured his handlers that President Truman was so eager for success that he would be willing to accept Soviet proposals as long as the USSR joined the United Nations.

Although White's advancement showed that he was under little suspicion, he constantly worried about exposure throughout his espionage career. In a decrypted Venona message of August 5, 1944, an NKGB officer reported to Moscow after meeting White that "JURIST" (White's code name) urged more caution in the relationship and proposed short, infrequent meetings in his car.[7] White had no cause for worry at that point. Even though Chambers had told the FBI about him in 1942, the warnings still went unheeded. In 1945, however, White's association with the Silvermaster Group would compromise him.

Elizabeth Bentley never met White, but as the courier for Silvermaster's agents she conveyed his information to the Soviets and knew his identity. When she volunteered to the FBI, she named White as one of the most important spies in the ring and provided details about the intelligence he gave the Soviets.

In 1946 Truman nominated White as the US representative to the newly established International Monetary Fund. His appointment was the last straw for J. Edgar Hoover, who had grown increasingly frustrated with Truman's soft stand on communists in the government. Hoover sent a memorandum to Truman's military aide detailing White's espionage. The secretary of state, James Byrnes, also received a copy and rushed to see the president. Truman was reportedly shocked by the information and checked on the nomination, only to learn that the Senate had just confirmed White.[8]

Escalating rumors of espionage dogged White, and he resigned from the International Monetary Fund in March 1947 after less than a year in the job. At the House Un-American Activities Committee hearings the next year, Chambers and Bentley both publicly identified him as a Soviet spy. In addition to the Hiss documents, Chambers had also stashed away a document in White's handwriting that provided conclusive proof of his espionage.

On August 13, 1948, White appeared before the committee to answer the accusations. In a prepared statement, he declared that "my creed is the American creed" and denied any involvement in espionage. Under intense questioning from Representative Nixon about his relations with Chambers, White insisted that "I do not recall having met the individual." White was emphatic and confident in his denials, and he apparently bamboozled the press, which gave him favorable reviews in the following day's news.[9] He returned to his summer home in Fitzwilliam, New Hampshire, and died suddenly of a heart attack three days after his testimony.

Four decades later, the declassification of the Venona messages conclusively proved White's espionage and revealed the Soviets' appreciation of his value as an intelligence reporter and agent of influence. However, the

Soviets' glowing assessment of his influence is questionable. Determining the value of agents of influence is often a difficult proposition. Policy is shaped by a legion of factors, and determining if a lone agent really influenced the final outcome is often impossible. Roosevelt and his inner circle had already formulated their policy toward a hawkish Japan before White attempted to manipulate them. In other cases White failed in attempts to influence US policy. Roosevelt rejected White's plan for postwar Germany and also another proposal inspired by the Soviet intelligence services for a multi-billion-dollar reconstruction loan for the USSR.

However, the record is clear on White's contribution as an intelligence producer. As an insider in the Roosevelt and Truman administrations, White was able to provide timely and accurate intelligence on US war plans, negotiating strategy, and policy intentions. He had few competitors as the Soviets' top spy in the 1930s and 1940s. If he could not provide the Soviets with insider knowledge on the full range of issues that interested the USSR, the NKGB had other well-placed spies who could.

THE SPY IN THE
WHITE HOUSE

LAUCHLIN CURRIE

*He [Zarubin, NKGB chief in America] has some
high-level agent in the White House.*

ANONYMOUS LETTER *to J. Edgar Hoover from an unknown
Soviet Embassy employee, August 7, 1943.*
Quoted by Benson and Warner, *Venona*

Imagine if the CIA had a spy inside the palace of the Iranian leader Mahmoud Ahmadinejad who could tell whether Iran had developed a nuclear weapon. Imagine a spy on the staff of the North Korean leader who could tip off the United States about his country's nuclear weapons capability. During Franklin D. Roosevelt's tenure as president, the Soviets had such a source in the White House. Lauchlin Currie worked in FDR's White House as a senior administrative assistant on economic affairs from 1939 until Roosevelt's death in 1945. He also passed secrets to the CPUSA the entire time.

Along with Harry Dexter White, Currie was among the brain trust of liberal economists who joined FDR's government. Currie was born in Nova Scotia, studied at the London School of Economics and Political Science, and received a PhD in economics from Harvard University, where he and White were teaching assistants. In 1934 Currie became a US citizen and began his government employment in White's Research Division at the

Treasury Department. On the eve of Roosevelt's third term, he was appointed a senior counselor to the White House.

In 1942 Currie was dispatched by Roosevelt to China, and upon return from the trip he fashioned an arms and aid package for the Chinese. Roosevelt then gave Currie a dual role, retaining him as a presidential adviser but also naming him to administer the Foreign Economic Administration, a wartime agency created to coordinate America's vast overseas economic activities, especially the Lend Lease program with the Soviet Union.

Currie's espionage career for the Soviets is far hazier than those of his fellow American spies. Only nine decrypted Venona messages deal with his spying, and they provide little insight about the wealth of information a spy with his access may have provided. The messages, however, include two examples of the secrets he passed that provide a glimpse of his access in the White House. In one case he advised the Soviets that the president told him that he was reluctant to recognize Charles de Gaulle's government until the French treated their colonies more fairly.[1] Currie also told the Soviets that Roosevelt would accept Stalin's demands regarding territorial gains in Poland and would also press Polish exiles about concessions to Moscow, information that gave the Soviets a green light to install a puppet regime.[2]

Sources like Currie are an intelligence officer's dream. Agent handlers normally work with spies who are layers away from top policymaking circles of their government. The handler must embark on a lengthy questioning of a spy to determine the subsources and methods by which the spy acquired the information so that analysts can determine its validity and importance. In Currie's case, the sourcing was simple and direct—he often acquired his information directly from the president of the United States.

Currie also provided the Soviets with a critical counterespionage nugget. As Elizabeth Bentley later told the FBI, in late 1944 Currie rushed to Nathan Silvermaster (see chapter 25) to tell him that the Americans were "on the verge of breaking Soviet codes."[3] Currie's knowledge of this highly compartmented information certainly demonstrated his unique access. However, somehow he got confused and thought the US code-breaking effort stemmed from the Office of Strategic Services' acquisition of a Soviet codebook from the Finns. The Soviets already knew about the codebook, because the president had ordered the office's chief, William Donovan, to return it to them as a demonstration of America's openness with its wartime ally. Because of this confusion, the Soviets apparently ignored Currie's tip-off until Kim Philby and William Weisband later revealed details of the Venona operation to the Soviets.

Like White, Currie was not a CPUSA member and cooperated with the Soviets on his own terms. He was among the agents Chambers identified to Assistant Secretary of State Adolf Berle, who wrote in his notes on the meeting that Currie "never went the whole way."[4] Bentley also confirmed to the FBI that Currie was cautious in his espionage dealings with the Soviets. Subsequent revelations in Vassiliev's notebooks indicate that the Soviet intelligence services bemoaned the fact that Currie would not meet directly with one of their officers so that his full potential as a source could be exploited.

Although Currie kept his distance from the NKVD, he eventually fell under suspicion. The anonymous letter to the FBI from inside the Soviet embassy had mentioned "a high-level agent in the White House," and Chambers and Bentley had both identified Currie by name. To protect Cur-

LAUCHLIN CURRIE was a Soviet mole inside FDR's White House from 1939 to 1945.
Library of Congress

rie the Soviets suspended contact with him once Philby had alerted them to Bentley's defection. By this time, however, Roosevelt had died and Currie had left the White House after Truman appointed his own team of advisers. The FBI finally interviewed Currie in 1947, but all he would admit was that he might have been indiscreet with fellow employees regarding compartmented information.

When Chambers and Bentley surfaced Currie's name publicly at the congressional hearing by the House Un-American Activities Committee, Currie was summoned to defend himself on August 13, 1948, the same day White appeared. Currie denied that he was a spy or even a communist. Like the majority of his fellow spies of the era, Currie escaped justice. The allegations of Chambers and Bentley were insufficient evidence to convict him, and the Venona messages that were eventually decrypted were too sensitive to be revealed in court. Currie went to Colombia on a mission for the World Bank in 1950 and spent the remainder of his life there, far beyond the reach of American justice.

Currie died in 1993, just two years before the public release of the Venona messages that revealed the espionage of "PAGE," his Soviet code name. Zealous supporters of Currie noted that the conversations and meetings he held with Soviet intelligence officers were a legitimate part of his White House duties. They selectively omitted the fact that Currie had never reported these meetings and was not representing the US government in them.[5]

To protect highly placed sources like Currie, the Soviet intelligence services needed a spy like Philby, a spy inside American counterespionage to warn of dangers to its networks. A promising candidate finally appeared on the NKGB's radar at the end of 1944.

THE SPY IN
US COUNTERESPIONAGE

JUDITH COPLON

The time is ripe for signing on "Sima" [Judith Coplon].

Message from an NKGB RESIDENT *to Moscow,*
December 5, 1944, decrypted by Venona

A spy inside the enemy's counterespionage service is the insurance policy that protects networks of sources. Kim Philby, as one example, not only had access to British but also to American, Canadian, and Australian counterspy efforts from his perch inside British intelligence. Because of the close cooperation between the United States and Great Britain, Philby was able to advise the NKGB about the defections of Igor Gouzenko and Elizabeth Bentley so it could suspend contact and save its spies from prosecution. He also received information from the highly compartmented Venona Project that he passed to the NKGB and enabled them to protect other sources.

The NKGB still had no spies inside the FBI with direct access to information that could endanger its espionage networks, and so it leapt on the opportunity when a Department of Justice employee with access to FBI files appeared ripe for recruitment. Judith Coplon was a Brooklyn native who proved to be a brilliant student at Barnard College, at that time the women's college of Columbia University. Once again, Columbia, where Chambers and

Bentley were first drawn to communism, had the ignominious distinction of breeding another top Soviet spy. Coplon was a member of the Young Communist League at the college and was fascinated with Russia, a fateful combination that would eventually lead her down the road to espionage.[1]

After graduating from Barnard in 1942, Coplon was hired as an analyst in the Economic Warfare Section of the Justice Department's New York City office. She befriended a female State Department employee who happened to be a Soviet agent and recommended her to the Soviet intelligence services. The recruitment was a breeze. In her first contact with the Soviets, the twenty-two-year-old analyst brimmed with enthusiasm at the prospect of sharing Justice Department secrets with the USSR.

Coplon was assigned to Washington and began work in the Foreign Agents Registration Section at the Justice Department on February 15, 1945, which was later to prove a critical date in her life. In the job Coplon now had access to FBI information on internal security investigations, Soviet organizations operating in the United States, and American communist leaders. For the Soviets, this was precisely the information they required from inside America's counterespionage service to protect their spy rings.

Coplon proved as much an overachiever as a spy as she had been as a Barnard student. She ignored Soviet warnings not to remove documents until she assessed the security situation in her new job.[2] She seemed obsessed with stealing as much as she could for the USSR, and one of her handlers advised Moscow that she "considers our work the main thing in her life" and that she decided against marrying her fiancé so she could focus on espionage.[3]

The information she gleaned tipped off the USSR that the FBI had shifted its focus away from fascists to the Soviets as the war drew to an end.[4] The FBI's new direction was also a wake-up call to KGB officers in New York, who had been accustomed until then to a benign environment where they could operate with impunity: "A review of this data shocked Soviet operatives at the New York Station who had previously dismissed the various US counterintelligence efforts as amateurish."[5] In response, the NKGB changed the code names of several agents and, in September 1945, Moscow Center issued a harsh warning to its residencies in America to tighten up their tradecraft. By then it was too late. Because of poor tradecraft, Elizabeth Bentley knew the identities of a host of Soviet spies and, two months after Coplon's warning, she would approach the FBI and begin unraveling the network.

The NKGB had already stopped the practice of assigning valuable spies to CPUSA intermediaries and instead handled Coplon directly. But the Soviet spy in American counterespionage was undone by the country's secret counterespionage weapon. Coplon was the first Soviet spy of the Golden Age who was arrested because of her identification in a decrypted Venona message.[6]

Even after the difficult decryption of Venona messages, the plain text translations were often vague and had to be assembled like a jigsaw puzzle and analyzed to identify the agents. In Coplon's case, however, deciphered Venona messages pinpointed her exactly. Two messages—dated December 31, 1944, and January 8, 1945—outlined her enthusiastic willingness to spy for the Soviets and mentioned her transfer from New York and exact Justice Department job. If this information did not suffice, one of the messages specified February 15, 1945, as the starting date of the new job.[7] No one else but Coplon fit this description.

The Venona team deciphered the messages identifying Coplon in 1948. Alarmed that a spy had been operating in its midst since 1944, the FBI immediately fielded discreet surveillance on Coplon to catch her in the act of spying and arrest her. As she traveled around Washington, FBI agents noted that she appeared to be checking to see if she was being followed, which was strange behavior for a Justice Department employee in her own capital. She ostensibly traveled to New York to see her parents every few weeks, but FBI surveillance discovered that she was meeting there with Vladimir Gubichev, a Russian employee at the United Nations.

After failing to obtain evidence against spies named by Whittaker Chambers and Elizabeth Bentley, the FBI wanted to ensure that the arrest and prosecution of Coplon would be airtight. Robert Lamphere, the FBI liaison to Venona who identified her from the deciphered messages, supervised the investigation. The FBI needed evidence of Coplon passing classified information to a foreign power to enhance the prosecution's case, so Lamphere baited the trap by ensuring that she received a fabricated FBI document with irresistibly juicy intelligence about its recruitment of a Soviet official.

The Venona information was too sensitive to be used as basis for an arrest warrant, and the Justice Department advised the FBI that information developed from the surveillance of Coplon was also insufficient justification. However, FBI agents could legally arrest her if they observed a felony in process—that is, Coplon passing classified documents to Gubi-chev. The FBI decided to arrest Coplon and Gubichev if they observed an exchange during her planned trip to New York on March 4, 1949. Years lat-er, in his account of Soviet espionage in America, Lamphere provided a vivid description of the arrest as hunter pursued prey through serpentine routes around various neighborhoods in New York City.[8] Coplon and Gubi-chev first met, then separated, and darted in and out of subways and buses on an evening journey that traversed almost the entire island of Manhattan. After a few hours, they finally met again.

The FBI agents believed that they spotted an exchange of documents and arrested both Coplon and Gubichev. They seized and emptied Coplon's purse on the spot. The young Soviet spy had taken Lamphere's bait. The false report was in her handbag, along with FBI "data slips" with classified information and a note advising her handlers that she was unable to filch a particular top-secret FBI document of interest to the Soviet intelligence services.[9]

The Soviets were outraged about Gubichev's arrest and claimed diplo-matic immunity, an issue that muddled the case from the outset. The State Department countered the Soviet claim and asserted that, "under United Nations rules, Gubichev had given up his diplomatic immunity when he signed the UN's oath of employment."[10] The United Nations had also sus-pended Gubichev from his position as soon as he was arrested and main-tained that his immunity only applied to official duties and not personal actions. In a "friend of court" brief, an outside attorney left the question unresolved, indicating that there were "cogent arguments on both sides of the issue."[11] Attorney General Tom Clark feared that the case against Coplon would be considerably weakened if she argued that she had been prevented from having access to Gubichev's testimony. Clark appealed to President Harry Truman to hold Gubichev for the trial and then deport him. Truman agreed, and Gubichev was deported a year after the pair was arrested.[12]

Because the involvement of Gubichev could complicate the prosecution of Coplon, the Department of Justice opted for two separate indictments. A grand jury in Washington indicted Coplon for espionage and the theft of classified documents, and another grand jury in New York indicted her and Gubichev for conspiracy to convey and receive classified information.

Coplon's judicial process would last almost two decades, and in the end she would never spend a single day in prison. The trials would set precedents regarding the prosecution of espionage cases in America. Alleged FBI missteps, misjudgment by the prosecution, adverse court rulings, and revelations unrelated to the case itself all combined to prevent Coplon's imprisonment.

Public opinion about the USSR had shifted considerably by the time Coplon first went on trial in April 1949. Chambers and Bentley had publicly revealed the extent of communist espionage at the House Un-American Activities Committee hearings, and the Alger Hiss trial was already under way. The Soviets had occupied Eastern Europe, and the Berlin blockade had been launched. Mao Zedong's rebels were on the verge of seizing power in China, further proof of the spreading danger of international communism. Although the climate in America was decidedly anticommunist, the FBI came under fire early in the first trial on the New York indictments. Coplon's attorney, Archie Palmer, argued that the defense was entitled to the FBI reports behind the data slips found in his client's purse in order to represent the accused. The argument presented a critical dilemma for the government and embodied the conflict that would haunt other espionage cases in the future. To prosecute an espionage case, the Justice Department would need to reveal US government secrets. If it refused to do so, the remaining evidence was often insufficient to convict the accused spy.

John Kelley, the government's prosecutor, countered the defense's appeal with comments that crystallized this dilemma: "In this modern world of espionage and counterespionage, the government will find it extremely difficult to prosecute a criminal if it must expose secrets."[13] Kelly's argument fell on deaf ears, and the judge ruled in Palmer's favor. Lamphere later recalled that he believed that the Justice Department would simply drop the case when faced with the prospect of publicly exposing the FBI's secret documents. He was shocked when it did not.[14]

Ironically, some of the documents proved more embarrassing to the FBI than damaging to national security. The files revealed that the FBI was monitoring famous Hollywood stars—the respected Helen Hayes, Paul Muni, Frederic March, and Edward G. Robinson, who starred in *Little Caesar*, a film lauded for its exposure of the pitfalls of a life of crime. Hoover and the FBI were pilloried in the press, and Truman was furious that hearsay and idle gossip had crept into official files. This information had little relevance to Coplon's case.

The tide turned against Coplon when the prosecution presented its case. On the stand, she mounted a lame defense, first trying to explain away the contents of "Pandora's purse," as her handbag was dubbed in the press. Coplon claimed that the FBI information in her purse was simply work she had taken home and, even more implausibly, background for a novel she was writing. The prosecution then revealed the note in which she advised the Soviets that she was unable to get a top-secret document, which effectively destroyed her alibi.

The other pillar of Coplon's shaky defense was designed to justify her contact with Gubichev. She alleged that she was in love with the Russian and had to meet him clandestinely because he was married. It was a sweet moment for the prosecution. In response to her claims of love for Gubichev, Kelley asked why she also had romantic trysts in a Baltimore hotel room with Howard Shapiro, a Justice Department attorney.

Coplon exploded on the stand and screamed at her lawyer. "You son of a bitch," she yelled at Palmer, "I told you this would happen. How could you let it happen with my mother in the courtroom?"[15] Coplon's defense was crushed. The jury quickly reached a verdict of guilty, and Coplon was given a sentence of forty months to ten years.

Coplon fared no better at her second trial in New York with Gubichev. She was sentenced to fifteen years, and Gubichev, in a deal worked out between the two governments, was found guilty but simply deported back to the USSR. His attorneys, however, had argued that the case should be dismissed because it was based on illegal search and seizure and evidence from wiretaps, charges that would plague the Coplon case in the future.

Despite convictions in two trials, the Coplon case was far from over. The New York verdict was reversed in December 1950. Although the appeals court believed that Coplon was guilty, Judge Learned Hand ruled that the government's arrest without a warrant was illegal and, as a result, so were its search and seizure. The classified documents found in Coplon's purse, the most damning evidence in the case, were thus worthless from a judicial standpoint. As a result of this ruling, a month after the trial Congress passed legislation allowing arrests without warrants in espionage cases, but the law could not be applied retroactively to Coplon.[16]

To confuse the case further, a year later the verdict of the Washington trial was upheld by the appeals court, which found the arrest legal and evidence sufficient for conviction, in direct opposition to the New York appeals court's decision. The Washington court, however, also decided that Coplon could request a hearing to determine if privileged telephone conversations with her attorney were tapped, which would entitle her to a new trial. The case was now muddled more than ever. Both sides petitioned the Supreme Court, which decided not to review the case. The Coplon case remained in limbo until 1967, when Attorney General Ramsay Clark decided that the government could not retry on both indictments.

Almost two decades after she was arrested, Judith Coplon was free. Between her first two trials, Coplon married Albert Socolov, one of her defense attorneys, and settled down in her native Brooklyn and raised a family of four children. She and her husband refused requests for interviews over the years, focusing instead on raising their children and managing two Mexican restaurants in New York. She died in February 2011, at eighty-nine years of age, without having spent a single day in jail.[17] One of the bitter ironies of the Golden Age of Soviet espionage was that the irrefutable Venona proof of Coplon's spying could never be used in court. Justice had to be sacrificed for national security.

The circus atmosphere at Coplon's trial captured the attention of the public just as had the drama of Hiss's trial. But they were but a prelude to the most sensational espionage trial in American history.

PART

THE
ATOMIC BOMB
SPIES: PRELUDE
TO THE COLD WAR

THE ATOMIC BOMB SPIES

I am the one to whom Fuchs gave the information.

Soviet agent HARRY GOLD's *confession to the FBI.*
Quoted by Albright and Kunstel, *Bombshell*

As the second half of the twentieth century dawned, the United States had emerged victorious from a global war as the world's foremost economic and military superpower. The nation's economic prosperity was reflected in feverish spending on new homes, cars, and time-saving gadgets that afforded Americans more leisure hours at ballparks and drive-in movies and allowed them to cluster at home in front of the newest entertainment phenomenon, the television set.

Life was good—or so it seemed. Beneath America's new prosperity lay a sense of anxiety. After four years of a world war, the country had immediately embarked on another conflict with its former ally, the Soviet Union. By 1950 the Soviets had installed puppet regimes in their neighboring countries, communists had seized power in China, and the North Atlantic Treaty Organization had been established as a bulwark against communist expansion. The Cold War had begun, and one of its most frightening aspects would be an arms race to acquire increasingly more lethal weaponry. Espionage played a vital role in this race, even before the Cold War began.

Only a few years after World War II ended, the Soviets dramatically leveled the playing field between the superpowers in the arms race. At the end of World War II America alone possessed the most awesome weapon in the history of humankind—the atomic bomb—and had demonstrated its willingness to use it. American omnipotence, however, was shattered in September 1949, when President Truman announced that the Soviets had successfully tested their own atomic bomb. In the 1950s frightened Americans would build bomb shelters in anticipation of an imminent Soviet attack, and schools would conduct air raid drills in which children huddled under their desks when sirens sounded.

The American public was alarmed because experts had calculated that the Soviets were years away from developing an atomic bomb. The Venona cryptographers, however, had deciphered a message in 1946 with the first hint of Soviet spies in the Manhattan Project. Over the next few years, they would decipher more Soviet intelligence messages that would reveal a massive espionage effort to acquire America's atomic bomb secrets. Their discovery would culminate in the most controversial espionage trial in American history and the only execution of American spies during peacetime.

The case of Julius Rosenberg and Ethel Rosenberg would haunt the American conscience for the next four decades and frame partisan debate between the left and right on Soviet communism. Anticommunist conservatives would vilify the Rosenbergs as traitors who passed the secret of the atomic bomb to the USSR, whereas liberals would claim that they were innocent scapegoats of Cold War hysteria. Even after the Venona messages revealed a half century later that the Rosenbergs had indeed spied for the Soviets, debate continues about the impact of their espionage and the severity of their sentence.

Atomic bomb espionage had its roots in the early 1940s, when the Soviet intelligence services began to notice scientific studies on uranium research in American and British journals.[1] The Soviets correctly concluded that the two allies were developing a bomb, and their suspicions were confirmed by Soviet moles in the British government. Anglo-American possession of the atomic bomb would make the two countries as much a threat to the USSR as Hitler's Nazis had been, so Stalin tasked his intelligence services to steal the secrets of his wartime allies and hasten the development of the Soviets' own weapon.

The Soviets already had agents suited and poised for the task. Klaus Fuchs, a German émigré to Great Britain, was a leading scientist on the separation of gaseous isotopes from uranium, a critical process in the development of a bomb, and he had been invited to work on the secret British nuclear project in 1941. After the Nazis invaded the USSR a few months later, Fuchs volunteered to the GRU because he believed that the Soviets needed the fruits of Anglo-American research to combat Hitler. As American and British cooperation on the project increased, Fuchs was dispatched to the United States and was eventually assigned to Los Alamos, the heart of the Manhattan Project. By that time, his case had been transferred to the NKGB, which had outmaneuvered the GRU in a turf battle for control of atomic weapons espionage.

Fuchs was now inside the most highly guarded US military facility of World War II. Access to the compound was restricted, and the mail was censored. The facility was ringed with armed soldiers, and some of the principal scientists were even escorted by personal bodyguards. The "need-to-know" principle was strictly enforced inside the US government. FBI director Hoover was even unaware of the project until, ironically, he inadvertently learned the secret from an American communist targeting Los Alamos to acquire spies within.

Fuchs, however, epitomized the security loopholes in the Anglo-American bomb project. Although he openly espoused communist views and had been a member of the German Communist Party, the need for scientific talent outweighed security concerns on both sides of the Atlantic.[2] As a result, routine background checks were cursory and, even when concerns about communist affiliation were highlighted, the warnings were dismissed. Security inside the facility itself was also lax. Chief scientist J. Robert Oppenheimer resisted measures regarding compartmentation of various aspects of the project. Spies inside Los Alamos could easily eavesdrop on classified conversations and even attend seminars on topics unrelated to their own work.

Still, because of the tight physical security at Los Alamos, Fuchs was unable to maintain contact with the Soviets, who had no idea that their agent was now inside Los Alamos, the heart of America's most important military project. Pressured by Stalin for information about the bomb, the NKGB dispatched a veteran courier, Harry Gold, to find their prize spy through his sister, who was then living in Massachusetts. The assignment of Gold would prove fatal to the entire atomic spy ring.

Gold was born in Switzerland of Jewish parents who had fled their native Russia. The family came to the United States in 1913. He was raised in Philadelphia, where he was shocked by anti-Semitic prejudice and gradually became attracted to Stalinist Russia as the hope for world Jewry. He became a chemist, and though he never formally joined the CPUSA, he was drawn into the underground and began stealing industrial secrets for the USSR in 1935. His first job was at the Pennsylvania Sugar Company, where he stole a dry ice formula that prevented ice cream from melting, a far cry from an atomic bomb.[3]

In February 1945, using the alias "Raymond," Gold eventually recontacted Fuchs through the scientist's sister.[4] Fuchs passed him information about the security of the Manhattan Project and progress on developing the bomb. His information included the important revelation that the Americans were now focused on plutonium instead of uranium-235 as bomb fuel and were studying implosion as a method to detonate the fuel. This information, which was supplemented by reports from other spies in the project, ultimately proved to be crucial to reducing the time in the Soviets' development of its own bomb. The NKGB was elated now that Fuchs was at Los Alamos and ensured that Gold set another meeting with him. The Soviets, however, would disregard basic security practices in their haste to steal atomic bomb secrets and thereby jeopardize some of their best spies on the project.

The steps for infiltrating spies like Fuchs into Los Alamos were simple because of inadequate personnel security measures. Meeting them and acquiring their secrets, however, posed considerable risk for the NKGB. Movements of Los Alamos scientists were restricted, and even on occasional forays away from the compound, security patrolled the nearby small town and visitors could easily attract attention. The NKGB could only meet its spies securely when they were able to travel either on extended leave or on short trips to nearby larger cities like Santa Fe and Albuquerque.

Fuchs was able to slip away from Los Alamos to meet Gold in Santa Fe on June 2, 1945. He passed the courier a description and sketches of the bomb and its components and informed him about the status of research on the ignition system and bomb core, two critical components of the weapon.

More important, Fuchs told Gold that the Americans planned an imminent test of the bomb before attacking Japan. Because of Soviet haste to satisfy Stalin's thirst for bomb secrets, the NKGB tasked Gold to meet another agent the following day in Albuquerque, a tradecraft error that would have fatal consequences for the atomic spy network.[5]

Fuchs returned to England in 1946 and continued to spy for the NKGB. Meanwhile, the Venona team decoded NKGB messages sent between 1944 and 1945 regarding a spy first encrypted "REST" and then renamed "CHARLES." A message from Moscow to the New York residency on April 10, 1945, indicated that CHARLES's information about the atom bomb "is of great value; . . . it contains information received for the first time about the electro-magnetic method of separation in ENORMOZ [the code name for the Manhattan Project]."[6] One of the reports attributed to REST was a scientific paper on using the gaseous diffusion process to obtain uranium. Robert Lamphere, the FBI's liaison to Venona, determined that the paper was written by Fuchs.

Someone else, of course, could have passed Fuchs's paper to the NKGB, but information in other messages further pinpointed him as agent REST/ CHARLES. By September 1949, soon after the Soviets tested their own bomb, the FBI was convinced that Fuchs was the spy and sent Lamphere to convey the bad news to his counterparts in London. In February 1950 the British arrested Fuchs, who by then had grown disillusioned with the Soviets and so confessed to his espionage. He was convicted and sentenced to fourteen years in prison, the maximum term under Great Britain's Official Secrets Act. The Soviets publicly denied Fuchs's espionage; but after his release nine years later, he quietly went off to East Germany, where he became a prominent scientist and member of the Communist Party Central Committee.

A decrypted Venona message included the information about the Soviets dispatching a courier, code-named ARNO, to recontact Fuchs through his sister. The FBI interviewed Fuchs before his trial to determine ARNO's identity. Fuchs claimed that he only knew the courier as "Raymond," but he was able to provide enough information to narrow down the FBI's list of suspects, which included Harry Gold. Gold had already come across FBI radar in the past as an acquaintance of Jacob Golos and had been summoned for grand jury questioning about his association with the spy ringleader.

The FBI questioned Gold in March 1950, just weeks after Fuchs's trial. He denied meeting Fuchs at first and claimed that he had never traveled to New Mexico. But when a search of his apartment turned up a map of Santa Fe, his resolve was broken. "I am the man to whom Fuchs gave the information," he admitted.[7] Nine days later, Gold confessed to the FBI agents that the KGB had asked him to perform one more task in New Mexico after he met Fuchs.

Gold then told the FBI that he had met another source in Albuquerque, a young army technician employed at Los Alamos whose address he identified on the Santa Fe map. Gold could not recall the technician's surname, but the spy's wife was named Ruth and the couple was Jewish. The spy had supplied Gold with a number of handwritten pages and sketches related to the atomic bomb.

Gold's revelation possibly matched the Venona decrypts about another source at Los Alamos code-named KALIBR. Was Gold's contact KALIBR? According to the KGB message, KALIBR was recruited by another agent code-named WASP to spy for the Soviets on the Manhattan Project. Other messages showed that KALIBR was providing the Soviets with information about security measures at Los Alamos and about experiments related to the bomb's detonation. More important, one of the messages indicated that KALIBR had been on leave in New York City in January 1945. On the basis of this information, the FBI identified those Manhattan Project staff members who had been on leave with residences in New York City, and it eventually pinpointed Army Sergeant David Greenglass as Gold's contact in Albuquerque.[8] The atomic spy ring had begun to unravel.

THE EXECUTED SPIES

THE ROSENBERGS

We are afraid of putting LIBERAL [Julius Rosenberg's code name]
out of action with overwork.

KGB *message to Moscow, December 5, 1944, decrypted by Venona.*

David Greenglass was arrested on June 15, 1950. The FBI was a step away from uncovering what its director, J. Edgar Hoover, would call "the crime of the century."[1] Greenglass admitted to the FBI that, during a visit to Albuquerque, his wife Ruth (code-named WASP) conveyed a proposal to spy for the NKGB from his brother-in-law, Julius Rosenberg. To protect his wife from prosecution, Greenglass cooperated with the FBI and confessed all he knew about his brother-in-law's spy ring. The admission would pit brother against sister, family against family, and the battle would be played out in one of the most famous trials of the twentieth century.

Julius Rosenberg and his wife Ethel were born and raised in New York's Lower East Side, a boiling cauldron of communist fervor in the 1930s and 1940s. Like his compatriots, Rosenberg was troubled by the rise of fascism in Europe and the Great Depression at home, so he embraced communism in his early years and joined the Young Communist League. He was so engrossed in his Communist Party work that he barely managed to graduate with a degree in electrical engineering from the City College of New York in February 1939. That same year he married Ethel Greenglass, who was a CPUSA member and an organizer of labor strikes.

Although Julius openly sold the communist newspaper, the *Daily Worker,* and collected dues for the party, his communist activities went unnoticed when the US Army Signal Corps hired him in 1939. Three years later he met Semyon Semyonov, a Soviet intelligence officer specializing in science and technology, at a Labor Day rally in New York's Central Park. Semyonov formally recruited the enthusiastic young communist Rosenberg at their third meeting.[2] Rosenberg's motivation, like scores of other CPUSA members of the era, was purely ideological, but he surpassed his comrades in his fanatic zeal to acquire secrets. Alexander Feklisov, his later Soviet handler, believed that Rosenberg passionately felt "a religious calling" to his spy work on behalf of the USSR.[3]

At the NKVD's direction, Rosenberg severed his overt ties to the CPUSA and became one of the Soviets' most prolific collectors of scientific intelligence and aggressive recruiters of new sources. As the principal agent of his growing network, Rosenberg worked so tirelessly in amassing US military and industrial secrets that even his grateful Soviet masters grew concerned: "We are afraid of putting LIBERAL [Julius Rosenberg's code name] out of action with overwork."[4]

Rosenberg was elated when he learned in the fall of 1944 that his brother-in-law had been assigned to a top-secret project in Los Alamos. Like the Rosenbergs, Greenglass had joined the Young Communist League, but, as he later admitted, he was less passionate about the cause: "Julius was a guy that really lived communism. To me it was like a peripheral thing."[5] Greenglass had graduated from a trade school and had become a machinist. After he was drafted into the army, he continued to trumpet his views to his annoyed fellow soldiers. In spite of his openly professed communism, he slipped through the lax security of the Manhattan Project and was assigned first to the Oak Ridge uranium production facility and then to Los Alamos. As Greenglass's biographer Sam Roberts noted, "It was a propitious moment. The Manhattan Project needed machinists. The Soviet Union needed another spy."[6]

Once Rosenberg learned of his brother-in-law's assignment, he excitedly raised the issue with his new Soviet handler, Alexander Feklisov, who was initially skeptical that the young and immature Greenglass would become an effective spy.[7] The Soviet intelligence services, however, were out of contact with their prize asset, Klaus Fuchs (see chapter 30), and gave Rosenberg the green light. The Rosenbergs huddled with Ruth Greenglass around the kitchen table of their cramped Lower East Side apartment as Julius lectured his sister-in-law about the moral justification of sharing atomic bomb secrets with the USSR. Ultimately, Julius convinced her to make an espionage proposal to her husband when she traveled to see him in New Mexico.[8]

Ruth Greenglass traveled to Santa Fe to join David while he was on leave in November 1944 and fulfilled her promise to Rosenberg. Although Ruth claimed that she had qualms about the proposal, Julius, who was four years older than the impressionable David, had served as his brother-in-law's communist guru. Greenglass accepted Rosenberg's offer and confirmed his willingness in a letter to his wife after the Santa Fe trip: "My darling, I most certainly will be glad to be part of the community project that Julius and his friends have in mind."[9]

When Greenglass returned to New York on leave in January 1945, he met with the Rosenbergs and provided an initial tranche of information about Los Alamos. Rosenberg told him that he might be contacted in Albuquerque by a Soviet courier. To assure David that the courier would be truly from the KGB, Rosenberg ripped the top of a Jell-O box in half, gave one part to Greenglass, and told him that the courier would show him the other half to demonstrate his bona fides.

In February 1945 the Army Signal Corps fired Rosenberg because of his CPUSA affiliation. As Venona decrypts later indicated, Moscow decided to suspend contact with Rosenberg now that the US government had

DAVID GREENGLASS, a machinist in the Manhattan Project at Los Alamos, was convinced to pass secrets to the Soviets by his brother-in-law, Julius Rosenberg. *Library of Congress*

focused on his party membership. Rosenberg's security problem, however, did not deter the KGB from acquiring atomic secrets from Greenglass. The KGB dispatched Harry Gold to meet both Fuchs and Greenglass in New Mexico. Gold had been given the torn Jell-O box half by the KGB and presented it to Greenglass. The young army sergeant matched it with his own half. The two pieces fit perfectly. The simple cardboard pieces now linked four Soviet spies—Fuchs, Gold, Greenglass, and, by association, Rosenberg. As Greenglass later admitted at the trial, he then provided Gold with "a sketch of a high explosive lens mold which was an experiment to study implosion effects."[10]

Moscow's concern for the security of Rosenberg's network escalated after Elizabeth Bentley's defection in November 1945. Feklisov, jittery that the FBI was now focusing on the Soviets since the war's end, took the risky move of visiting Rosenberg's apartment to warn him about Bentley. Feklisov was less than reassured when Rosenberg told him that he had known Jacob Golos and often identified himself as "Julius" over the phone to a woman, undoubtedly Bentley, who answered whenever he telephoned Golos's home.

Rosenberg was unfazed by Feklisov's warning and continued to exercise poor tradecraft by meeting his sources in his apartment to gather intelligence. By the end of 1948, Moscow Center suspected that his apartment may have been bugged by the FBI and warned its American residency to rein him in and order him to cease the meetings.[11]

By that time Greenglass had been discharged from the army. Although he had no access, the NKGB urged him to become a student at the University of Chicago in order to recruit former Los Alamos colleagues who were now working there. Greenglass never pursued this suggestion and instead formed a company with Rosenberg. But their relationship soon began to sour as Julius spent more time spying than on the family business. The partnership fizzled, and David found work as a mechanic in a Brooklyn company that assembled radar stabilizers for tank weapons.[12]

Soviet concern about the Rosenberg ring escalated to outright panic after Fuchs and Gold were arrested, because Gold could now lead the FBI to Greenglass and his in-laws. By early 1950 the Soviet intelligence services were planning to exfiltrate the Rosenbergs and Greenglasses from the United States.[13] But Greenglass hedged. His wife, Ruth, was pregnant and had also suffered serious burns in a kitchen fire that precluded travel in the immediate future. By the time she recovered and the couple could flee, the FBI was ready to pounce. Greenglass was arrested, and he fingered the Rosenbergs. A month later, on July 17, Julius Rosenberg was arrested for conspiracy to commit espionage. Three weeks later, his wife Ethel joined him in prison.

Greenglass was not alone in identifying the Rosenbergs. As early as 1947, Gardner's Venona cryptographers had broken out messages pointing to the Rosenberg ring. By early 1950 the Venona team was deciphering messages from 1944 that shed further light on the identity of a source code-named ANTENNA (later changed to LIBERAL) who was passing the KGB reams of technical secrets.

In a September 21, 1944, message decrypted by Venona, the NKGB residency informed Moscow that "LIBERAL recommended the wife of his wife's brother, Ruth Greenglass," and revealed that Ruth's husband worked at Los Alamos.[14] In another deciphered message dated November 27, 1944, the residency explicitly used the name "Ethel" in describing LIBERAL's wife: "Information on LIBERAL's wife. Surname that of her husband, first name Ethel. 29 years old. Married five years. Finished secondary school. A FELLOWCOUNTRYMAN [CPUSA member] since 1938. Sufficiently well developed politically. Knows about her husband's work."[15]

Even if the NKGB believed that its encrypted traffic was secure, basic communications tradecraft argues against including a true name in an operational message that could identify an active or even potential source. Code names are used specifically as another layer of security in the event that hostile intelligence services are able to read intercepted traffic or if a paper copy of the message inadvertently falls into enemy hands. Ironically, the KGB encrypted President Franklin D. Roosevelt, clearly not one of its spies, as "KAPITAN," but it provided no extra layer of security to one of its most prolific agents. Instead of using the true names "Ethel" and "Ruth Greenglass" in operational messages, the KGB could have easily sent these true names via diplomatic pouch or in separate correspondence cross-referenced to the original operational message.

Although the Venona information pinpointed the Rosenbergs, it could not be used in court and the FBI needed other evidence to convict the couple. David Greenglass's decision to betray his in-laws and testify against them would be critical to the prosecution. As one of the prosecutors, Assistant District Attorney James Kilsheimer, put it, "Without his confession, I doubt there would have been a case."[16]

Another City College graduate recruited by Julius, Morton Sobell, was also arrested and would stand trial with Julius and Ethel as part of the "Rosenberg Ring." Sobell had worked for the Navy Bureau of Ordnance and then at General Electric as an engineer on military contracts. Sobell managed to flee to Mexico, but he was seized by Mexican agents and delivered into the hands of the FBI. Like the Rosenbergs, Sobell vehemently denied the espionage charges.

The spy trial of the century opened on March 6, 1951, in a decidedly anticommunist climate. Since the dramatic revelations of Soviet espionage at the House Un-American Activities Committee hearings in 1948, Alger Hiss had been exposed as a spy and convicted of perjury and Judith Coplon had been convicted on espionage charges. In a demagogic speech to a West Virginia women's' club in 1950, Senator Joe McCarthy captured the limelight with his shocking allegation that more than 200 Soviet spies worked in the State Department. Although the charges were never proven and McCarthy was later discredited, he had inflamed America's fears of Soviet subversion before the Rosenberg trial.

The primary prosecutor of the Rosenberg case, Irving Saypol, had won a string of anticommunist convictions, including one in the second perjury trial of Hiss. Saypol initially pushed for the death sentence for the couple as a lever to pressure the defiant Julius into a plea bargain. If Julius admitted his guilt and named his confederates, he would receive a lighter sentence and there would be a more favorable disposition of his wife's case. But Julius remained unshakable in his refusal.

The death sentence maneuver in the Rosenberg case would be employed against many future Cold War spies to win plea bargains in exchange for lesser charges for their accomplices. Another harbinger of later Cold War spy cases was the dilemma between using classified government information in open court to bolster the case against the Rosenbergs and the potential harm to national security from exposing those secrets. The government, however, was eager to convict the Rosenbergs in order to deter others from spying, and so the chairman of the Atomic Energy Commission declassified parts of Greenglass's testimony, which was the centerpiece of the prosecution's case.

Greenglass's testimony about his recruitment by Rosenberg and his delivery of atomic bomb sketches was reinforced by other witnesses. Ruth Greenglass proved more convincing on the stand than her husband in her detailed and articulate testimony. Harry Gold, who was sentenced to thirty years imprisonment at his own trial later that year, detailed his NKGB courier duties to the jury. He specifically focused on his collection of Greenglass's information in Albuquerque and the damning password he used with the Los Alamos spy: "I come from Julius."

Even Bentley joined the fray. Although she had never met Rosenberg, she recalled an incident when her Soviet handler and lover, Jacob Golos, had driven her to the Lower East Side and got out of the car to receive materials from an unidentified male whose description fit Rosenberg's. She added that she often answered phone calls at Golos's home from a male identifying himself as Julius. A commercial photographer then testified that he had taken passport photographs of the Rosenbergs, which the prosecution presented as proof that the couple was preparing to flee the country.

In response to these accusations, Rosenberg's attorney, Emanuel Bloch, mounted a poor defense. Bloch's primary argument was that Greenglass had fabricated the story of his in-laws' involvement in his crime in order to retaliate for conflicts over their joint business venture. Rosenberg took the stand to bolster the argument with a detailed account of Greenglass's thirst for revenge over their failed business venture but did little else to help his case. Once Rosenberg had invoked the Fifth Amendment in response to a question about his Communist Party membership, he lost credibility with the jury.[17] Ethel Rosenberg also took the stand and hurt their case even more with her thinly disguised contempt for the proceedings.[18]

The accumulated weight of evidence, the Rosenbergs' unconvincing and even contemptuous testimony, and the intense anticommunism of the day all left the outcome in little doubt. Julius and Ethel Rosenberg and Morton Sobell were found guilty. Sobell was sentenced to thirty years in prison. David Greenglass, because of his cooperation with the FBI, was sentenced to only fifteen years. The most controversial sentences were meted out to the Rosenbergs.

Judge Irving Kaufman, who harbored ambitions of a nomination to the Supreme Court, labeled the Rosenbergs' crime a "diabolical conspiracy to destroy a God-fearing nation."[19] Kaufman claimed that the couple had not only betrayed the bomb to the Russians but had also "caused the communist aggression in Korea, with the resultant casualties exceeding 50,000, . . . and who knows but that millions more of innocent people may pay the price of your treason."[20] Kaufman may have been eager to prove that he was tough on communism, but his accusation about the Rosenbergs' responsibility for the Korean War was considered a stretch even by the ardent anticommunists of the day.

Spying in wartime was a crime punishable by death under the 1917 Espionage Act, and Kaufman sentenced the couple to die in the electric chair in May 1951. No American has been sentenced to death for espionage since then.

Bloch, the defense attorney, condemned the sentence and angrily countered that Tokyo Rose and Axis Sally, propagandists for Japan and Germany during the war, had only received ten to fifteen years for treason, and Klaus Fuchs, a scientist with far more insider expertise than Greenglass and the Rosenbergs, was only sentenced to fourteen years by the British. He also argued that, even if they were guilty, the Rosenbergs had spied for a wartime ally and the intent of the espionage law was to punish those who spied for an enemy.[21]

As the judicial appeals process continued for the next two years, protests against the sentence erupted around the globe. The Rosenbergs' two young

JULIUS AND ETHEL ROSENBERG
after their trial for espionage. While conclusive evidence of Julius's espionage emerged over the next forty years, the extent of Ethel's involvement remains a mystery. *Library of Congress*

sons, Robert and Michael, were paraded at rallies sporting signs that read "Don't Kill My Mommy and Daddy." Appeals for clemency bombarded the White House from European leaders and even the pope. The Soviet intelligence services launched a covert propaganda campaign to save their spies, and, in a hypocritical maneuver, their Eurocommunist stooges orchestrated rallies for the Rosenbergs to divert attention from the Soviets' anti-Semitic purge of the Czechoslovak government at the time.[22]

But this global outcry had no impact on US courts. The verdicts were upheld in appellate courts, and the Supreme Court refused to hear the case in October 1952. President Dwight D. Eisenhower refused pleas for executive clemency the following February. In one final effort to save Julius and Ethel, another appeal was made to the Supreme Court. This time the appeal was based on a clause in the Atomic Energy Act of 1946 stipulating that the death sentence or life imprisonment for disclosure of atomic secrets should only be imposed upon a jury's recommendation. Because the jury in the Rosenberg trial did not recommend the death sentence, Judge Kaufman's sentencing might be invalid.[23] Justice William O. Douglas granted a stay of execution for the Supreme Court to hear the appeal, but the justices upheld the sentence and voted six to three to revoke Douglas's stay. The Rosenbergs had run out of time.

During the appeals process, the Rosenbergs continued to maintain their innocence and refused to cooperate with the FBI. They actively engaged in the campaign to reverse their sentences but did themselves more harm than good. Ethel remained strident and contemptuous and Julius never budged from his rigid commitment to communism. On the eve of their executions, they still remained intransigent. Ethel regaled her husband by singing "Good Night, Irene," and Julius, the communist ideologue, paradoxically crooned to her "The Battle Hymn of the Republic."

Tearful supporters of the Rosenberg cause held a vigil outside Sing Sing Prison in Ossining, New York, on June 19, 1953, the night of the executions. Paul Robeson, the heralded opera singer who openly supported the USSR, led the crowd in a soft rendition of "Swing Low, Sweet Chariot." Julius Rosenberg was strapped into the electric chair first and the sentence was carried out swiftly. In a grisly scene immediately afterward, Ethel remained alive in the chair after the first shock waves passed through her body. The executioners had to send two more jolts through her until a puff of steam wafted from her head.

Ethel Rosenberg's execution still remains controversial. Although conclusive evidence of Julius's espionage emerged during the next forty years, the extent of Ethel's involvement remains a mystery. According to Venona decrypts, Ethel was a committed communist knowledgeable and supportive of her husband's espionage. But aside from these sketchy NKGB messages, the only evidence of Ethel's involvement in Julius's spying was

provided by the Greenglasses. According to their testimony, Ethel supported Julius in urging Ruth to make the recruitment pitch to David and was
present when Julius gave him his contact instructions for New Mexico.
Ruth Greenglass also told the FBI that Ethel had typed up her husband's
scribbled notes on the bomb for passage to the NKGB, and David corroborated her story. Four decades later, however, David changed his story and
claimed that he did not remember Ethel typing his notes but just assumed
that his wife Ruth's version was accurate.[24] The prosecution presented no
other evidence of Ethel Rosenberg's espionage activities at the trial.

Support for Ethel's death sentence was far from unanimous in the government. J. Edgar Hoover, despite his staunch anticommunism, even dis-
puted the sentence, claiming that the execution of a mother who would
leave two orphaned sons would harm the FBI's efforts against Soviet subversion.[25] Her sentence also seems unduly harsh when measured against
the fate of future Cold War spies, whose espionage activity was conclusively proven but whose punishments were far lighter.

Because the Rosenbergs were executed for their espionage, debate in the
ensuing decades over their guilt or innocence was even more emotional
than in the Alger Hiss case. As in the Hiss debate, support for the Rosenbergs' innocence gathered momentum throughout the next two decades,
first after McCarthyism was discredited and later after the Vietnam War
and Watergate engendered broad mistrust of public institutions.

However, no new evidence surfaced to support their innocence. On the
contrary, beginning in the 1980s, a series of revelations further proved the
Rosenbergs' guilt. Ironically, most of these revelations emerged from the
Soviet side. The first revelation came from no less an authority than former Soviet leader Nikita Khrushchev. In an expanded version of his memoirs published in 1990, Khrushchev claimed that he "heard from both
Stalin and Molotov that the Rosenbergs provided very significant help in
accelerating the production of our atomic bomb."[26] The KGB defectors
Oleg Gordievskiy and Vasili Mitrokhin also confirmed the Rosenbergs'
guilt. Finally, Rosenberg's NKGB handler, Alexander Feklisov, provided a
wealth of detail about the operation in his memoir, *The Man behind the
Rosenbergs,* although he downplayed the value of the information Julius
received from Greenglass and insisted that Ethel played a minimal role in
her husband's espionage.

By that time Feklisov's revelations barely caused a stir. The declassification of the Venona messages in 1995 and 1996 included the NKGB cables that clearly identified Julius and Ethel Rosenberg. The messages silenced even the most stalwart believers in the Rosenbergs' innocence. In 2008, after years of denying his own espionage, the Rosenbergs' codefendant Morton Sobell, then ninety-one years old, admitted that he and the Rosenbergs stole military secrets for the Soviet Union. As a result, the Rosenberg sons finally acknowledged that they, too, now believed that their father was a Soviet spy.[27]

Yet the overwhelming evidence in these revelations still has not ended controversy about the Rosenbergs' fate. Although the vast majority of commentators acknowledge the Rosenbergs' espionage, some nonetheless question the importance of the secrets they passed and thus the severity of their sentence. Some authoritative voices believed that the damage to US national security was substantial. The Atomic Energy Commission considered Greenglass's sketch of a high explosive lens mold and his work on implosion experiments to be of great value to the Soviets. Richard Rhodes, the leading historian of the American bomb, claimed that Greenglass's information regarding explosive experiments contributed significantly to the development of the Soviets' own weapon.[28] Greenglass's information had primarily allowed the Soviets to avoid the trial-and-error mistakes that American scientists had made and thus had accelerated the development of their own atomic bomb.

Others, however, dispute the Rosenbergs' contribution. In their view, David Greenglass was merely a vocational school graduate with a primitive understanding of the bomb's complexity, and his information was scarcely comparable to the secrets passed by Klaus Fuchs, a scientist directly involved in atomic bomb research. Feklisov claimed that Greenglass's sketch of the bomb was "a childish scribble—it was meaningless."[29] Although his account is clearly biased, Feklisov supported his argument by citing physicists who deemed Greenglass's sketch a "rough caricature of the atomic bomb mechanism, full of mistakes and without access to details to understand or reproduce it."[30] Even the head of the Manhattan Project, General Leslie Groves, believed that "the data that went out in the case of the Rosenbergs was of minor value."[31]

Judging Greenglass's information in isolation, those who minimize the Rosenbergs' atomic bomb espionage may be right, but they miss a key point about intelligence. Information from spies must be corroborated before policymakers can use it to shape policy. The more important the issue, the more compelling is the need for corroboration. And no issue was as vital to the USSR at the dawn of the post–World War II era as the atomic bomb.

Joseph Stalin's intelligence chief, Lavrentiy Beria, was skeptical about the atomic bomb information and insisted on confirmation of reporting from Fuchs and other sources on American progress in the Manhattan Project. Anatoliy Yakovlev, a science and technology intelligence officer in the United States, noted that "from the very beginning, Beria suspected the materials contained disinformation. He thought that the enemy was trying to get us involved in huge expenses and efforts that had no future."[32]

Beria's suspicion was fueled by the Soviets' lack of contact with Fuchs for almost a year. Beria suspected that the German-born scientist had been caught and directed to feed the Soviets false information. Greenglass's information may have lacked technical sophistication and detail, but its primary value was to corroborate some of the intelligence from Fuchs and other sources. For this reason the Soviet intelligence services, pressured by Beria for this corroboration, took the risk of using a key courier like Harry Gold to meet both Fuchs and Greenglass in New Mexico. The Greenglass information passed by Rosenberg to the Soviets was perhaps of little value on its own, but it played a key role as one piece of a complex puzzle that was eventually solved by the Soviets and led to their development of an atomic bomb.

One Soviet advocate of the importance of Greenglass's information was, perhaps, even more authoritative than Khrushchev, Beria, Feklisov, or any of the defectors who discussed the Rosenberg case. Igor Kurchatov, the head of the Soviet atomic bomb program, asserted that the "data received from spies were of immense, invaluable importance for our state and our science."[33] Kurchatov's comment was undoubtedly sincere because his life depended on the project—the Soviet scientist knew that Stalin would have shot him if he failed to produce the bomb.

In addition, information that has come to light only recently reveals that Rosenberg recruited not one but two sources in the Manhattan Project. In addition to Greenglass, Rosenberg enlisted his friend Russell McNutt, an engineer and communist sympathizer who worked for the Kellex Company, which was contracted in 1942 to construct a uranium gas diffusion facility at the Manhattan Project's facility in Oak Ridge. McNutt, who was only known by his code name FOGEL (later changed to PERSIAN), was among the first Soviet sources inside the project and passed information about the structural designs of the facility, although he later rejected KGB pressure to work at Oak Ridge itself.[34]

The controversy over Rosenberg's atomic bomb espionage has overshadowed the damage done by his entire spy network. Greenglass worked on America's most secret and most critical military project, but he was only one of many spies in the Rosenberg ring. Rosenberg and his network passed volumes of information on conventional US weapons systems to the Soviet intelligence services that had a long-term impact extending into the first decade of the Cold War. At its peak, Rosenberg's network had eight agents, including engineers and aviation scientists who provided information on a broad spectrum of US military research and development.[35]

According to Feklisov, the Rosenberg network passed the Soviets more than 20,000 pages of classified documents. Among them was the entire 12,000-page design manual for America's first jet fighter, the P-80 Shooting Star.[36] Rosenberg's spies also passed the NKGB detailed information about US computer technology, radar systems, and jet engine designs that enabled the Soviet military to quickly narrow the gap with its Cold War adversary in the conventional weapons arena.[37]

Rosenberg himself stole blueprints for a proximity fuse, a device designed to detonate bombs upon approach to a target at a point where maximum damage can be inflicted. He later stole the fuse itself and passed it to Feklisov as a Christmas present in 1944. Two of his key agents on conventional weapons systems were equally productive. Alfred Sarant and Joel Barr, electrical engineers who had been recruited by Rosenberg, worked on military radar projects in the Army Signal Corps and the Western Electric Company. From 1943 to 1945 Sarant and Barr gave Rosenberg more than 9,000 pages of classified materials on more than a hundred US weapons programs.[38]

According to Feklisov, the pair gave the Soviet intelligence services the blueprints for America's most advanced microwave radar system and the M-9 gun director, an analog computer "that predicted a moving object's future position based on radar input and then automatically aimed and fired an artillery gun."[39] The Soviets engineered their own version and, together with Rosenberg's stolen proximity fuse, used the technology in their missile systems. A Soviet surface-to-air missile, the SA-2, contained the technology and successfully shot down Francis Gary Powers's U-2 on May Day 1960, an incident that heightened tensions between the superpowers.[40]

Sarant and Barr managed to escape the tightening FBI net around Rosenberg and his fellow spies. They eventually reached the Soviet Union, where they resettled under new identities and fathered the Soviet microelectronics industry.[41] Thus Rosenberg's espionage network flourished long after its ringleader's execution.

The damage done to US national security by the Rosenberg network was significant. But was it significant enough to warrant even Julius Rosenberg's execution? The Rosenberg case is a glaring example of the impact of the political and social context of the times on the punishment meted out to spies. The fear and hostility toward the USSR that gripped Americans in the early years of the Cold War influenced one lone judge to sentence the Rosenbergs to death, and a significant part of the American public supported this decision. Three decades after the Rosenbergs' execution, a US Navy warrant officer, John Walker, would share nuclear submarine secrets with the KGB that could have endangered the country if war had broken out. He escaped the death penalty and is serving a life term in prison. By the time of his spying, the fear and hostility had dissipated, and arrests of American spies had become a routine feature of the Cold War.

The Rosenberg affair was also a harbinger of the role domestic politics would play in future espionage cases in the United States. Debate over the Rosenbergs' innocence or guilt, and the justice of injustice of their sentence, reflected more the partisan politics of conservatives and liberals than objective assessments of evidence. In the decades to come, espionage would continue to be a political football between parties in power and the opposition, with one side using a spy to prove that the other was weak on national security issues. This trend would come full circle in the 1990s at Los Alamos, when charges of espionage against a Chinese-born nuclear scientist, Wen Ho Lee, would spark Republican accusations of Democratic blindness to the threat from the People's Republic of China.

The Rosenbergs' executions marked the end of the ideologically motivated spying of the Golden Age of Soviet espionage in America. Some who supported the death sentence naively believed that their executions would serve as a deterrent and mark the end of all espionage against America.

They were, of course, wrong. In the next decades of the Cold War, Americans with access to secrets would continue to spy for the Soviets and other foreign powers, but very few would do so out of ideological sympathy for communism.

The Rosenbergs were executed for passing the NKGB a small yet important piece of the atomic bomb puzzle, whereas a more important Soviet spy inside the Manhattan Project never spent a single day in prison. In the case of atomic bomb espionage, justice proved to be truly blind.

THE ATOMIC BOMB SPY
WHO GOT AWAY

THEODORE HALL

I was worried about the dangers of an American monopoly
of atomic weapons if there should be a postwar depression.
To help prevent that monopoly, I contemplated a brief encounter
with a Soviet agent, just to inform them of the existence of
the A-Bomb project.

THEODORE HALL's *comments to the authors of* Bombshell

Theodore Alvin Hall's "brief encounter" with the Soviet intelligence services took place and evolved into an espionage relationship that lasted on and off for almost nine years. During this period Hall was "the only American scientist known to have given the Soviet Union details on the design of an atomic bomb."[1] He was the youngest of the known spies of the Soviet Golden Age of espionage in America, and he died at seventy-four years of age without having spent a day in jail for his crime.

Hall shared a common background with many of his fellow spies of the era. His parents were Russian Jews who fled the homeland for the United States. His father, a furrier, married an Eastern European immigrant's daughter and the newlyweds settled in the Washington Heights area of northern Manhattan. Hall was born Theodore Holzberg, but the family name would be changed at his elder brother's urging when Ted was eleven years old. When his father's business flourished, the family moved to their own house in the suburbs, where they lived until the Great Depression forced them to move back to Manhattan. The Halls were a typical family of the age, with one exception. Young Theodore was a child genius.

Although boys his age studied the batting averages of their favorite New York Yankees, Ted Hall was more fascinated by Albert Einstein's theory of relativity and other wonders of the world of physics. He skipped three grades in elementary school, whizzed through a high school for the intellectually gifted, and entered Queens College when he was merely fifteen years old.

Hall was not only fascinated by science. His brother Edward, eleven years his senior, was attracted to communism while a student at the City College of New York, a hotbed of radicalism in the 1930s and 1940s.[2] The younger Hall idolized Edward, and by the age of eleven years he was reading the *Communist Manifesto* and other socialist tracts suggested by his older brother. Two years later he would join the leftist American Student Union. Ironically, the founder of the union's chapter at City College was Julius Rosenberg.[3] The two never met, even though years later their stolen secrets would land on the same desk in NKGB headquarters.

After two years at Queens College, Hall transferred to Harvard University, which was eager at the time to attract the best young scientific brains in the nation regardless of their age. Hall even dominated the whiz kids at Harvard and was immediately placed into his junior year. Although he excelled in his science studies, he also remained interested in international affairs and was troubled by the rise of fascism in Nazi Germany.

Hall's interest in communism intensified after he was assigned to a dormitory known as "Moscow on the Charles" because a handful of its students vented their nonconformism in socialist activities rather than collegiate pranks. He quickly developed two paramount passions, science and communism, that would converge a few years later in espionage.

For all his genius, Hall was young and impressionable. He had looked up to Ed Hall as a father figure and mentor, but his brother was away in the US Army Air Corps. Hall filled the void by befriending one of his Harvard roommates, Saville Sax, a new mentor who would play a pivotal role in both their futures. Sax and Hall came from similar roots. Sax's parents were Russian émigrés, and his father had prospered in the upholstery business in America. The family had embraced the communist revolution, and Sax's mother headed the local Russian War Relief office.

Hall's accomplishments in physics at Harvard led to a job offer from the Manhattan Project. After Sax learned of the offer, he suggested to Hall that, once he was inside the project, he should pass information to the Soviets. Sax did not need to make this suggestion. Hall was already considering it.[4]

In January 1944, eighteen-year-old Hall began work inside the nation's most vital military project and fully intended to betray its secrets. His work entailed measuring uranium fission under the impact of high-energy neutrons, a key procedure to unleash the chain reaction that would detonate an atomic bomb. Despite his youth, he excelled and was soon assigned to experiment on implosion, the method that the Manhattan Project had ultimately decided was the key to successful detonation of the bomb.

The restrictive environment at Los Alamos left few outside activities to divert scientists and plenty of time to ponder the impact of their research. All were aware of the awesome destructive power of the weapon they were developing. Many were concerned that America's monopoly on the bomb could destabilize a world already wracked by war and believed that international controls over the weapon were necessary. Others believed that the Soviet Union had a right to the bomb to create a postwar strategic balance. Their views further convinced Hall that he was planning the right course. Reflecting on his beliefs a half century later, he claimed that "as I worked at Los Alamos and understood the destructive power of the atomic bomb, I asked myself what might happen if World War II was followed by a depression in the United States while it had an atomic bomb?"[5]

While on leave in New York in October 1944, Hall contacted Sax to figure out a way to spy for the Soviets. Both of them made ham-handed attempts to approach the Soviet intelligence services, and Sax even tried to meet Earl Browder, the head of the CPUSA, but he got no further than the receptionist with his farfetched tale. Sax and Hall were initially dismissed as possible double agents sent by the FBI until Hall managed to meet Sergey Kurnakov, an NKGB agent working as a journalist.

Kurnakov's later report on his meeting described Hall as a youthful version of the tweedy professor, tall, gangly, and disheveled, but brilliant. Kurnakov was initially suspicious of Hall's story about work on a classified military project, so he tested the boy by asking him if he realized what he

THEODORE HALL spied for the Soviets off and on for almost nine years and was not publicly exposed until the 1990s. *Los Alamos National Laboratory, US Department of Energy*

was doing by giving away America's secrets. Hall replied that "there's no country except for the Soviet Union which could be entrusted with such a terrible thing."[6] Hall also realized that the Soviets might find his story hard to swallow, so he backed it up with documentary information. He handed Kurnakov a report that he had written about work at Los Alamos and a list of scientists at the facility.

Despite fears of an FBI provocation, the NKGB residency was under considerable pressure to produce intelligence on the Manhattan Project.

On November 12, 1944, the residency sent a buoyant message to Moscow about Hall. This message provided a glowing appraisal of Hall's talents, access, and ideological motivation.[7] The message also included Hall's true name and indicated that he was the son of a furrier and had graduated from Harvard. Although the NKGB subsequently assigned, respectively, the code names MLAD (the Russian root for "young") and STAR ("old") to Hall and Sax, the security measure was too late. In the spring of 1950, the Venona team would decipher the NKGB's damning message with Hall's true name.

Moscow decided that Sax would be Hall's courier. The NKGB was already taking unnecessary risks using its veteran courier Harry Gold to contact both David Greenglass and Klaus Fuchs in New Mexico. Saddling Gold with yet another Los Alamos spy was stretching security beyond acceptable limits, and Sax had perfect cover to visit his friend in New Mexico. In December 1944 Sax traveled to Albuquerque, where Hall handed him a two-page report on Los Alamos's implosion research that was highly evaluated by Soviet scientists. As Albright and Kunstel note in *Bombshell,* "What Ted Hall gave his Harvard roommate that day was a bold new concept for assembling a critical mass so rapidly that all risk of a fizzle would be eliminated. The idea would become the key to the invention of the plutonium bomb."[8]

Just a few months later, the Soviet intelligence services provided their chief, Lavrentiy Beria, with a comprehensive report on America's pursuit of the atomic bomb. Hall's information formed a substantial part of this report and was corroborated by information from David Greenglass. Fuchs, in his February 1945 meeting with Harry Gold, would later provide more details about plutonium and the implosion method for detonating the bomb that would confirm the information from the other two spies.

Just as the Soviet intelligence services could rely on multiple, well-placed sources on political and economic topics, it now enjoyed similarly unique advantages on America's primary military project. Beria's concerns about American disinformation were now alleviated thanks to separate sources reporting from inside the project. As noted in *Bombshell,* "this was a rare phenomenon, unique in American history. Three individuals unknown to each other decided for reasons of political philosophy to commit espionage at the same time, in the same place, giving approximately the same kind of information to the same foreign government."[9]

By the spring of 1945 Sax had been replaced as a courier by Lona Cohen, a seasoned Soviet intelligence veteran. Lona was an American citizen and CPUSA member recruited into the NKVD by her husband, Morris Cohen, who had served as a Soviet agent in the Spanish Civil War. The couple would become the most famous "mom and pop" operatives in KGB history. After Klaus Fuchs was arrested, the Cohens fled the United States and emerged four years later in Britain as the Krogers, a couple of quirky antiquarian book dealers. They were arrested in 1961 and sentenced to more than twenty years in prison. In 1969 they were released in a spy exchange and returned to Moscow, where they trained a future generation of KGB illegals and were glorified as "heroes of the Soviet Union."

While working with Hall, Lona Cohen demonstrated the ingenuity that later won her KGB honors. Meeting an agent in the isolated and closely monitored environment around Los Alamos was a nerve-wracking task. The Soviet intelligence officer had to devise a solid cover story for his or her presence in the far reaches of New Mexico and be ready to confidently answer questions if confronted by security officers that even patrolled the larger cities of Santa Fe and Albuquerque. For their meeting in the spring of 1945 in Albuquerque, Lona decided that, if asked, she would explain that she had tubercular problems and was searching for places to live in the dry New Mexico climate. Fortunately, she was never challenged en route to the meeting.

Hall passed to Lona crumpled pages of reports that she stuffed among tissues in a Kleenex box to smuggle back on the long train ride to her Soviet controllers in New York. These pages contained details on the workings of the American bomb. To Lona's dismay, security officers were checking passengers boarding the train as she arrived at the platform. The quick-thinking agent delayed boarding until the last minute, fumbled opening the zipper of her suitcase and searching for her ticket inside, and, in a bold move, asked a security officer to hold her Kleenex box while she looked. She "found" the ticket, answered a few routine questions about her travel, and boarded the train. For one brief moment an unsuspecting security agent held in his hands the evidence of major Soviet espionage against America. Lona Cohen's story would be recounted in the corridors of the KGB for years, an epic tale testifying to the wits and courage of a model officer.[10]

Hall's pages in the Kleenex box and the other information that he passed to the NKGB in 1944 and 1945 were far more valuable to the Soviets than Greenglass's sketches and description of the bomb. Hall was the first to tip the Soviets to Los Alamos's experiments on the bomb's implosion method, a project in which he was a key figure. According to Albright and Kunstel, "without the implosion principle, it seems likely the Soviets would have failed in their first desperate attempts to catch up to the Americans on the bomb. Not realizing the pitfalls of plutonium, the USSR might well have rushed blindly into building a bomb based on the older, cruder concept of a gun-type design."[11]

World War II ended a few months later after atomic bombs were dropped on Hiroshima and Nagasaki. Hall was discharged in June 1946, and that fall he joined other Manhattan Project scientists at the University of Chicago. He no longer had access to secrets and, since the defections of Bentley and Chambers, the Soviets had suspended contact with scores of their spies. Hall continued to pursue his two passions: science and communism. He pursued a PhD in physics, he married a Chicago girl with similar political views, and they both openly joined the Communist Party. His friend and one-time courier, Saville Sax, had flunked out of Harvard twice and decided to join Hall in Chicago, but their spying days seemed to be over.

In 1948, however, the Soviet intelligence services returned. The Soviets had learned that the Americans were researching a new generation of bombs at the University of Chicago. Morris Cohen was tapped to recontact

Hall and persuaded him to sever his overt ties to the party and infiltrate the project. Not only did Hall agree, but a Venona message decrypted years later suggested that he recruited two fellow scientists at Chicago whose identities have never been discovered.[12]

When the Soviets exploded their own atomic bomb in August 1949, Hall decided his work was done and his spying days were over. His decision was fortuitous because the following spring the Venona team deciphered the message that identified him as a willing recruit for the Soviet intelligence services.

The FBI had no other evidence except the Venona message and no penetrations of Soviet intelligence that could have shed further light on Hall's spying. After Harry Gold was arrested and admitted to receiving atomic secrets from a soldier at Los Alamos, FBI agents initially believed that Hall might be the culprit until Gold fingered Greenglass. Because the NKGB had wisely isolated Hall from the other atom bomb spies, none of them could provide any evidence against him in a trial. His decision to quit spying had also precluded any possibility that the FBI could catch him in the act of passing secrets.

The FBI then resorted to a tactic that it would use repeatedly when faced in future spy cases with no evidence usable in court. FBI agents simply confronted Hall, hoping that he would crack under questioning. But this "Hail Mary" attempt did not work. Hall denied any involvement in espionage. The only other person who could have identified him was Sax, who was not about to incriminate himself. Sax was also questioned by the FBI and followed his friend's example by denying any cooperation with the NKGB. The trail went cold and Hall remained free.

A few weeks after Hall's meeting with the FBI, Julius and Ethel Rosenberg were convicted and sentenced to death. Hall was well aware that he had given the Soviets far more than the Rosenbergs and must have wondered when and if the other shoe might drop. His case remained open at the FBI, but without a shred of evidence other than the Venona decrypts, agents were transferred to higher-priority cases and the investigation languished.

Hall moved to New York to work at the Sloan-Kettering Cancer Institute, where he immersed himself in a new field, microbiology. He occasionally met Soviet intelligence officers, though he had little to offer them. In 1953 he finally ceased all contact with the Soviets. A decade later, he and his family moved to England, where he pursued a career in microbiology at Cambridge University. He never abandoned his passion for communism, and he balanced his scientific pursuits with participation in rallies to ban the bomb and end the war in Vietnam.

Hall lived in quiet obscurity for more than thirty years, forgotten by the FBI and KGB. In a 1994 interview, Morris Cohen referred to the mysterious agent MLAD (Hall's KGB code name): "I assume that even in a hundred years his name won't be exposed."[13] He was wrong. Fifty years after Hall volunteered to spy for the Soviets, the declassified Venona decrypts included messages about Hall's espionage and Sax's collaboration. Hall's name was blacked out of the original release of the messages, but his identity was soon discovered.

Hall was not arrested. The Venona messages, once considered too sensitive to be revealed in court, were now insufficient to prosecute Hall. By this time, even those with direct knowledge of Hall's treachery were unable to provide evidence. His friend Sax, his recruiter Kurnakov, and his courier Lona Cohen had all died. Although the justice system ignored Hall, the *Washington Post* published an article in February 1996 identifying him as agent MLAD, and the media began pressing him for his side of the story.

In 1997 Hall wrote a long letter to Albright and Kunstel, which has since been published in *Bombshell*.[14] In this letter Hall stopped just short of admitting espionage but acknowledged mistakes in his youth: "In 1944 I was nineteen years old—immature, inexperienced and far too sure of myself. I recognize that I could easily have been wrong in my judgment of what was necessary, and that I was indeed mistaken about some things, in particular my view of the nature of the Soviet state." Still, he remained unrepentant. While admitting that he was a different person from the youthful scientist he once was, he wrote "I am no longer that person, but I am by no means ashamed of him."

In 1999 Hall died from the renal cancer that had plagued him for ten years. He was never arrested and never spent a day in jail. Theodore Hall and Julius Rosenberg were both guilty of espionage, but fate treated them very differently.

Other Manhattan Project spies of the Soviet Golden Age of espionage were mentioned only by their code names in the Venona traffic and remained unknown for years. Like Ted Hall, they escaped punishment for their betrayal. In just the past few years, however, the identities of a few more Soviet spies who worked on the atomic bomb have been revealed. Surprisingly, the identity of one of these spies was disclosed by the president of Russia.

THE SPY FROM THE
CORNFIELDS

GEORGE KOVAL

Koval was a trained agent, not an American civilian. He was
that rarity, which you see a lot in fiction but rarely in real life—
a sleeper agent. A penetration agent. A professional officer.

JOHN EARL HAYNES *on* GEORGE KOVAL.
Quoted by Walsh, "George Koval"

Six decades after the end of the Manhattan Project, a rare event occurred in espionage history. On November 2, 2007, Russian prime minister Vladimir Putin posthumously honored Soviet citizen George Koval with the Hero of the Russia Federation Medal, the nation's highest civilian honor, and acknowledged Koval's contribution to the Soviet Union's development of an atomic bomb. In the Kremlin's press release on this unusual event, Putin noted that Koval, operating under the code name DELMAR, provided information that "helped speed up considerably the time it took for the Soviet Union to develop an atomic bomb of its own, thus ensuring the pres-ervation of strategic military parity with the United States."[1] According to Putin's admission, Koval was able to obtain this critical information because he was "the only Soviet intelligence officer to penetrate the US secret atomic facilities producing the plutonium, enriched uranium, and polonium used to create the atomic bomb."[2]

Nations rarely acknowledge those who have spied for them, even with the passage of years and especially in the extremely secretive Russia. Putin's calculated public revelation had less to do with historical enlightenment than with politics. Putin had consistently touted the past achievements of the intelligence services as part of his nationalist agenda. A former KGB officer himself, Putin headed the Federal Security Service (Federal'naya Sluzhba Bezopasnosti, FSB). After embarking on a political career that led to the presidency of Russia, Putin significantly increased the budget, authorities, and morale of the nation's intelligence services and used them as instruments to solidify his power.

In addition, Putin presented the Koval award a month before parliamentary elections in December 2007, and the event was timed not only to promote patriotic pride and public support for his spy services but also to ensure victory for his party, United Russia, which did triumph handily with about 65 percent of the vote nationwide. Just a few months earlier, Putin had also publicly trumpeted his pledge to restore Russian military power after a decade of steep post-Soviet decline, which may explain his recognition of the achievements of an officer from the GRU, Russia's military intelligence service. To laud the civilian service as well, the Russian government awarded a similar medal soon after to George Blake, a Soviet spy in British intelligence who had escaped prison after his arrest for espionage.

Both medals were awarded a few months after Britain's Queen Elizabeth had presented a medal to Oleg Gordievsky, the senior KGB officer who had spied for years on behalf of the British and had defected in 1985. Some observers suggested that the Russian awards were a rejoinder to the United Kingdom, which had roiled bilateral relations by accusing Russian intelligence of involvement in the poisoning of the Putin regime critic Alexander Litvinenko in London.[3] Whatever the political reason behind Putin's decision, he did acknowledge an important event in the history of Russian espionage against America. Koval's achievement was unique. Despite the extensive network of Soviet spies stealing American secrets in the 1930s and 1940s, no other known staff officer of Russian intelligence has ever obtained employment with a security clearance inside a US government agency.[4]

Koval's story began in an unlikely venue for an espionage tale, the heartland of America's corn belt in Sioux City, Iowa, a central hub for the tristate area of southwest South Dakota, northwest Iowa, and northeast Nebraska.

In the second great wave of immigration to the United States, millions of Russians and Eastern Europeans came to America's shores and fanned out across the country. Iowa's farmlands, meatpacking plants, and coal mines attracted many of them with the promise of employment and a better life. This new wave of immigrants included Jewish craftsmen and merchants like Koval's father Abraham, a carpenter by trade, who had fled the czar's ruthless persecution of their brethren in Russia and set up cultural organizations and synagogues in their newly adopted land to preserve their heritage.

Abraham Koval and his wife Ethel, the daughter of a rabbi, left their small town near Minsk in Byelorussia and settled in Sioux City in 1910. Three sons were born to the couple in America. George, the middle son, was born on Christmas Day 1914.[5] Just months after George's birth, the leftist Industrial Workers of the World, nicknamed the "Wobblies" in popular parlance, organized one of their "free speech fights" in Sioux City to organize agricultural and industrial laborers into their union. And they found sympathy among some of the European immigrants in the area who had already been supporters of socialism in their native countries.

Among these supporters was George's mother Ethel, who had belonged to an underground revolutionary socialist group back in Russia and had passed on her beliefs to her family.[6] As a teenager, George was a brilliant student as well as an outspoken advocate of communism. He graduated from a local high school with honors at the age of fifteen years, and a year later he served as a young delegate to a Communist Party conference in Iowa. In September 1931 he was arrested for occupying the office of a municipal official and demanding that he find shelter for two women evicted from their homes.[7] His FBI file would later reflect his comments to schoolmates that his family planned to return to Russia where the government was building a "utopia" for Jews.

Koval was telling his classmates the truth. He went on to study electrical engineering at the University of Iowa. But in 1932, in the midst of the Great Depression, the Kovals decided to return to Russia. The "utopia" about which George had regaled his friends was Birobidzhan, a sparsely populated region in the far eastern reaches of Russia near the Chinese border. The settlement of thousands of Soviet Jews to Birobidzhan was in reality a Stalinist creation designed to attract Jews to farming and better integrate them into Soviet society. This remote area had been selected as the enclave to resettle Jews away from more populated areas in Russia where the gentile population despised and repressed them and also to check the expansion of China and Japan into the Russian Far East.[8] The dream of a Jewish utopia, however, was destroyed by the brutal Stalinist purges of the late 1930s, in which the Jewish leadership of Birobidzhan was denounced as Trotskyites and was suppressed.

But the purges were years away when the Kovals joined the many pro-Soviet Jews who dreamed of the socialist paradise and left behind the economic misery of Depression-era America. Abraham Koval was the secretary of the Sioux City Branch of ICOR, the Yiddish acronym for the "Association for Jewish Colonization in the Soviet Union," which facilitated his family's return to Russia. The Kovals joined an ICOR commune in Birobidzhan, where Abraham continued to work as a carpenter and his sons labored at various jobs. In 1934 young George went to Moscow to study chemical engineering at the Mendeleyev Institute of Chemical Technology. While at the university, he met and married a fellow student, but they were together only a short time before the course of George's future was changed dramatically.

George graduated with honors in 1939, and by that time he had already attracted the interest of the GRU. Like any good intelligence service, the GRU undoubtedly scouted the country's universities for new talent, an especially pressing need after Stalin's purges of the Red Army in the 1930s. Koval would have been an irresistible candidate. He had an unblemished record and excelled in the sciences at a time when the Soviet Union intensively sought new technologies to develop its military capabilities against increasing Nazi aggression. Many of these new technologies had been developed in the United States, and George Koval had been born and bred in heartland America, spoke native English, and could maneuver in the country without raising an iota of suspicion.

More important, Koval, unlike the many Soviet spies in America who had emerged through the ranks of the Communist Party of the United States, was barely known to other communist comrades in the United States or tainted by the atrocious tradecraft they practiced. He was trained directly by professionals to be an "illegal" intelligence officer, and he would conduct espionage against the land of his birth for eight years, from 1940 to 1948.

As Koval would reveal to Arnold Kramish, a former colleague in the Manhattan Project, "I was drafted into the [Soviet] army in 1939 to cover up my disappearance from Moscow."[9] By October 1940 Koval returned to America as a fully trained GRU illegal. He worked for Raven Electric, a supplier of electrical products located in New York City, far from his native Iowa. His cover legend was simple and was designed to arouse absolutely no interest. He claimed that he was unmarried, was an orphan, had been raised by an aunt, and was a man of modest means who never traveled—all elements of a bland biography that was complemented by his naturally easygoing personality and sincere enthusiasm for America's pastime, baseball. More important, he abandoned his vocal support of communism and largely kept his political views to himself, most assuredly on the advice of his GRU trainers.

Koval's intelligence mission was to gather information on American chemical research and development, especially regarding toxins that might have military applications. Living the life of a law-abiding citizen, Koval registered for the draft even though his GRU controllers hoped he would win a deferment because he would lose his access to chemical information. The Soviet intelligence services in general had little interest in US enlisted men because they had limited access to information of value. George Koval would prove to be the exception.

Koval was drafted into the US Army as a private in February 1943. After basic training, he was sent to the Citadel to study electrical engineering and then assigned to a new unit, the Army Specialized Training Program, which was intended to provide qualified enlisted men with specialized technical training at American colleges and universities. He was also then sent to the City College of New York, the alma mater of Julius Rosenberg, to further develop his engineering skills. From that hotbed of socialism, Koval was reassigned in August 1944 to an innocuous-sounding unit called the Special Engineer Detachment.

The Special Engineer Detachment was part of the Manhattan Project. The Soviet Union had now infiltrated a professionally trained intelligence officer into America's most secret military endeavor. Because of his job responsibilities, Koval gained broader access to elements of the atomic bomb program than any other Soviet spy inside the Manhattan Project.

Although Los Alamos was the primary facility where the atomic bomb was to be designed, other aspects of the program were dispersed among sites throughout the United States. Klaus Fuchs, Greenglass, and Hall were all inside Los Alamos, but Koval was assigned to the Oak Ridge, Tennessee, facility, which was responsible for enriching uranium and producing plutonium, the two most critical elements in the atomic bomb program. At the time, Manhattan Project scientists were focusing on the development of two different types of bombs, one based on enriched uranium and the other on plutonium.[10]

Both chemical elements are radioactive, and thus the facility required a strict regimen of safety measures. Koval was granted unique access to the facility because of his position as a health physics officer responsible for monitoring radiation levels throughout the entire complex. As Kramish noted when interviewed years later, "he had access to everything."[11] As part of these duties, Koval was responsible for maintaining the inventory of experimental substances for potential bomb fuels. After a few months at Oak Ridge, Koval was granted leave, which allowed him to contact his GRU handler and pass descriptions of the entire complex and its functions and, in particular, data about the production of enriched uranium and plutonium. When he was interviewed decades later about his GRU career, Koval was still proud that he was the only Soviet intelligence officer who held a sample of American-produced plutonium in his hands.

The production processes for uranium and plutonium on which Koval reported were as crucial to the project as the bomb design under development at Los Alamos. Uranium was in short supply and plutonium had proven too unstable for the bomb design developed at Los Alamos. The material would simply fizzle out and fail to produce the chain reaction required for detonation. Project scientists experimented with another radioactive element, polonium, for use as the neutron "initiator" to trigger the desired chain reaction to detonate the plutonium bomb. Polonium for this trigger, dubbed "Urchin," was produced at Oak Ridge and another project site in Hanford, Washington. The material was then sent for refinement to a facility in Dayton, where the polonium-based trigger was produced.

In June 1945 Koval was transferred to serve as a health officer at the Dayton facility, where he learned detailed information about the polonium solution to the "fizzle" problem. According to Kramish, the use of the polonium trigger was "one of the most secret parts of the Manhattan Project."[12] In July of that year the polonium trigger "passed a crucial test; . . . the world's first atomic bomb exploded at a site called Trinity within the bombing range in Alamogordo, New Mexico."[13] Just a month later, the uranium-based atomic bomb was dropped on Hiroshima and, within a few days, the plutonium-based bomb activated by the polonium trigger fell on Nagasaki.

By the end of 1945 Koval had passed the secret of the polonium trigger to the Soviets. He not only reported to the GRU that the Americans were producing polonium for use as the trigger in the plutonium bomb but also provided the monthly volume of polonium production at Oak Ridge. A few months later he supplemented this by outlining the process used by Manhattan Project scientists to produce polonium.[14]

On August 29, 1949, the USSR surprised the world with the detonation of its first atomic bomb at the Semipalatinsk Test Site in Kazakhstan. This device was a plutonium weapon, and years later the Soviets revealed that the device employed a polonium-based trigger. No less an authority than the Russian Atomic Energy Ministry—in its 1995 study, *The Creation of the First Soviet Nuclear Bomb (Sozdanie pervoy sovetskoy yadernoy bomby* in Russian)—confirmed that intelligence provided directly to program head Igor Kurchatov included a detailed description of the polonium trigger.[15]

In 2007, when Putin posthumously awarded Koval the nation's highest civilian medal, Russian news accounts revealed that the polonium trigger for the first Soviet bomb was prepared according to the "recipe" provided by their agent Delmar, that is, George Koval.[16] The relatively recent revelations about Koval are largely based on Russian accounts that are, to some degree, designed to laud the accomplishments of Russian intelligence. But Koval's American colleagues in the Manhattan Project have confirmed the broad access he enjoyed to the program. Besides, he was both a professionally trained intelligence officer and a scientist who would have foraged for secrets and recognized those of most importance. Also, considering the slipshod security at Manhattan Project facilities, his acquisition of the polonium trigger secret is certainly plausible. He most likely did obtain and pass the key information to the Soviets, and, along with secrets from other atomic bomb spies, it contributed to the Soviets' detonation of its first atom bomb an estimated five years ahead of schedule.

The bombs produced by the Manhattan Project ended the war. Thousands of servicemen, including Koval, were demobilized and returned home to resume their lives. He was honorably discharged from the army in February 1946 and returned to New York to continue his studies in electrical engineering. He shunned offers to continue classified work in Dayton because he believed the security situation in the United States would become more difficult. His fellow GRU officer, Igor Gouzenko, had defected in Canada and made startling revelations about Soviet espionage, especially in the Manhattan Project. A month after Koval's discharge, a British scientist involved in the atom bomb program, Alan Nunn May, was arrested as a result of Gouzenko's information.

Koval decided instead to complete his bachelor's degree at City College in February 1948. A few months later, he told friends that he had received an offer to work on the construction of a power station in Europe. In October 1948 he sailed for Europe aboard an ocean liner and simply vanished for decades.

By the time Koval departed, his initial suspicions about increasing security in the United States were more than justified. Besides the Gouzenko revelations, the accusations of widespread Soviet espionage by Elizabeth Bentley and Whittaker Chambers were now public, the House Un-American Activities Committee had launched its hearing on the issue, and decipherment of Venona messages were unearthing an increasing number of Soviet spies, a development the Soviets had learned from their spy in the project, William Weisband.

However, this increased scrutiny alone might not have prompted Koval's departure. The Soviet intelligence services tenaciously held on to their productive spies. Thus, even after David Greenglass was discharged from the army and lost his access, the NKGB tried to redirect him to study at the University of Chicago to target scientists working there on classified military research. Soviet intelligence also recontacted Theodore Hall to direct him to the same university. Koval had not only been productive but was also a trained professional staff officer of the GRU. He would not have left the United States unless Moscow had discovered a specific threat to his security and warned him to escape.

One of the Russian chroniclers of Koval's story, Andrey Shitov, claims that a Soviet defector told the FBI that the GRU illegal chief in the early 1940s was based in a New York company dealing in electronic products and, as a result, Koval and Raven Electric were investigated by the FBI.[17] Years later, colleagues in Oak Ridge and Dayton and acquaintances from Sioux City confirmed that they had been interviewed by the FBI in about

1949 or 1950. This investigation turned up information about Koval and his family's procommunist views during their Iowa days and their subsequent emigration to Russia.

Interviews with Koval's colleagues in the Manhattan Project would have clarified his access for the FBI and enabled an assessment of the secrets he might have given away and the damage caused. Information from a defector, supplemented by the Koval family history and the fact of their return to the Soviet Union, would have strengthened the case against agent "Delmar." The final piece of evidence, circumstantial though it might be, was Koval's mysterious disappearance.

Some commentators on the Koval case have criticized the FBI for keeping the Koval case secret from the American public in an effort to prevent embarrassment over its failure to protect American secrets.[18] Although hints of a government cover-up are always titillating, the truth is probably far more mundane.

The FBI could hardly be blamed for the stream of scientists with communist views who infiltrated the Manhattan Project. General Leslie Groves, who directed the project, was wary of the FBI and depended on army counterintelligence to conduct security checks on project personnel. Besides, the demand for qualified technical personnel was so intense that scientific ability often overrode security concerns, as evidenced in the case of Klaus Fuchs and a legion of other scientists who were hired in spite of their communist beliefs.

The FBI certainly got off to a late start pursuing Soviet spies in the United States, but the Soviets were allies at the height of their espionage against America and the FBI was understandably more focused on spying by the Axis powers and on widespread Depression-era crime. Besides that, the FBI for obvious reasons does not comment on open investigations, and the Koval case remained open for years because the suspect had vanished. The FBI was also coping not only with the Koval investigation but also with hundreds of more active leads that surfaced in the deciphered Venona messages. Koval's case, much like that of Ted Hall, eventually languished in the FBI's files while the spy hunters pursued these other leads and dealt with newly emerging espionage threats in the early days of the Cold War. The FBI, however, reportedly did attempt to search for Koval in Western Europe and Latin America with the help of the

CIA.[19] They came up with nothing, because Koval had long since been in the Soviet Union.

Koval lived a quiet life after his return to the Soviet Union. Ironically, though he was honored by the president of Russia himself after his death, Koval's secret achievements brought him more misery than glory in his postwar life in the Soviet Union.

In June 1949 Koval was issued a terse notification of his honorable discharge from the Red Army, which, for security reasons, made no mention of his outstanding contribution to his country. He returned to his scientific studies, and in two years he earned the Soviet equivalent of a doctorate at the Mendeleyev Institute. But the gaping hole in his résumé prevented him from finding a university job. As he himself later claimed in correspondence with Kramish, "life in the Soviet Union was such that my activities, instead of bringing me awards, had an opposite, very strong negative effect on my life." When he left the Soviet military in 1949, Koval added, "I received discharge papers as an untrained rifleman with the rank of private—with nine years of service in the armed forces!" His seemingly undistinguished military record and his foreign background "made me a very suspicious character."[20]

Exasperated, Koval finally appealed to the GRU for help, and his old masters did respond. In March 1953 the head of the GRU intervened with the Ministry of Higher Education, and Koval was soon hired by his alma mater, but only as a lab assistant. He eventually managed to obtain a faculty position and spent the next forty years there teaching and writing several scientific papers.

Koval remained unheralded for almost the rest of his life until the GRU welcomed him to a closed ceremony at its headquarters in 2000 and awarded him a medal for his service to military intelligence. Within a few years details about his intelligence exploits began to emerge in the Russian media, though he was still identified only by his code name. Vladimir Lota, the author of *The GRU and the Atom Bomb,* interviewed Koval several times for his book and wanted to identify "agent Del'mar" by his true name, but Koval refused.[21] He finally changed his mind in a conversation with the author on his ninety-second birthday. A month later, in January 2006, Koval died.

George Koval is only one of the many Soviet spies of the era whose identities have come to light in recent years thanks to the partial opening of KGB files and intensive research by historians. More identifications will likely come in the future as these historians shed further light on this dark period in the story of espionage against America. Even if more spies inside the Manhattan Project are identified, the evidence now available proves that the Soviet intelligence services had stolen secrets about the most vital elements of America's most significant military effort in World War II.

ESPIONAGE IN THE COLD WAR AND BEYOND

The exposure of Soviet spy networks after World War II finally wakened a slumbering America to the espionage threat. At the dawn of the Cold War, the FBI significantly increased its counterespionage efforts against the Soviets and their allies. Besides that, almost two centuries after its birth, the United States finally established a peacetime intelligence service with the creation of the CIA in 1947.

The CIA was only part of the huge growth in America's national security apparatus during the Cold War. As a result, the number of American citizens with access to government secrets significantly increased, which consequently complicated the problem of finding spies among them. In addition to the FBI's scrutiny of Soviet activities, the US government established stricter security measures to protect its classified information and monitor signs of espionage among federal employees with security clearances. Unfortunately, in many cases, these security measures were only loosely observed and spies went undetected.

In other cases security measures were simply outdated. The Truman administration instituted a program for US government employees that required the swearing of a loyalty oath and undergoing a background investigation to determine communist sympathies. By that time, however, America's flirtation with Soviet communism had passed. Communism attracted few Americans after the revelations of Stalinist purges, the Soviets' heavy-handed imposition of control in Eastern Europe, and the exposure of Soviet subversion inside the United States. Americans would continue to spy for the USSR, but their motivations had drastically changed from the ideological commitment of earlier espionage networks. Meanwhile, the FBI and other investigative agencies limited their security programs to narrow investigations of an employee's communist sympathies instead of his or her overall suitability for work in sensitive positions.

Since the Revolutionary War, Americans had spied for a broad spectrum of motives. Some, like Benjamin Church and Edward Bancroft, passed secrets to the enemy because of outright greed, whereas others, like Benedict Arnold, betrayed secrets because of a complex brew of motives including money, ego, and revenge. Still others spied out of loyalty to a cause, such as the vast majority of Civil War spies and the Soviet spies of the 1930s and 1940s, who were lured by the promise of a communist utopia. From the onset of the Cold War, Americans continued to spy for these same reasons, but the overwhelming majority of them were more interested in dollars than doctrine and betrayed their country for purely financial motives. According to a Department of Defense study on espionage by Americans between 1947 and 2001, "Americans most consistently have cited money as the dominant motive for espionage and over time money has increased in predominance among motives. . . . Of individuals who professed a single motive for espionage, one-fourth of the civilians and three-fourths of the military claimed they had spied for money."[1]

Alexander Feklisov, the Soviet handler of the Rosenbergs, nostalgically bemoaned the passing of the ideological spy in his memoirs: "The time for national missions and civic loyalties had returned and the great ideological spies finally disappeared from the scene. After that, payment became the norm."[2] His colleagues in the Soviet intelligence services, however, quickly adjusted and recruited a number of military enlisted men to exchange secrets for money in the first decade of the Cold War. The exposure of these spies eventually convinced US security officials to focus on sudden or unexplained wealth as an indicator of espionage activity and to conduct background investigations on overall suitability, not merely the existence of communist sympathies.

Security measures like background investigations and monitoring potential indicators of employee problems or espionage are essential to combating foreign espionage, but ultimately the best method to catch spies in one's own ranks is to have spies in the enemy's counterintelligence apparatus. Although John Jay's Committee on Detecting and Defeating Conspiracies made some fledgling attempts in this regard, the United States placed little emphasis on penetrating hostile intelligence services until the Cold War. During the height of Soviet espionage in the 1930s and 1940s, defectors like Walter Krivitsky had alerted the US government to spy networks in America, but the FBI never exploited these defectors for leads to other disaffected colleagues who might have been recruited to identify American spies.[3]

During the Cold War, however, the FBI's pursuit of Soviet intelligence officers was an essential aspect of its counterespionage program. The CIA, though its primary duty was intelligence collection, was also responsible for recruiting officers in foreign intelligence services who could reveal their countries' spies in the US government. The highest priority on the CIA's list was the recruitment of Soviet intelligence officers. Throughout the Cold War, FBI and CIA sources inside the counterespionage services of the Soviet Union and its allies would unmask a number of spies in the US government.

Despite increased security measures and offensive counterespionage attempts to penetrate hostile intelligence services, America remained plagued by its chronic tendency toward disbelief that its citizens in positions of trust would betray the nation's secrets. As noted above, during the Cold War every US government agency involved in national security, with the exception of the coast guard, fell victim to espionage. Ironically, even the FBI and CIA, the two primary agencies charged with combating foreign espionage, failed to detect spies in their own ranks because of this tendency toward disbelief.

In 1985 Edward Lee Howard, an operations officer fired by the CIA, betrayed America's best source inside the USSR to gain his revenge. A White House review of the CIA's handling of this case noted the "fundamental inability of managers of the Soviet Division to think the unthinkable, that a [CIA] Directorate of Operations employee would engage in espionage."[4] Even after the Howard case, the CIA still refused to think the "unthinkable" about a more damaging spy in its midst. In 1994 Aldrich

Ames, a CIA officer who worked in the heart of counterintelligence on the Soviet Union, was arrested after betraying to the KGB dozens of American sources inside the USSR. Ames had remained undetected for nine years, despite mediocre performance reports, heavy drinking, and signs of unexplained wealth.

The CIA, however, was not alone in its disbelief. The FBI remained largely impregnable to Soviet espionage during the 1930s and 1940s and had investigated scores of espionage suspects throughout the US government. However, for years FBI counterespionage had no hint that one of its own, Robert Hanssen, was spying for Russia. Like Ames, Hanssen worked in counterespionage on the Soviet Union and provided his masters with virtually the US government's entire playbook to protect the nation's secrets from the USSR.

Ames and Hanssen, like many other spies during and after the Cold War, were eventually caught due to a combination of their own tradecraft mistakes and US counterespionage measures that were far more professional than the amateurish ones of pre–Cold War America. Before the Cold War, American spies were often exposed primarily due to their own gross tradecraft errors, as in the cases of Benedict Arnold and Rose O'Neal Greenhow, or due to defectors from their cause, as in the case of the Soviet spies of the 1930s and 1940s. Other espionage and sabotage attempts were frustrated by the shoddy tradecraft of their controllers, as in the case of the German spymasters in World War I and World War II. The Soviets and their allies exercised more efficient tradecraft in dealing with their Cold War spies. Although many of these spies remained undetected for years, like their predecessors, they too eventually made costly security mistakes and were caught.

The punishment for Americans caught spying evolved during the Cold War. Thanks to the decryption of Soviet messages in the Venona Project, a vast number of spies were identified; but the very sensitivity of the project precluded use of the information in open court. This dilemma continued through the first half of the Cold War as intelligence agencies successfully argued against prosecution in many spy cases to avoid revelations of government secrets in espionage trials.[5] In 1977, however, President Jimmy Carter's attorney general, Griffin Bell, reversed this policy and advocated a balanced approach that would allow prosecution while preserving classified information. Procedures to achieve this balance were introduced—such as closed hearings and limiting disclosure to only the judge, jury, and attorneys—and some of these procedures were subsequently included in congressional legislation on espionage law.[6]

The severity of punishment meted out for espionage also changed after the controversial Rosenberg trial. No other American citizen convicted of espionage was executed after the Rosenbergs. The damage caused by a handful of these spies was arguably similar or even more serious than the harm done by the Rosenbergs. The information supplied by John Walker to the Soviets, according to an affidavit at his trial from the director of naval intelligence, had "potential . . . war-winning implications for the Soviet side."[7] Walker was ultimately sentenced to life imprisonment and still sits in jail for his crime, but Julius Rosenberg sat in the electric chair for his.

The difference was that Julius Rosenberg and his wife Ethel were both symbols and arrested spies. Their case symbolized the sharp divide between conservatives and liberals on communism, and their trial galvanized both sides into impassioned debate. For liberals, the Rosenbergs were iconic victims of a paranoid, right-wing witch hunt. For conservatives, they were symbols of an insidious foreign menace threatening America's way of life. The Rosenbergs were ultimately executed as much for what they represented as what they did. By the time of Walker's arrest, however, America had grown accustomed to Cold War espionage. The exposure of Soviet Bloc spies had become as routine a part of the Cold War as arms negotiations and saber rattling summit meetings.

Although the Soviet Bloc dominated espionage against America during the Cold War, in the 1980s a new trend emerged that continues to the present day. Arrests of spies revealed that, aside from the members of the Soviet Bloc, other nations, among them both allies and adversaries, were stealing America's secrets. According to the Department of Defense study cited above, almost one-third of the American spies arrested in the 1980s committed espionage for other countries besides the Soviet Union.[8]

The arrest of CIA officer Larry Wu Tai Chin in 1985 for espionage on behalf of the People's Republic of China heralded a massive espionage effort against the United States that has mushroomed in the ensuing decades. Since Washington established diplomatic relations with Beijing,

Chinese intelligence has flooded America with students, scientists, businesspeople, and émigrés from all walks of life to harvest America's political, military, economic, and scientific secrets. Communist China, of course, had long been an adversary of the United States. A more shocking espionage case surfaced in the same year with the arrest of US Navy analyst Jonathan Pollard for passing secrets to Israel, America's most stalwart ally in the Middle East and recipient of enormous amounts of US military and economic assistance.

On the eve of the 1990s, the Berlin Wall fell. Within two years, communist regimes in Eastern Europe toppled, Germany reunified, and the Soviet Union ceased to exist. The superpower conflict that had defined the world order for almost half a century was over. Still, peace had not come. During the 1990s the United States deployed troops against warlords in Somalia and dictators in Iraq, Serbia, and Haiti. Terrorism gradually replaced the Soviet Union as the greatest threat to US national security. A shadowy terrorist group known as al-Qaeda (Arabic for "the base") sprouted from the jihadist forces that had fought the Soviets in Afghanistan and attacked Americans both at home and abroad.

The new geopolitical order and the new threats were not the only dramatic changes of the decade. Globalization, the growing socioeconomic and cultural interdependence of peoples and corporations, added a new twist to the espionage threat. In the globalized economy, corporate information became as important to a nation's security as military or political secrets. America, the only remaining superpower when the dust of the Cold War cleared, was the primary target. According to an estimate by the American Society for Industrial Security, in 1996 alone the theft of US business proprietary information amounted to more than $2 billion a month.[9] In response to the increasing theft of corporate secrets, Congress passed the Economic Espionage Act in 1996, which made the theft or misappropriation of trade secrets a criminal offense.

By the end of the twentieth century, globalization also began to challenge traditional concepts of loyalty to a state, and increasing numbers of Americans spied not for money or ideological beliefs but because of foreign attachments and dual allegiances. More than half the spies arrested in the 1990s claimed that dual allegiance drove them to cooperate with foreign powers.[10] Continuing the trend from the 1980s, an increased number of these spies with dual loyalties committed espionage on behalf of countries other than Russia, among them a growing number of allies. According to the former national counterintelligence executive, Joel Brenner, as of 2007, "there are now 140 foreign intelligence services that try to penetrate the United States or US organizations abroad, and for many of them, we are their number one target."[11]

Although this ever-increasing number of nations spy against the United States, the nation still remained unable to resolve the dilemma between maintaining security in the national defense and ensuring civil liberties. Even after the vast Soviet penetration of US national security, some Americans still remained wary of possible abuses while pursuing spies. Unfortunately, their suspicions were revived when spy mania once again prevailed over spycatching in the early days of the Cold War.

The excesses of Lafayette Baker and Attorney General Mitchell Palmer were repeated in the 1950s when Senator Joe McCarthy waved lists of communists who allegedly worked in the US government in front of news cameras and defamed civil servants with baseless charges that surfaced no major Soviet spies. McCarthy was eventually discredited, but his smear campaign again made Americans suspicious of government efforts to catch spies. Those suspicions were fueled again during the turbulent 1960s and 1970s. As opposition to the Vietnam War mounted, the FBI's director, J. Edgar Hoover, launched COINTELPRO (Counterintelligence Program) to investigate possible links between foreign powers and antiwar protesters and civil rights activists. The protests were ultimately proven to be homegrown dissent and not the chicanery of foreign subversives. Over the course of a century, Baker's police, Palmer's raids, McCarthy's lists, and Hoover's COINTELPRO unmasked no major spies in the US government. Their messianic hunt for subversives ultimately backfired and, paradoxically, exacerbated the threat of foreign espionage by discrediting counterespionage and diverting resources from the pursuit of real spies in the government.

The same suspicions about counterespionage have persisted to the present day and have had a major impact on America's war to combat terrorism. More than a decade after the catastrophic terrorist attacks of September 11, 2001, the US government is still grappling with the dilemma between upholding civil liberties and ensuring the defense of its citizens from terrorism. This dilemma is reflected in heated debates over the interrogation, detention, and prosecution of captured terrorists and also over government attempts to monitor communications to identify terrorists and prevent future attacks.

The immediacy of terrorist threats highlights the urgency of resolving the dilemma now to counter both espionage and terrorism. During the Cold War, American counterespionage often failed to catch spies who penetrated almost every agency of the US government. Until the Soviet Bloc's spies were discovered, they passed secrets that could have shifted the balance in a war with the Soviet Union. Fortunately, the United States never went to war, and the Soviets never had the opportunity to fully exploit the advantages gained from their Cold War spies. Once these spies were unmasked, the United States had time to adopt countermeasures to offset the damage from American secrets in the hands of the USSR.

Now, however, America is at war and no longer has the time to develop countermeasures against terrorist espionage. Terrorists can exploit information from their spies to pinpoint the security vulnerabilities of potential targets, gauge America's knowledge of terrorist tactics, and ultimately use this insider information to launch immediate attacks.

Terrorist spies can work in almost any profession that provides the access to prepare for an attack—a cafeteria worker picking up snippets of information in a mess hall, a crossing guard with knowledge of school bus schedules, or, as exposure of a June 2007 plot against John F. Kennedy International Airport in New York demonstrated, an airline employee with the motive and access to inflict significant damage. Even more devastating would be a terrorist spy inside the US government, especially its intelligence community, where he or she could acquire secrets that would make possible a catastrophic terrorist attack that would pale by comparison with Cold War espionage losses.

Another threat that could prove even more dangerous to US national security than terrorism is cyber espionage. Computers and Internet communications have revolutionized every field of human endeavor, ranging from improvements in medical science to facilitation of criminal activity. Espionage is no exception. A century and a half ago, Civil War spies used primitive yet ingenious means to hide scraps of paper with military information in the tresses of Southern belles or secret compartments in food baskets. Nazi spies rolled up the blueprints of America's most advanced weapon, the Norden bombsight, in an umbrella to transport them to Germany. By the time of the Cold War, technological advances in cryptography facilitated national defense communications; but a single spy, John Walker, enabled the Soviets to read classified US Navy communications on a daily basis.

Even the millions of messages to which the Soviets were privy through Walker pale by comparison with the potential theft of terabytes of data that can be gleaned through cyber intrusion. Information gained through traditional espionage is usually piecemeal, consisting of bits of intelligence provided by individual spies that must be assembled like pieces of a jigsaw puzzle to obtain a clear picture of an adversary's plans, intentions, and capabilities.

In contrast, the information that a single spy can download to a thumb drive and spirit away to his masters could fill in such a puzzle more quickly and more comprehensively. Remote cyber intrusion without the intervention of a spy offers even more advantages by eliminating the elements of human weakness that plague traditional espionage—the typical spy's inaccurate memory, tradecraft lapses, falsehoods, and other emotional factors.

Hacking—that is, gaining unauthorized access to information systems— was originally the province of computer hobbyists motivated by mischief making or financial gain. The number of hacking incidents in recent years has skyrocketed. Between 2006 and 2011 the US Computer Emergency Response Team of the Department of Homeland Security reported an astounding 650 percent rise in cyber intrusions.[12]

The US government has become a major target of hackers ranging from lone wolf computer experts to foreign governments that have also capitalized on cyber intrusions as a means of conducting espionage. Among these governments, China has been the most aggressive in gaining access to government systems in the United States and other nations. As the director of national intelligence, James Clapper, noted in testimony to the US Senate, "the Chinese made a substantial investment in this area. They have a very large organization devoted to it. And they're pretty aggressive. . . . This is just another way in which they glean information about us and collect on us for technology purposes. And so, it's a very formidable concern."[13]

China has reportedly gleaned the equivalent of millions of pages of sensitive US government information through cyber espionage, from passwords of State Department users to designs for costly weapons systems.[14] China, however, is not alone among governments employing cyber espionage. Russia, a country with a long tradition of excellence in mathematics, has generated some of the world's leading computer hackers. Among the more troubling hacking incidents in recent years, Russian intelligence was suspected of cyber intrusion into the military information systems of Georgia before and during its August 2008 incursion into the country.

In addition to this cyber espionage, however, the Russians were also suspected of disrupting the computer communications of the Georgian government and military to reduce its ability to resist the attack and brought down civilian websites to instill panic in the populace. This incident of "cyberwarfare"—that is, the penetration of computer systems not for espionage but sabotage—was considered the first "integration of offensive cyber operations into political-military strategy."[15] Such cyberattacks could also be perpetrated by terrorists if they developed the capability and could threaten a host of vital infrastructure systems in the United States, including the banking industry, telecommunications, electrical grids, and air traffic control.

Some skeptics argue that fears of the impact of cyber intrusions are overblown.[16] The rapid advances in computer technology and the increasing number and sophistication of computer attacks appear to indicate otherwise. The comments of such observers suggest a gnawing sense of disbelief, the same disbelief that has led to many of the stories of espionage against America presented here. The lessons from these stories of past American spies from the Revolutionary War to the Cold War should serve to overcome this disbelief and illuminate the directions for an unknown future where imminent threats like terrorism and cyberattacks jeopardize the nation's security. There has been no moment in American history more urgent to apply these lessons than now in order to prevent spying by those dedicated to destroying the American way of life.

Notes

INTRODUCTION

1. Redmond, "America Pays the Price."
2. Ibid.
3. Dulles, *Craft of Intelligence*, 19.
4. The ideologically committed American spies who refused payment are discussed in detail in parts IV and V of the present volume. One of the leading couriers of espionage information, Elizabeth Bentley, was particularly incensed when her Soviet handler offered her money and lashed back at him: "What kind of racket is this when they pay you to do your duty?" Bentley, *Out of Bondage*, 247. Another courier, Harry Gold, was irked by Soviet attempts to provide him with money and gifts. Although Gold could barely make ends meet, he even refused expenses and paid for his extensive travel as a courier from his own funds. Hornblum, *Invisible Harry Gold*, Kindle edition, chap. 3, location 1266.
5. Dulles, *Craft of Intelligence*, 52.
6. Keegan, *Intelligence in War*, 24.
7. Commager and Morison, *Growth of the American Republic*, 283.
8. The trial and execution launched an era of intense debate between anti-Soviet conservatives and liberals who believed that the Rosenbergs were innocent victims of a right-wing witch hunt. However, over the years revelations from a host of sources—including decrypted Soviet cable traffic in the Venona Project, KGB defectors, and even Rosenberg's handler—have proven conclusively that Julius provided Soviet intelligence with classified information on the atomic bomb. Debate still continues in some quarters about the significance of the information passed by Julius and the extent of his wife Ethel's involvement, topics that are discussed in detail in chapter 31 of this volume. See Benson and Warner, *Venona*; Gordievsky and Andrew, *KGB*, 315–16, 379–81; Andrew and Mitrokhin, *Sword and the Shield*, 128; and Feklisov and Kostin, *Man behind the Rosenbergs*.

9. Haynes, Klehr, and Vassiliev, *Spies,* 62.
10. Keegan, *Intelligence in War,* 6.

CHAPTER 1

1. Zinn, *People's History,* 60.
2. Ibid., 77.
3. Crews, "Spies and Scouts."
4. Thompson, *Secret New England,* xi–xii.
5. Bakeless, *Turncoats,* 32.
6. For further information on Revere and the Mechanics, see Cummings, "Paul Revere," 3–14; Fischer, *Paul Revere's Ride,* Kindle edition, chap. 5, location 1003; Bakeless and Bakeless, *Spies of the Revolution,* 42–50; and Rafalko, *Counterintelligence Reader,* 1:2–3.
7. Revolutionary espionage and conspiracy were often fueled by alcohol. Taverns have long been convenient venues for spy meetings and were the seedbeds of patriotic intrigue before and during the war. The Continental Congress often met in the City Tavern in Philadelphia, and the local Sons of Liberty in New York City drank together at Fraunces Tavern, now a historic landmark. Militiamen in Lexington gathered at Buckman's Tavern, and Revere's "Mechanics" frequented the Green Dragon in Boston, where all would take an oath of secrecy before discussions. The founding fathers themselves were no strangers to the world of alcohol—Sam Adams was a brewer and saloonkeeper and John Hancock and John Adams were both distillers.
8. Isaacson, *Benjamin Franklin,* 308–9. Franklin stung his son with his accusation that "you, who are a thorough courtier, see everything through the government's eyes." Van Doren, *Benjamin Franklin,* 483.
9. Rafalko, *Counterintelligence Reader,* 1:1.
10. Bakeless, *Turncoats,* 125.
11. Jay's brother James also contributed to colonial intelligence by developing invisible inks to hide secret correspondence. Rafalko, *Counterintelligence Reader,* 1:24.
12. Allen, *George Washington, Spymaster,* 169.
13. Rafalko, *Counterintelligence Reader,* 1:11.
14. Bakeless, *Turncoats,* 162.

CHAPTER 2

1. For further information on Church, see Allen, *George Washington, Spymaster,* 35–37; Bakeless and Bakeless, *Spies,* 60–75; Bakeless, *Turncoats,* 9–24; Rafalko, *Counterintelligence Reader,* 1:3–9; and Cummings, "Paul Revere," 7.
2. Rafalko, *Counterintelligence Reader,* 1:5.
3. Ibid., 1:6.
4. Ibid.
5. Dulles, *Craft of Intelligence,* 206.
6. Rafalko, *Counterintelligence Reader,* 1:7.

7. Bakeless and Bakeless, *Spies of the Revolution,* 74–75.
8. French, *General Gage's Informers,* 181.
9. Rafalko, *Counterintelligence Reader,* 1:9.
10. Bakeless and Bakeless, *Spies of the Revolution,* 72.
11. Quoted by Bakeless, *Turncoats,* 146.
12. Thompson and Campbell, "General Gage's Spies," 19.

CHAPTER 3

1. The company was managed by Augustin Beaumarchais, who, as a diversion from his commercial interests, was also a dramatist and wrote *The Barber of Seville* and *The Marriage of Figaro,* on which the famous operas are based.
2. Schaeper, *Edward Bancroft,* Kindle edition, chap. 3, location 1411–31.
3. Ibid., chap. 2, 1117–37.
4. For in-depth studies of the Bancroft case, see Schaeper, *Edward Bancroft,* which is the most comprehensive treatment to date. Also see Vaillancourt, "Edward Bancroft"; O'Toole, "Intrigue"; Miller, *Spying for America,* 48–51; and Allen, *George Washington, Spymaster,* 87–91.
5. For a comprehensive examination of Bancroft's study, see Schaeper, *Edward Bancroft,* chap. 1, 291–455.
6. Schaeper, *Edward Bancroft,* chap. 4, 1873.
7. Rafalko *Counterintelligence Reader,* 1:22.
8. Although many analysts associate "covert action" with any clandestine activity, the term has a very precise definition today: clandestine activities conducted overseas to influence policies or events in support of national policy objectives. As defined in Executive Order 12333, issued by President Ronald Reagan in 1981, the activities are to be planned and conducted such that the role of the US government is not apparent or acknowledged publicly.
9. Allen, *George Washington,* 93.
10. For further details on Bancroft's clandestine communications and use of the dead drop, see O'Toole, "Intrigue," 75; Schaeper, *Edward Bancroft,* chap. 6, 2745–58; and Vaillancourt, "Bancroft," A59.
11. Vaillancourt, "Bancroft," A61.
12. Miller, *Spying for America,* 51.
13. Schaeper, *Edward Bancroft,* chap. 7, 3065.
14. Fortescue, *Correspondence of King George,* 3:481–82.
15. Schaeper, *Edward Bancroft,* chap. 7, 3180.
16. Ibid., chap. 6, 2457–60.
17. O'Toole, "Intrigue," 79.
18. Charlevois, "Nothing to Hide," 85.
19. Vaillancourt, "Bancroft," A63.
20. Charlevois, "Nothing to Hide," 87. Miller and O'Toole support the theory that Franklin knew of and exploited Bancroft's spying to deceive the British. A handful of authors have suggested that Franklin himself was a British spy, but most historians have convincingly disproven this theory.
21. Miller, *Spying for America,* 61.

CHAPTER 4

1. Wallace, *Traitorous Hero*, 7.
2. Quoted by Van Doren, *Secret History*, 146.
3. Wallace, *Traitorous Hero*, 56.
4. Campbell, "Benedict Arnold," 86.
5. Ibid., 89.
6. Brandt, *Man in the Mirror*, 116.
7. Wallace, *Traitorous Hero*, 151.
8. Van Doren, *Secret History*, 188.
9. Campbell, "Benedict Arnold," 101.
10. Quoted by Sparks, *Writings of George Washington*, 7:523.
11. Quoted by Taylor, *Some New Light*, 55.
12. Wallace, *Traitorous Hero*, 232.
13. Van Doren, *Secret History*, 194.
14. Amory, "John André," A1–A2.
15. Van Doren, *Secret History*, 210.
16. Quoted by Amory, "John André," A4.
17. Quoted ibid., A3.
18. Van Doren, *Secret History*, 300.
19. Amory, "John André," A9.
20. Pennypacker, *George Washington's Spies*, 162.
21. Brandt, *Man in the Mirror*, 224.
22. Allen, *George Washington, Spymaster*, 127.
23. Quoted by Sparks, *Writings of George Washington*, 7:533.
24. Flexner, *Traitor and Spy*, 393.
25. Rafalko, *Counterintelligence Reader*, 1:20.
26. Wallace, *Traitorous Hero*, 314.
27. Quoted by Van Doren, *Secret History*, 159.
28. Middlekauff, *Glorious Cause*, 545.
29. Morpurgo, *Treason at West Point*, 135.
30. Quoted by Pennypacker, *George Washington's Spies*, 181.
31. Sale, *Traitors*, 61.

CHAPTER 5

1. "Jefferson clearly conceived of it as an intelligence mission. . . . He planned it to its finest detail, and he chose soldiers rather than scientists to carry it out." Ameringer, *US Foreign Intelligence*, 34–35.
2. Miller, *Spying for America*, 88.
3. Ameringer, *US Foreign Intelligence*, 48.
4. Kane, *Spies for the Blue and Gray*, 10.
5. Stern, *Secret Missions*, 11.
6. "Stay-behinds" refer to covert operatives of a nation who literally "stay behind" in a country when a state of war exists between that country and the operative's nation. Citizens of the stay-behind's nation are usually expelled or depart the

enemy country once war is declared. The stay-behind's mission is to collect intelligence inside enemy territory and/or conduct sabotage or other subversive activities. Often the stay-behind is an actual citizen of the enemy country or can pass as one.

7. Stern, *Secret Missions*, 18.
8. Fishel, *Secret War*, 54.
9. Ibid., 27.
10. Fishel, "Mythology."
11. Bakeless, *Spies of the Confederacy*, 120.
12. Kane, *Spies for the Blue and Gray*, 49–50.
13. Bakeless, *Spies of the Confederacy*, 94.
14. Markle, *Spies and Spymasters*, 19.

CHAPTER 6

1. Markle, *Spies and Spymasters*, 5.
2. Fishel, *Secret War*, 113.
3. Morison, *Oxford History of the American People*, 2:414.
4. Fishel, *Secret War*, 104.
5. Ibid., 222–24.
6. Sears, *Civil War Papers of George B. McClellan*, 453.
7. Another innovator in all-source intelligence was Brigadier General James Garfield, who was to become the twentieth president of the United States and the second chief executive after Lincoln to be assassinated. While serving as chief of staff to the commanding general of the Army of the Cumberland, Garfield operated as a one-man all-source intelligence shop. He gained mastery at consolidating information on enemy troop numbers and movements and presenting comprehensive analyses to his commander.
8. As Edwin Fishel notes, once again progress in intelligence was forgotten once the war ended: "It [all-source intelligence] passed from the scene with the end of the Civil War, not to be re-invented until the Second World War. It was legislated into permanence in the National Security Act of 1947, which established the Central Intelligence Agency." Fishel, *Secret War*, 299.
9. Pinkerton, *Spy of the Rebellion*, Kindle edition, location 2017–40.
10. An excellent analysis of the letter is presented by Daigler, "Shaping of American Counterintelligence."
11. Pinkerton, *Spy of the Rebellion*, location 2028.
12. Daigler, "Shaping of American Counterintelligence," 45.

CHAPTER 7

1. For further details on Webster, see Axelrod, *War between the Spies*, 123–28; Kane, *Spies for the Blue and Gray*, 62–78; Markle, *Spies and Spymasters*, 21–22, 69–70; and Miller, *Spying for America*, 116–19.
2. Kane, *Spies for the Blue and Gray*, 66–67.

CHAPTER 8

1. Blackman, *Wild Rose*, xi. For other studies of Greenhow, see Axelrod, *War between the Spies*, 44–62; Bakeless, *Spies of the Confederacy*, 4–13, 58–60; Fishel, *Secret War*, 58–68; Kane, *Spies for the Blue and Gray*, 12–27; Markle, *Spies and Spymasters*, 154–67; and Miller, *Spying for America*, 107–11.
2. Bakeless, *Spies of the Confederacy*, 9–10; Kane, *Spies for the Blue and Gray*, 14.
3. Fishel, *Secret War*, 58.
4. Quoted by Kane, *Spies for the Blue and Gray*, 25.
5. Blackman, *Wild Rose*, 3–7; Kane, *Spies for the Blue and Gray*, 22.
6. Blackman, *Wild Rose*, 184–87.
7. Ibid., 186.
8. Greenhow, *My Imprisonment*, Kindle edition, location 1068.
9. Miller, *Spying for America*, 115; Rafalko, *Counterintelligence Reader*, 1:60.
10. Bakeless, *Spies of the Confederacy*, 50.
11. Fishel, *Secret War*, 64–65.
12. Ibid.
13. Pinkerton arrested another female spy, Belle Boyd, whose alleged spy exploits were widely heralded during and after the Civil War, even though most are unproven. Boyd had no spy network, used no tradecraft, and in fact brazenly trumpeted her espionage to the press. Her love for the limelight hardly qualifies her as a spy, and Pinkerton only arrested her after she herself had told the press about her spying against Union troops.
14. Fishel, *Secret War*, 65.
15. Ibid., 66.

CHAPTER 9

1. Fishel, *Secret War*, 24–25. Also see Mogelever, *Death to Traitors*; Kane, *Spies for the Blue and Gray*, 79–81; Markle, *Spies and Spymasters*, 6–7; and Miller, *Spying for America*, 121–24.
2. Mogelever, *Death to Traitors*, 50.
3. Fishel, *Secret War*, 56–57.
4. Miller, *Spying for America*, 121.
5. Baker's techniques are discussed in detail by Daigler, "Shaping of American Counterintelligence," 46–47; and by Mogelever, *Death to Traitors*, 88–91.
6. Bakeless, *Spies of the Confederacy*, 8.
7. For further details on secessionist clerks, see Fishel, *Secret War*, 57.
8. Baker's postwar role in two major events in US history far overshadowed his counterespionage work. Although other agencies did most of the legwork, Baker led the investigation and capture of John Wilkes Booth and his coconspirators for the assassination of Abraham Lincoln. Ironically, he was later embroiled in controversy regarding rumors that he himself may have been part of the cabal to kill Lincoln. The second event occurred when, after Lincoln's death, Baker lied to Congress in his attempts to assist radicals win the impeachment case against President Andrew Johnson.

CHAPTER 10

1. Markle, *Spies and Spymasters*, 99. For more information about Conrad, see Axelrod, *War between the Spies*, 86–93; Bakeless, *Spies of the Confederacy*, 64–87; Markle, *Spies and Spymasters*, 99–101; and Miller, *Spying for America*, 149–53.
2. Markle, *Spies and Spymasters*, 100.
3. Miller, *Spying for America*, 152.
4. Quoted by Bakeless, *Spies for the Confederacy*, 323.

CHAPTER 11

1. Varon, *Southern Lady*, 253–56; for further biographical information on Van Lew, see 9–10, 17–34. For discussions of Van Lew's espionage work, also see Ryan, *Yankee Spy*; Axelrod, *War between the Spies*, 104; Fishel, *Secret War*, 551–55; Markle, *Spies and Spymasters*, 56, 179–87; and Leonard, *All the Daring of a Soldier*, 50–57.
2. Ryan, *Yankee Spy*, 10.
3. Varon, *Southern Lady*, 255.
4. Ibid., 181.
5. Most accounts of Van Lew's espionage refer to her as "Crazy Bet" or "Mad Lizzie" because she supposedly feigned the role of an unbalanced woman so the Confederates would dismiss her as a threat to the cause. In Elizabeth Varon's biography, however, the author makes a convincing case that Van Lew's social status and not any pretended craziness was the key to her espionage success. According to Varon, Van Lew's contemporaries, especially Confederate officials, never viewed her as a daffy spinster. In addition, Varon notes that the myth was created mistakenly by a chronicler of her story who only knew Van Lew in her later years when she was understandably distraught over her impoverishment after the war. Varon, *Southern Lady*, 253–56.
6. Ryan, *Yankee Spy*, 8.
7. Kane, *Spies for the Blue and Gray*, 178.
8. Van Lew did keep a diary, which recorded her strong antislavery views, her work caring for Union prisoners, and developments in the war. She constantly worried that the journal would be discovered and noted that she was frequently watched by Confederate detectives. The parts of the diary that remain have been reproduced by Ryan, *Yankee Spy*.
9. Axelrod, *War between the Spies*, 104.
10. In her biography of Van Lew, Varon notes that little documentary evidence regarding the Mary Bowser story exists but speculates that Mary Richard, a slave whom Van Lew sent north for schooling, may be identical to Bowser. Varon, *Southern Lady*, 165–68.
11. Ryan, *Yankee Spy*, 12.
12. Rose, "Civil War," 76. Rose—which is a pseudonym for Kenneth Daigler, a former counterintelligence expert at the Central Intelligence Agency—also notes that Bowser was inducted into the US Army Intelligence Hall of Fame at Fort Huachuca, Arizona, on June 30, 1995. Rose's article is an enlightening and compelling study of a topic rarely treated in Civil War histories.

13. Markle, *Spies and Spymasters,* 58.
14. For a full account of Edmonds's spy career, see Reit, *Behind Rebel Lines.*

CHAPTER 12

1. Miller, *Spying for America,* 196.
2. Ibid., 197.

CHAPTER 13

1. Shirer, *Rise and Fall of the Third Reich,* 177–84.
2. Miller, *Spying for America,* 217.
3. Rintelen did collect occasional intelligence of value. As one example of political intelligence, he tipped off Germany that Italy was buying munitions from America and would probably join the Allies, an analysis that subsequently proved correct. Witcover, *Sabotage at Black Tom,* 86.
4. For more details, see Witcover, *Sabotage at Black Tom,* 118–19; and Rafalko, *Counterintelligence Reader,* 1:101.
5. Warner, "Kaiser Sows Destruction," 3.

CHAPTER 14

1. For an in-depth study of the interagency rivalries, see Fox, "Early Days of the Intelligence Community."
2. Ibid., 9.
3. Ibid., 14–16.
4. Gilbert, Finnegan, and Bray, *In the Shadow of the Sphinx,* 7.
5. Quoted by Jensen, *Price of Vigilance,* 115.

CHAPTER 15

1. Ibish, *Report on Hate Crimes,* 7.
2. Franklin D. Roosevelt arrived at his home, across the street from Palmer's, as the bomb went off. As he ran into his home to check on his children's safety, Roosevelt spotted pieces of the terrorist's corpse on his doorstep, a traumatic episode that must have affected his own approach to subversion as president. Miller, *Spying for America,* 231.
3. Ibid., 232.

CHAPTER 16

1. Miller, *Spying for America,* 240.
2. Ibid., 244.
3. Rowan, *Secret Agents,* 214.
4. Kahn, *Hitler's Spies,* 85–87.
5. For a comprehensive treatment of the Rumrich case, see Batvinis, *Origins,* 3–28. The Rumrich case is also discussed by Leon Turrou, the FBI agent who led the

investigation, and by Rowan; see Turrou, *Nazi Spies,* 33–63; and Rowan, *Secret Agents,* 106–27.

6. Batvinis, *Origins,* 12.
7. Rowan, *Secret Agents,* 122.
8. Batvinis, *Origins,* 28.
9. Ibid., 14.
10. A US representative from New York, Samuel Dickstein, read Griebl's name into the *Congressional Record* as a Nazi spy. In an ironic twist Dickstein himself would become a spy for the Soviet Union years later. Turrou, *Nazi Spies,* 200.
11. FBI, "Byte Out of History."
12. The full directive is given by Rafalko, *Counterintelligence Reader,* 1:173.
13. Ibid., 1:177–78.

CHAPTER 17

1. Miller, *Spying for America,* 254.
2. Pardini, *Legendary Norden Bombsight,* 294.
3. The security measures are detailed in ibid., 41.
4. A number of studies of German intelligence in the United States cover the Lang case: Farago, *Game of the Foxes,* 37; Johnson, *Germany's Spies,* 17–20; Kahn, *Hitler's Spies,* 330; and Wighton and Peis, *Hitler's Spies and Saboteurs,* 24–31.
5. Wighton and Peis, *Hitler's Spies and Saboteurs,* 27.
6. "*Goering* considers the Norden bombsight the most important thing in the world. In 1938 I memorized the blueprints and carried them over to Germany in my head. I got 10,000 marks for that job." Sayers and Kahn, *Sabotage,* 27.
7. Wighton and Peis, *Hitler's Spies and Saboteurs,* 28.
8. Ibid., 28–29.
9. Kahn, *Hitler's Spies,* 331.

CHAPTER 18

1. For more information on the Sebold case, see Batvinis, *Origins,* 226–56; Johnson, *Germany's Spies,* 30–32; Sayers and Kahn, *Sabotage,* 23–41; and Wighton and Peis, *Hitler's Spies and Saboteurs,* 31–39.
2. Batvinis, *Origins,* 228.
3. Wighton and Peis, *Hitler's Spies and Saboteurs,* 34.
4. Batvinis, *Origins,* 249.
5. For more details, see Batvinis, *Origins,* 226.
6. Miller, *Spying for America,* 270.
7. Batvinis, *Origins,* 233

CHAPTER 19

1. After a group of German army officers attempted to assassinate Hitler in July 1944, Canaris and a number of other senior officers considered disloyal to the regime were arrested and executed.

2. Dobbs, *Saboteurs*, 9. Dobbs's book is a comprehensive study of the German sabotage operation. Operation Pastorius is also discussed by Johnson, *Germany's Spies*, 61–72; and Wighton and Peis, *Hitler's Spies and Saboteurs*, 41–80.
3. Dobbs, *Saboteurs*, 59–60.
4. Ibid., 122.
5. The FBI convinced Dasch to plead guilty so his confession would remain secret and he could thus prevent Nazi reprisals against his mother and relatives who were still living in Germany. Hoover allegedly promised Dasch he would be released in six months (Dobbs, *Saboteurs*, 189–90). Johnson maintains that Dasch was hoodwinked so that Hoover could divert criticism for unlawful tactics against left-wing groups by taking all the credit for exposing the German sabotage ring (Johnson, *Germany's Spies*, 102).
6. For further information, see Willing, "William Colepaugh." Gimpel also wrote a memoir based on the operation; see Gimpel, *Agent 146*.
7. Willing, "William Colepaugh," 55.
8. Kahn, *Hitler's Spies*, 539.
9. Farago, *Game of the Foxes*, 333.
10. Kahn, *Hitler's Spies*, 523.

CHAPTER 20

1. Bearse and Read, *Conspirator*, 51. Other studies of Kent's case include Clough, *State Secrets;* and Snow, *Case of Tyler Kent*.
2. Gordievsky and Andrew, KGB, 226–27; Volkman, *Espionage*, 169. Bearse and Read also believe Kent spied for the Russians; see Bearse and Read, *Conspirator*, 35–41.
3. Bearse and Read, *Conspirator*, 10.
4. Quoted by Clough, *State Secrets*, 178–79.
5. Ibid., 29.
6. Persico, *Roosevelt's Secret War*, 24.
7. The theory is presented by Volkman, *Espionage*, 171–74.
8. Johnson, *Germany's Spies*, 83–84.
9. Miller, *Spying for America*, 271.
10. Kent's later years are detailed by Bearse and Read, *Conspirator*, 264–74.

CHAPTER 21

1. Rowan, *Secret Agents*, 76.
2. Hynd, *Betrayal*, 93.
3. Sayers and Kahn, *Sabotage*, 68.
4. For further details on Thompson, see Hynd, *Betrayal*, 62–72; Rowan, *Secret Agents*, 95–99; and Deacon, *Kempeitai*, 173–75.
5. Hynd, *Betrayal*, 53.
6. Another staff member of the navy, John Walker, spied for the Soviet Union for eighteen years and was perhaps the most damaging spy in American history. Like Thompson, Walker also tried—and succeeded—to lure his friends into espionage and even persuaded his brother and his son to join his spy ring.

7. Deacon, *Kempeitai,* 175.
8. Rowan, *Secret Agents,* 99.
9. For further details on Farnsworth, see Deacon, *Kempeitai,* 176–77; Hynd, *Betrayal,* 44–51; and Rowan, *Secret Agents,* 100–105.
10. Hynd, *Betrayal,* 48.
11. Deacon, *Kempeitai,* 176.
12. Rowan, *Secret Agents,* 105.
13. Matthews, *Shadows Dancing,* 29.
14. Ibid., 181.

CHAPTER 22

1. Brownell and Billings, *So Close to Greatness,* 278.
2. Allen Weinstein and Alexander Vassiliev coined the term "Golden Age" to describe Soviet espionage in America in their landmark study of the era; see Weinstein and Vassiliev, *Haunted Wood.*
3. Andrew and Mitrokhin, *Sword and the Shield,* 42.
4. OGPU is the Russian acronym for the Joint State Political Directorate, the USSR's civilian intelligence organization from 1923 until 1934, when it was incorporated into the NKVD, the acronym for the National Commissariat for Internal Affairs. The name of the Soviet civilian intelligence service was changed a number of times after its ancestor, the Cheka, was established after the Bolshevik Revolution. In 1934 the OGPU became the GUGB, the Main Directorate of State Security, which was within the NKVD. In 1943 the name of the security service was changed to the NKGB, the People's Commissariat of State Security, and then became the Ministry of State Security in 1946. All these were forerunners to the KGB, which was established in 1954.
5. Bentley, *Out of Bondage,* 176.
6. Romerstein and Breindel, *Venona Secrets,* 45.
7. Weinstein and Vassiliev, *Haunted Wood,* 5.
8. Benson and Warner, *Venona,* xvii–xviii.

CHAPTER 23

1. The secrets of Soviet espionage against America have been revealed in comprehensive detail not only by the declassification of Venona decrypts of Soviet intelligence cables but also in a host of other accounts. Weinstein and Vassiliev were granted access to Soviet intelligence archives for their excellent study of the issue; see Weinstein and Vassiliev, *Haunted Wood.* The Soviet defectors Oleg Gordievsky and Vasili Mitrokhin, who also had access to KGB archives, corroborated many details in other accounts and, on the US side, FBI agent Robert Lamphere provided a wealth of detail about FBI investigations and behind-the-scenes interagency deliberations on Soviet espionage; see Andrew and Mitrokhin, *Sword and the Shield;* and Lamphere, *FBI–KGB War.* Further revelations were uncovered by Vassiliev thanks to his unique access to KGB archives; much of the information he recorded from the documents into notebooks was included by Haynes, Klehr, and Vassiliev, *Spies.*

2. Peake, "Venona Progeny."
3. Benson and Warner, *Venona*, xv.
4. Ibid., xxi.
5. Haynes and Klehr, *Venona*, 339. The Centre for Counterintelligence and Security Studies has compiled a list of 541 sources; see Centre for Counterintelligence and Security Studies, "American Agents."
6. West, *Venona*, 34.
7. The intelligence historian Michael Warner framed the debate surrounding Truman's knowledge of Venona in "Did Truman Know about Venona?" *Center for the Study of Intelligence,* Bulletin 11 (Summer 2000): 2–4.
8. Haynes, Klehr and Vassiliev, *Spies,* 398.
9. Ibid., 400.
10. Ibid., 402.
11. Ibid., 405.
12. Ibid., 402.
13. The outing is briefly described by Weisband's son, William, in an interview with PBS *Nova Online,* www.pbs.org/wgbh/nova/venona/fami_weisband.html.

CHAPTER 24

1. For a detailed study of the Gouzenko case, see Knight, *How the Cold War Began.*
2. For the details about the defection, see ibid., 14–43.
3. Ibid., 2–3.
4. Quoted by Andrew and Mitrokhin, *Sword and the Shield,* 137.

CHAPTER 25

1. Bentley had initially gone to the FBI office in New Haven, Connecticut, in August 1945 but refrained from mentioning her knowledge of Soviet espionage activities. Instead she lodged "a vague complaint" about someone who approached her and claimed to be a federal official. Haynes and Klehr, *Early Cold War Spies,* Kindle edition, chap. 3, location 1360.
2. Kessler, *Clever Girl,* 48. In addition to Kessler's biography, for further details about Bentley's background, see her autobiography, Bentley, *Out of Bondage;* and Olmsted, *Red Spy Queen.*
3. Bentley, *Out of Bondage,* 4.
4. Kessler, *Clever Girl,* 39.
5. Bentley, *Out of Bondage,* 27.
6. For more details on the Silvermaster ring, see Weinstein and Vassiliev, *Haunted Wood,* 157–71.
7. Weinstein and Vassiliev, *Haunted Wood,* 87.
8. For the details of the Soviet efforts to remove Bentley as the controller of their spy rings, see ibid., 97–103.
9. Ibid., 95.
10. Bentley, *Out of Bondage,* 233.
11. Ibid., 243.

12. Weinstein and Vassiliev, *Haunted Wood,* 100.
13. Bentley, *Out of Bondage,* 247.
14. Ibid., 255.
15. Ibid., 279.
16. Weinstein and Vassiliev, *Haunted Wood,* 98.
17. Gorsky wrote in a cable to NKGB headquarters that "only one remedy is left—a drastic one—to get rid of her." His message is among the KGB archives cited by Weinstein and Vassiliev, *Haunted Wood,* 102.
18. Benson and Warner, *Venona,* 226.
19. Haynes and Klehr, *Early Cold War Spies,* chap. 3, Kindle location 1191.
20. The libel suits and criticism are discussed in detail by Kessler, *Clever Girl,* 190–94, 260–65.
21. Haynes, Klehr, and Vassiliev, *Spies,* 543.

CHAPTER 26

1. Weinstein, *Perjury,* 70.
2. Weinstein and Vassiliev, *Haunted Wood,* 38–44; Ehrman, "Alger Hiss Case," 2–4.
3. Weinstein and Vassiliev, *Haunted Wood,* 47.
4. Isaac Don Levine, the journalist who arranged Chambers's meeting with Berle, claimed that Berle tried to inform Roosevelt but got a cold shoulder. Levine, *Eyewitness,* 197. Berle claimed that he repeated Chambers's allegations to a White House aide, Marvin McIntyre, and not to Roosevelt. *New York Times,* August 31, 1948; Berle and Jacobs, *Navigating the Rapids,* 598.
5. Chambers, *Witness,* 470.
6. Winchell, *Winchell Exclusive,* 149.
7. Miller, *Spying for America,* 351.
8. National Security Agency, Venona decrypt, March 30, 1945, message, release 3, www.nsa.gov/public_info/_files/venona/1945/30mar_kgb_interviews_gru_agent.pdf.
9. Ehrman, "Alger Hiss Case," 12.

CHAPTER 27

1. Andrew and Mitrokhin, *Sword and the Shield,* 109.
2. Weinstein and Vassiliev, *Haunted Wood,* 18.
3. Ibid., 21.
4. Rees, *Harry Dexter White,* 79.
5. Ibid., 158.
6. For a detailed treatment of White's dealings with Pavlov, see Schechter and Schechter, *Sacred Secrets,* 22–26.
7. National Security Agency, Venona decrypt of August 4–5, 1944, message, release 3, www.nsa.gov/public_info/_files/venona/1944/4aug_harry_dexter_white.pdf.
8. Romerstein and Breindel, *Venona Secrets,* 51–52.
9. Rees, *Harry Dexter White,* 416.

CHAPTER 28

1. National Security Agency, Venona decrypt of June 24, 1944, message, www.nsa
   .gov/public_info/_files/venona/1944/24jun_covername_pazh.pdf.
2. Haynes and Klehr, *Venona*, 146–47. Currie's information was included in the same
   June 24, 1944, message cited in note 1.
3. Andrew and Mitrokhin, *Sword and the Shield*, 130.
4. Chambers, *Witness*, 468.
5. The most zealous supporter was Roger Sandilands, a professor and former student
   of Currie, who advanced the idea that Currie's dealings with the Soviets were
   sanctioned and dismissed the evidence of espionage. The historians John Earl
   Haynes and Harvey Klehr rebut Sandilands's arguments in detail; see Haynes and
   Klehr, *In Denial*, Kindle edition, location 1921–2034.

CHAPTER 29

1. Mitchell and Mitchell, *Spy Who Seduced America*, 19; Haynes, Klehr, and Vassiliev,
   Spies, 287–88.
2. Weinstein and Vassiliev, *Haunted Wood*, 279.
3. Ibid.
4. Ibid.
5. Ibid.
6. Benson and Warner, *Venona*, xxv.
7. National Security Agency, Venona decrypt of December 31, 1944, and January 8,
   1945, messages, release 3, www.nsa.gov/public_info/_files/venona/1944/31dec_
   flora_sovschin.pdf and www.nsa.gov/public_info/_files/venona/1945/8jan_judith_
   coplon.pdf.
8. Lamphere, *FBI–KGB War*, 108–10.
9. Ibid., 110.
10. Ibid.
11. Mitchell and Mitchell, *Spy Who Seduced America*, 54.
12. Ibid.
13. Ibid., 103.
14. Lamphere, *FBI–KGB War*, 118.
15. Ibid., 119.
16. For the details of the various trials, see Lamphere, *FBI–KGB War*, 110–24;
    and Mitchell and Mitchell, *Spy Who Seduced America*, 189–283.
17. Roberts, "Judith Coplon."

CHAPTER 30

1. Albright and Marcia Kunstel, *Bombshell*, 74.
2. The security measures, including their inadequacies, are discussed in detail by
   Rafalko, *Counterintelligence Reader*, 2:86–98.
3. Weinstein and Vassiliev, *Haunted Wood*, 176.
4. The details of Gold's attempts to reestablish contact with Fuchs are included in
   a KGB message. National Security Agency, Venona decrypt of November 16, 1944,

message, release 3, www.nsa.gov/public_info/_files/venona/1944/16nov_klaus_ fuchs_harry_gold.pdf.

5. Ibid., 210–11.

6. National Security Agency, Venona decrypt of April 10, 1945, message, release 3, www.nsa.gov/public_info/_files/venona/1945/10apr_atomic_bomb_info.pdf.

7. Albright and Kunstel, *Bombshell*, 218.

8. Lamphere, *FBI–KGB War*, 175–76.

CHAPTER 31

1. See Spartacus Educational, "Rosenberg Trial," www.spartacus.schoolnet.co.uk/ USArosenbergT.htm.

2. Feklisov and Kostin, *Man behind the Rosenbergs*, 96. Feklisov, who served for six years in the United States, was Rosenberg's primary Soviet case officer. His decision to publicize Rosenberg's spy exploits was designed to vindicate Julius Rosenberg but only served to add to the overwhelming evidence of his agent's espionage activities that surfaced after his execution. Feklisov's account also gives a rare glimpse into the close bonds developed between spy and handler.

3. Ibid., 105.

4. National Security Agency, Venona decrypt of December 5, 1944 message, release 3, www.nsa.gov/public_info/_files/venona/1944/5dec_various_agents.pdf.

5. Quoted by Roberts, *Brother*, 45.

6. Ibid, 81.

7. Feklisov and Kostin, *Man behind the Rosenbergs*, 133.

8. Ruth Greenglass's account of the meeting which she admitted to the FBI is discussed by Lamphere, *FBI–KGB War*, 196–97.

9. Quoted by Andrew and Mitrokhin, *Sword and the Shield*, 128.

10. Quoted by Albright and Kunstel, *Bombshell*, 139.

11. Moscow's concerns about Rosenberg's poor security and suspicions about the FBI's bugging of his apartment are outlined in a KGB message of December 1948 cited by Weinstein and Vassiliev, *Haunted Wood*, 222.

12. Ibid., 328.

13. KGB planning for the exfiltration is discussed by Weinstein and Vassiliev, *Haunted Wood*, 330–31.

14. National Security Agency, Venona decrypt of September 21, 1944, message, release 1, www.nsa.gov/public_info/_files/venona/1944/21sep_recruitment_by_ rosenbergs.pdf.

15. National Security Agency, Venona decrypt of November 27, 1944, message, release 1, www.nsa.gov/public_info/_files/venona/1944/27nov_mrs_rosenberg.pdf.

16. Quoted by Roberts, *Brother*, 236.

17. Radosh and Milton, *Rosenberg File*, 241.

18. Ibid., 260.

19. Quoted by Caute, *Great Fear*, 167.

20. Quoted by Miller, *Spying for America*, 354.

21. Radosh and Milton, *Rosenberg File*, 452.

22. Ibid., 348–49.

23. Caute, *Great Fear,* 68.
24. Roberts, *Brother,* 483.
25. Radosh and Milton, *Rosenberg File,* 279–80.
26. Khrushchev, *Khrushchev Remembers,* 194.
27. "Rosenberg Sons Admit Father Was Spy," CNN News, September 18, 2008, www .cnn.com/2008/CRIME/09/18/rosenberg.sons.ap/index.htm. Despite the vast amount of revelations confirming the Rosenbergs' espionage activity, some pockets of disbelief still exist. E.g., the National Committee to Reopen the Rosenberg Case still presents arguments supporting the Rosenbergs' innocence on its website, http://ncrrc.org.
28. Rhodes, *Dark Sun,* 187–93.
29. Interview in the *New York Times,* March 16, 1997, cited at www.cnn.com/ US/9703/16/rosenbergs.
30. Feklisov and Kostin, *Man behind the Rosenbergs,* 262.
31. Radosh and Milton, *Rosenberg File,* 449.
32. Albright and Kunstel, *Bombshell,* 164.
33. Quoted ibid., 270.
34. The information about McNutt was included in Vassiliev's notebooks and revealed by Haynes, Klehr, and Vassiliev, *Spies,* 34–39.
35. Haynes, Klehr, and Vassiliev, *Spies,* 339.
36. Feklisov and Kostin, *Man behind the Rosenbergs,* 127.
37. For further details on the spy ring's production, see Usdin, "Tracking Julius Rosenberg's Lesser Known Associates."
38. Feklisov and Kostin, *Man behind the Rosenbergs,* 119.
39. Usdin, "Tracking Julius Rosenberg's Lesser Known Associates," 15.
40. Feklisov and Kostin, *Man behind the Rosenbergs,* xvii.
41. For a detailed account of the key roles of Sarant and Barr in the USSR, see Usdin, *Engineering Communism.*

CHAPTER 32

Hall's comments on the book *Bombshell: The Secret Story of America's Unknown Atomic Spy Conspiracy,* by Joseph Albright and Marcia Kunstel, were included in a statement sent to the authors of *Bombshell* and were cited on page 288 of the book. *Bombshell* is the most comprehensive account of Theodore Hall's espionage activity and his role in building the atomic bomb, and this chapter draws heavily on their account. Albright and Kunstel conducted more than sixteen days of interviews with Hall.

1. Albright and Kunstel, *Bombshell,* 9.
2. Ed Hall ended his flirtation with communism, became an aeronautical engineer, and went on to play a leading role in the development of the US intercontinental ballistic missile program.
3. Albright and Kunstel, *Bombshell,* 38.
4. Ibid., 61.
5. Ibid., 90.
6. Weinstein and Vassiliev, *Haunted Wood,* 336.

7. National Security Agency, Venona decrypt of November 12, 1944, message, release 1, www.nsa.gov/public_info/_files/venona/1944/12nov_possible_new_recruit.pdf.
8. Albright and Kunstel, *Bombshell,* 114.
9. Ibid., 156.
10. The story, recounted by KGB officer Anatoliy Yakovlev in an internal KGB bulletin, is included by Albright and Kunstel, *Bombshell,* 152.
11. Ibid., 127.
12. Andrew and Mitrokhin, *Sword and the Shield,* 148. According to John Earl Haynes, Harvey Klehr, and Alexander Vassiliev, the basis for this claim is weak; see Haynes, Klehr, and Vassiliev, *Spies,* 124.
13. Albright and Kunstel, *Bombshell,* 277.
14. Ibid., 288–89.

CHAPTER 33

1. President of Russia, "President Vladimir Putin Handed Over to the GRU [Military Intelligence] Museum the Gold Star Medal." Although Putin revealed Koval's identity, details of the spy's exploits had already appeared in the Russian press. In *GRU i atomnaya bomba* [The GRU and the atomic bomb], Vladimir Lota, an unabashed supporter of Russian military intelligence, extols the achievements of DELMAR, Koval's code name. In another detailed account, the journalist Andrey Shitov—"Agent Del'mar vykhodit na svyaz'" [Agent Delmar comes into contact]—claimed that he had obtained two of the investigative files in Koval's FBI case, which had long since been declassified.
2. President of Russia, "President Vladimir Putin Handed Over to the GRU [Military Intelligence] Museum the Gold Star Medal."
3. Associated Press, "Russia Honors Its Cold War Spies."
4. During the Cold War, a Soviet Bloc national, Karl Koecher, of the Czechoslovak intelligence service, managed to be hired as a translator for the Central Intelligence Agency and compromised one of its best sources in the Soviet Foreign Ministry, Alexander Ogorodnik.
5. There was some confusion about Koval's exact birth date because some official documents listed it as December 25, 1913, but both school records and an official declaration of his father list the year as 1914.
6. Lota, "Ego zvali Del'mar" [They called him Delmar].
7. Shitov, "Agent Del'mar."
8. "Stalin's Forgotten Zion: An Illustrated History 1928–1996," www.swarthmore.edu/Home/News/biro/index2.html.
9. Walsh, "George Koval."
10. Ibid.
11. Broad, "Spy's Path."
12. Shitov, "Agent Del'mar."
13. Walsh, "George Koval."
14. Lota, "Ego zvali Del'mar." According to Lota's article, Koval's report was well detailed: "The polonium is sent to New Mexico where it's used to make an atomic

bomb. The polonium is produced from bismuth. As of 1 November 1945 the volume of plutonium produced was 300 curies per month, but that has now been raised to 500."

15. Lota, "Ego zvali Del'mar." According to the ministry study, the Soviets had obtained from stolen secrets the general description of the bomb, its measurements and mass as well as ten of the basic components used in the device. A very detailed description was provided for the construction of the polonium and beryllium source of the neutron "initiator," which consisted of a hollow beryllium sphere with fifteen wedge-shaped grooves in which the polonium was located.

16. Lota, "Ego zvali Del'mar."

17. Shitov, "Agent Del'mar."

18. Doyle, "US Embarrassed." See also "A Non-Definitive History: Koval, George Abramovich," DocumentsTalk.com, www.documentstalk.com/wp/koval-george-abramovich-1913-2006-delmar.

19. Lota, "Ego zvali Del'mar."

20. Walsh, "George Koval."

21. Lota, "Ego zvali Del'mar."

CONCLUSION

1. Herbig and Wiskoff, *Espionage,* xii.

2. Feklisov and Kostin, *Man behind the Rosenbergs,* 66.

3. Benson and Warner, *Venona,* xviii.

4. Weiner, Johnston, and Lewis, *Betrayal,* 54.

5. For a detailed discussion of this evolution, see Herbig and Wiskoff, *Espionage,* 6–11.

6. Ibid., 10.

7. Quoted by Church, "Justice."

8. Herbig and Wiskoff, *Espionage,* 74.

9. Poteat, "Downside of Globalization," 13.

10. Herbig and Wiskoff, *Espionage,* 69.

11. Brenner, "Strategic Counterintelligence."

12. Grow and Hosenball, "Special Report."

13. Clapper, "Testimony."

14. Grow and Hosenball, "Special Report."

15. Haddick, "This Week at War."

16. Morozov, "Cyber Scare."

BIBLIOGRAPHY

Albright, Joseph, and Marcia Kunstel. *Bombshell: The Secret Story of America's Unknown Atomic Spy Conspiracy.* New York: Random House, 1997.

Allen, Thomas G. *George Washington, Spymaster.* Washington, DC: National Geographic Society, 2004.

Ameringer, Charles. *US Foreign Intelligence.* Lanham, MD: Lexington Books, 1990.

Amory, Robert. "John André, Case Officer." *Studies in Intelligence,* 5, no. 3 (Summer 1961): A1–A15.

Andrew, Christopher. *For the President's Eyes Only: Secret Intelligence and the American Presidency from Washington to Bush.* New York: HarperCollins, 1995.

Andrew, Christopher, and Vasili Mitrokhin. *The Sword and the Shield: The Mitrokhin Archive and the Secret History of the KGB.* New York: Basic Books, 1999.

Associated Press. "Russia Honors Its Cold War Spies." November 12, 2007. www.msnbc.msn.com/id/21758424/ns/world_news-europe/.

Auger, Helen. *Secret War of Independence.* New York: Brown, 1956.

Axelrod, Alan. *The War between the Spies: A History of Espionage during the American Civil War.* New York: Atlantic Monthly Press, 1982.

Bakeless, John. *Spies of the Confederacy.* New York: Lippincott, 1970.

———. *Turncoats, Traitors and Heroes: Espionage in the American Revolution.* New York: Lippincott, 1959.

Bakeless, Katherine, and John Bakeless. *Spies of the Revolution.* New York: Scholastic Book Services, 1962.

Baker, Lafayette C. *A History of the United States Secret Service.* Westminster, MD: Heritage, 1970. First published 1867 by L. C. Baker.

Batvinis, Raymond J. *The Origins of FBI Counterintelligence.* Lawrence: University Press of Kansas, 2007.

Bearse, Ray, and Anthony Read. *Conspirator: The Untold Story of Churchill, Roosevelt and Tyler Kent, Spy.* New York: Doubleday, 1991.

Beirne, Francis F. *Shout Treason: The Trial of Aaron Burr*. New York: Hastings, 1959.

Benson, Robert L., and Michael Warner, eds. *Venona: Soviet Espionage and the American Response 1939–1957*. Washington, DC: National Security Agency and Central Intelligence Agency, 1996.

Bentley, Elizabeth. *Out of Bondage*. New York: Devin-Adair, 1951.

Berle, Beatrice Bishop, and Travis Neal Jacobs. *Navigating the Rapids, 1918–1971: From the Papers of Adolf A. Berle*. New York: Harcourt, 1973.

Black, Conrad. *Franklin Delano Roosevelt: Champion of Freedom*. New York: PublicAffairs, 2003.

Blackman, Anne. *Wild Rose: Rose O'Neale Greenhow, Civil War Spy*. New York: Random House, 2005.

Bohlen, Charles E. *Witness to History*. New York: W. W. Norton, 1973.

Brandt, Claire. *Man in the Mirror: A Life of Benedict Arnold*. New York: Random House, 1994.

Brenner, Joel. "Strategic Counterintelligence." Speech before the American Bar Association Standing Committee on Law and National Security, March 29, 2007. www.dni.gov/speeches/20070329_speech.pdf.

Broad, William. "A Spy's Path: Iowa to A-Bomb to Kremlin Honor." *New York Times*, November 12, 2007. www.nytimes.com/2007/11/12/us/12koval.html.

Brownell, Will, and Richard N. Billings. *So Close to Greatness: A Biography of William C. Bullitt*. New York: Macmillan, 1987.

Campbell, Kenneth J. "Benedict Arnold, America's First Defector." In *Secret New England: Spies of the Revolution*, edited by Edmund R. Thompson. Kennebunk, ME: Association of Former Intelligence Officers, 1991.

Carlson, John Roy. *Under Cover: My Four Years in the Nazi Underworld of America*. New York: E. P. Dutton, 1943.

Caute, Douglas. *The Great Fear: The Anti-Communist Purge under Truman and Eisenhower*. New York: Simon & Schuster, 1978.

Centner, James L. *Codename: Magpie—The Final Nazi Espionage Mission against the US in WW II*. North Charleston, SC: Booksurge, 2006.

Centre for Counterintelligence and Security Studies. "American Agents Working for the Soviets, 1930s–1950s." www.cicentre.com/?pages=cases_venona.

Chambers, Whittaker. *Witness*. New York: Random House, 1952; Washington, DC: Regnery, 1987. Citations refer to the Regnery edition.

Charlevois, J. J. "Nothing to Hide." *Studies in Intelligence* 9, no. 2 (Spring 1965): 85–88.

Church, George. "Justice for the Principal Agent." *Time*, September 8, 1986. www.time.com/time/magazine/article/0,9171,962236-1,00.html.

Clough, Bryan. *State Secrets: The Kent-Wolkoff Affair*. London: Hideaway, 2005.

Cohen, Stan, Don DeNevi, and Richard Gay. *They Came to Destroy America: The FBI Goes to War against Nazi Spies and Saboteurs before and during World War II*. Missoula, MT: Pictorial Histories, 2003.

Commager, Henry Steele, and Samuel Eliot Morison. *The Growth of the American Republic*, 6th ed. New York: Oxford University Press, 1969.

Congreve, William. *The Mourning Bride. In The Completed Plays of William Congreve*, edited by Herbert Davis. Chicago: University of Chicago Press, 1967.

Conrad, Thomas N. *A Confederate Spy.* Westminster, MD: Heritage Books, 2009. First published 1892 by J. S. Ogilive.

Cook, Fred. *The Unfinished Story of Alger Hiss.* New York: William Morrow, 1958.

Cooper, H. H. A., and Lawrence J. Redlinger. *Catching Spies.* Boulder, CO: Paladin Press, 1988; New York: Bantam Books, 1990.

Craig, R. Bruce. *Treasonable Doubt: The Harry Dexter White Spy Case.* Lawrence: University Press of Kansas, 2004.

Crews, Ed. "Spies and Scouts, Secret Writing, and Sympathetic Citizens." *Journal of the Colonial Williamsburg Foundation,* Summer 2004. www.history.org/foundation/journal/Summer04/spies.cfm.

Cummings, Richard. "Paul Revere and the Mechanics." In *Secret New England: Spies of the Revolution,* edited by Edmund R. Thompson. Kennebunk, ME: Association of Former Intelligence Officers, 1991.

Current and Future Worldwide Threats: Hearings before the United States Senate Committee on Armed Services, 112th Cong. Testimony of James Clapper, Director of National Intelligence, March 10, 2011. http://armed-services.senate.gov/Transcripts/2011/03%20March/11-11%20-%203-10-11.pdf.

Daigler, Kenneth. "The Shaping of American Counterintelligence: Protecting Washington during the Civil War." *Intelligencer* 15, no. 1 (Fall–Winter 2005): 41–48.

Dasch, George J. *Eight Spies vs. America.* New York: McBride, 1959.

Davis, James Kirkpatrick. *Spying on America: The FBI's Domestic Counterintelligence Program.* New York: Praeger, 1982.

Deacon, Richard. *Kempeitai: The Japanese Secret Service Then and Now.* Tokyo: Tuttle, 1983.

DeBrosse, Jim. "Russian Spy Lived in Dayton, Stole Secrets." *Dayton Daily News,* February 15, 2010, www.daytondailynews.com/news/dayton-news/russian-spy-lived-in-dayton-stole-secrets-548624.html.

DeToledano, Ralph. *Seeds of Treason.* New York: Funk & Wagnalls, 1950; Belmont, MA: Western Islands, 1965.

——. *Spies, Dupes and Diplomats.* New York: Duell, Sloan and Pearce, 1952; New Rochelle, NY: Arlington, 1967.

Dobbs, Michael. *Saboteurs: The Nazi Raid on America.* New York: Alfred A. Knopf, 2004.

Doyle, Leonard. "US Embarrassed as Putin Honours Spy Who Came in from the Cornfields." *The Independent.* November 13, 2007. www.independent.co.uk/news/world/europe/us-embarrassed-as-putin-honours-spy-who-came-in-from-the-cornfields-400112.html.

Dulles, Allen. *The Craft of Intelligence.* New York: Harper & Row, 1963. Guilford, CT: Lyons, 2006. Citations refer to the Lyons edition.

Edmonds, S. Emma E. *Nurse and Spy in the Union Army.* Ann Arbor: University of Michigan Press, 2005. First published 1865 by W. S. Williams.

Ehrman, John. "The Alger Hiss Case." *Studies in Intelligence,* no. 10 (Winter–Spring 2001): 1–13.

Espionage Cases: 1975–2004. Monterey, CA: Defense Personnel Security Research Center, 2004.

Ewers, Justin. "New Evidence of a Soviet Spy in the US Nuclear Program." *US News & World Report,* January 2, 2009, www.usnews.com/news/national/articles/2009/01/02/new-evidence-of-a-soviet-spy-in-the-us-nuclear-program/photos.

Farago, Ladislav. *The Game of the Foxes.* New York: David McKay, 1971.

FBI. "A Byte Out of History: Spies Caught, Spies Lost, Lessons Learned." www.fbi.gov/news/stories/2007/december/espionage_120307.

Feis, William. *Grant's Secret Services.* Lincoln: University of Nebraska Press, 2002.

Feklisov, Alexander. Interview by *New York Times,* March 16, 1997. www.cnn.com/US/9703/16/rosenbergs.

Feklisov, Alexander, and Sergei Kostin. *The Man behind the Rosenbergs: By the KGB Spymaster Who Was the Case Officer of Julius Rosenberg, Klaus Fuchs, and Helped Resolve the Cuban Missile Crisis.* New York: Enigma Books, 2004.

Fischer, David Hackett. *Paul Revere's Ride.* New York: Oxford University Press, 1994.

Fishel, Edwin. "The Mythology of Civil War Intelligence." *Civil War History* 10, no. 4 (December 1964): 344–67.

———. *The Secret War for the Union: The Untold Story of Military Intelligence in the Civil War.* Boston: Houghton Mifflin, 1996.

Flexner, James. *The Traitor and the Spy: Benedict Arnold and John André.* Boston: Little, Brown, 1975.

Ford, Corey. *A Peculiar Service: A Narrative of Espionage in and around New York during the American Revolution.* Boston: Little, Brown, 1965.

Fortescue, Sir John. *The Correspondence of King George the Third.* London: Macmillan, 1928.

Fox, John F. "Early Days of the Intelligence Community: Bureaucratic Wrangling Over Counterintelligence, 1917–1918." *Studies in Intelligence* 49, no. 1 (2005): 9–17.

Freidel, Frank. *Franklin D. Roosevelt: A Rendezvous with Destiny.* Boston: Little, Brown, 1990.

French, Allen. *General Gage's Informers.* Ann Arbor: University of Michigan Press, 1932.

Gilbert, James L., John P. Finnegan, and Ann Bray. *In the Shadow of the Sphinx: A History of Army Counterintelligence.* Fort Belvoir, VA: US Department of the Army, 2005.

Gimpel, Erich. *Agent 146: The True Story of a Nazi Spy in America.* 1957. New York: Berkley, 2003. First published 1957 as *A Spy for Germany* by Robert Hale in London.

Gordievsky, Oleg, and Christopher Andrew. *The KGB: The Inside Story of Its Foreign Operations from Lenin to Gorbachev.* London: Sceptre, 1991.

Gouzenko, Igor. *The Iron Curtain,* edited and translated by Andy C. O'Brien. New York: E. P. Dutton, 1948.

Greenhow, Rose. *My Imprisonment and the First Year of Abolition Rule at Washington.* Kindle edition. First published 1863 by Robert Bentley.

Grow, Brian, and Mark Hosenball. "Special Report: In Cyber-Spy vs. Cyber-Spy, China Has the Edge." Reuters, April 14, 2011. www.reuters.com/article/2011/04/14/us-china-usa-cyberespionage-idUSTRE73D24220110414.

Haddick, Robert. "This Week at War: Lessons from Cyber War I." *Foreign Policy,* January 28, 2011. www.foreignpolicy.com/articles/2011/01/28/this_week_at_war_lessons_from_cyberwar_i.

Haynes, John Earl, and Harvey Klehr. *Early Cold War Spies: The Espionage Trials That Shaped American Politics*. New York: Cambridge University Press, 2006.

———. *In Denial: Historians, Communism and Espionage*. San Francisco: Encounter Books, 2003. Kindle edition.

———. *Venona: Decoding Soviet Espionage in America*. New Haven, CT: Yale University Press, 1999.

Haynes, John Earl, Harvey Klehr, and Alexander Vassiliev. *Spies: The Rise and Fall of the KGB in America*. New Haven, CT: Yale University Press, 2009.

Herbig, Katherine L., and Martin F. Wiskoff. *Espionage against the United States by American Citizens 1947–2001*. Monterey, CA: Defense Personnel Security Research Center, 2002.

Hiss, Alger. *In the Court of Public Opinion*. New York: HarperCollins, 1957.

Hoover, J. Edgar. *Masters of Deceit*. New York: Henry Holt, 1958; New York: Pocket Books, 1961.

Hornblum, Allen M. *The Invisible Harry Gold: The Man Who gave the Soviets the Atom Bomb*. New Haven, CT: Yale University Press, 2010.

Hyde, H. Montgomery. *The Atom Bomb Spies*. New York: Atheneum, 1980.

Hynd, Alan. *Betrayal from the East: The Inside Story of Japanese Spies in America*. New York: Robert M. McBride, 1943.

Ibish, Hussein, ed. *Report on Hate Crimes and Discrimination against Arab Americans: The Post–September 11 Backlash*. Washington, DC: American-Arab Anti-Discrimination Committee, 2003.

Isaacson, Walter. *Benjamin Franklin: An American Life*. New York: Simon & Schuster, 2003.

Jeffreys-Jones, Rhodri. *Cloak and Dollar: A History of American Secret Intelligence*. New Haven, CT: Yale University Press, 2002.

Jensen, Joan. *The Price of Vigilance*. New York: Rand McNally, 1968.

Johnson, David Alan. *Betrayal: The True Story of J. Edgar Hoover and the Nazi Saboteurs Captured during World War II*. New York: Hippocrene Books, 2007.

———. *Germany's Spies and Saboteurs*. Osceola, WI: MBI, 1998.

Kahn, David. *Hitler's Spies: German Military Intelligence in World War II*. New York: DaCapo Press, 1978.

Kane, Harnett. *Spies for the Blue and Gray*. New York: Ace Books, 1954.

Keegan, John. *Intelligence in War: Knowledge of the Enemy from Napoleon to Al Qaeda*. New York: Alfred A. Knopf, 2003.

Kent, Tyler. "Speech at the Fourth Institute of the Historical Review Conference." September 1982. www.ihr.org/jhr/v04/v04p173_Kent.html.

Kessler, Lauren. *Clever Girl: Elizabeth Bentley, the Spy Who Ushered in the McCarthy Era*. New York: HarperCollins, 2003.

Khrushchev, Nikita. *Khrushchev Remembers,* translated and edited by Jerrold L. Schechter and Vyacheslav V. Luchkov. Boston: Little, Brown, 1990.

Knight, Amy. *How the Cold War Began: The Gouzenko Affair and the Hunt for Soviet Spies*. Toronto: McClelland & Stuart, 2005.

Kotani, Ken. *Japanese Intelligence in World War II,* translated by Chiharu Kotani. Oxford: Osprey, 2009.

Lamphere, Robert. *The FBI–KGB War.* New York: Random House, 1986.

Leonard, Elizabeth. *All the Daring of the Soldier: Women of the Civil War Armies.* New York: Penguin, 1999.

Levine, Isaac Don. *Eyewitness to History: Memoirs of a Foreign Correspondent for Half a Century.* New York: Hawthorn, 1973.

Lloyd, Mark. *The Guinness Book of Espionage.* New York: DaCapo Press, 1994.

Lomask, Milton. *Aaron Burr: The Conspiracy and Years of Exile, 1805–1836.* New York: Farrar, Straus & Giroux, 1982.

Lota, Alexander. "Ego zvali Del'mar" [They Called Him Delmar]. *Krasnaya Zvezda,* July 25, 2007. http://vrazvedka.com/smi/lota/delmar.html.

———. *GRU i atomnaya bomba* [The GRU and the Atomic Bomb]. Moscow: Olma Press, 2002.

Markle, Donald. *Spies and Spymasters of the Civil War.* New York: Barnes & Noble, 1994.

Masters, Jonathan. "Confronting the Cyber Threat." *Council on Foreign Relations,* May 23, 2011. www.cfr.org/technology-and-foreign-policy/confronting-cyber-threat/p15577U.S.

Matthews, Tony. *Shadows Dancing: Japanese Espionage against the West, 1939–1945.* New York: St. Martin's Press, 1993.

Middlekauff, Robert. *Glorious Cause: The American Revolution 1763–1789.* New York: Oxford University Press, 2005.

Mitchell, Marcia, and Thomas Mitchell. *The Spy Who Seduced America: Lies and Betrayal in the Heat of the Cold War—the Judith Coplon Story.* Montpelier, VT: Invisible Cities, 2002.

Miller, Nathan. *Spying for America: The Hidden History of US Intelligence.* New York: Dell, 1989.

Mogelever, Jacob. *Death to Traitors: The Story of General Lafayette C. Baker, Lincoln's Forgotten Secret Service Chief.* New York: Doubleday, 1960.

Morozov, Evgeny. "Cyber Scare: The Exaggerated Fears Over Digital Warfare." *Boston Review,* July–August 2009. http://bostonreview.net/BR34.4/morozov.php.

Morpurgo, J. E. *Treason at West Point: The Arnold–Andre Conspiracy.* New York: Mason Charter, 1975.

Morris, Richard B. *John Jay: The Making of a Revolutionary.* New York: Harper & Row, 1975.

———. ed. *Seven Who Shaped Our Destiny: The Founding Fathers as Revolutionaries.* New York: HarperCollins, 1978.

Morison, Samuel Eliot. *The Oxford History of the American People.* 3 vols. New York: Oxford University Press, 1965; New York: Mentor, 1972. Citations refer to the Mentor edition.

Mortimer, Gavin. *Double Death: The True Story of Pryce Lewis, the Civil War's Most Daring Spy.* New York: Walker, 2010.

Nagy, John A. *Invisible Ink: Spycraft of the American Revolution.* Yardley, PA: Westholme, 2010.

National Security Agency. Official Venona website. www.nsa.gov/public_info/declass/venona/index.shtml.

National Security Agency. Venona decrypt of December 5, 1994, message, release 3, www.nsa.gov/public_info/_files/venona/1994/5dec_flora_wovschin.pdf

Neely, Jack. "George Koval: Oak Ridge's Master Spy." *Metropulse,* July 29, 2009. www.metropulse.com/news/2009/jul/29/george-koval-oak-ridges-master-spy/.

Olmsted, Kathryn. *Red Spy Queen: A Biography of Elizabeth Bentley.* Chapel Hill: University of North Carolina Press, 2002.

O'Toole, G. J. A. "Intrigue in Paris." In *Secret New England: Spies of the Revolution,* edited by Edmund R. Thompson. Kennebunk, ME: Association of Former Intelligence Officers, 1991.

Palmer, Dave R. *George Washington and Benedict Arnold: A Tale of Two Patriots.* Washington, DC: Regnery, 2006.

Pardini, Albert. *The Legendary Norden Bombsight.* Atglen, PA: Schiffer, 1999.

Paul, Joel Richard: *Unlikely Allies: How a Merchant, a Playwright and a Spy Saved the American Revolution.* New York: Riverhead, 2009.

Peake, Hayden B. "The Venona Progeny." *Naval War College Review* 53, no. 3 (Summer 2000). http://web.archive.org/web/20060820054409/http://www.nwc.navy.mil/press/review/2000/summer/re2-su0.htm.

Pennypacker, Morton. *George Washington's Spies on Long Island and in New York.* Brooklyn: Long Island Historical Society, 1939; Cranbury, NJ: Scholar's Bookshelf, 2005. Citations refer to Scholar's Bookshelf edition.

Persico, Joseph. *Roosevelt's Secret War: FDR and World War II Espionage.* New York: Random House, 2001.

Philbrick, Herbert. *I Led Three Lives.* New York: Grosset & Dunlap, 1952.

Pincher, Chapman. *Traitors.* New York: Penguin, 1987.

Pinkerton, Allen. *Spy of the Rebellion.* Kindle edition. New York: G. W. Carleton, 1883.

Poteat, S. Eugene. "The Downside of Globalization: The Surge in Economic and Industrial Espionage." *Intelligencer* 15, no. 2 (Fall–Winter 2006–7): 11–18.

Powers, Thomas. *Intelligence Wars: American Secret History from Hitler to Al Qaeda.* New York: New York Review of Books, 2002.

President of Russia. "President Vladimir Putin Handed Over to the GRU [Military Intelligence] Museum the Gold Star Medal and Hero of Russia Certificate and Document Bestowed on Soviet Intelligence Officer George Koval." Press release, November 2, 2007. http://archive.kremlin.ru/eng/text/news/2007/11/150176.shtml.

Radosh, Ronald, and Joyce Milton. *The Rosenberg File.* New Haven, CT: Yale University Press, 1997.

Rafalko, Frank, ed. *Counterintelligence Reader.* 4 vols. Washington, DC: National Counterintelligence Center, 2001.

Redmond, Paul. "America Pays the Price for Openness." *Wall Street Journal,* June 2000. www.apfn.net/messageboard/7-09-03/discussion.cgi.46.html.

Rees, David. *Harry Dexter White: A Study in Paradox.* New York: Coward, McCann & Geoghegan, 1973.

Reit, Seymour. *Behind Rebel Lines: The Incredible Story of Emma Edmonds, Civil War Spy.* New York: Gulliver, 1988.

Revere, Paul. "Letter to Jeremy Belknap." Massachusetts Historical Society. www.masshist.org/objects/cabinet/april2002/reveretranscription.htm.

Rhodes, Richard. *Dark Sun: The Making of the Hydrogen Bomb.* New York: Simon & Schuster, 1995.

Richelson, Jeffrey T. *A Century of Spies: Intelligence in the Twentieth Century*. New York: Oxford University Press, 1995.

Riebling, Mark. *Wedge: The Secret War between the FBI and CIA*. New York: Alfred A. Knopf, 1994.

Roberts, Sam. *The Brother: The Untold Story of the Rosenberg Case*. New York: Random House, 2001.

———. "Judith Coplon, Haunted by Espionage Case, Dies at 89." *New York Times*, March 1, 2011. www.nytimes.com/2011/03/02/us/02coplon.html.

Romerstein, Herbert, and Eric Breindel. *The Venona Secrets: Exposing Soviet Espionage and America's Traitors*. Washington, DC: Regnery, 2000.

Rose, Alexander. *Washington's Spies: The Story of America's First Spy Ring*. New York: Bantam, 2006.

Rose, P. K. "The Civil War: Black American Contributions to Union Intelligence." *Studies in Intelligence, Winter* 1998–99, 73–80.

Rout, Leslie, and John F. Bratzel. *Shadow War: German Espionage and US Counter-espionage in Latin America during World War II*. Frederick, MD: University Publications, 1986.

Rowan, Richard. *Secret Agents against America*. Garden City, NY: Doubleday, 1939.

Ryan, David D. *A Yankee Spy in Richmond: The Civil War Diary of "Crazy Bet" Van Lew*. Mechanicsburg, PA: Stackpole Books, 1996.

Sale, Richard T. *Traitors: The Worst Acts of Treason in American History from Benedict Arnold to Robert Hanssen*. New York: Berkley, 2003.

Sayers, Michael, and Albert E. Kahn. *Sabotage: The Secret War against America*. New York: Harper & Brothers, 1942.

Schaeper, Thomas J. *Edward Bancroft: Scientist, Author, Spy*. New York: Yale University Press, 2011. Kindle edition.

Schechter, Jerrold, and Leona Schechter. *Sacred Secrets: How Soviet Intelligence Operations Changed American History*. Washington, DC: Brassey's, 2002. Reprinted in paperback, 2003; citations refer to this edition.

Schneir, Walter. *Final Verdict: What Really Happened in the Rosenberg Case*. New York: Melville House, 2010.

Sears, Stephen W., ed. *The Civil War Papers of George B. McClellan: Selected Correspondence 1860–1865*. New York: DaCapo Press, 1989.

Sheehan, Neil. *A Fiery Peace in a Cold War: Bernard Schriever and the Ultimate Weapon*. New York: Vintage Books, 2010.

Sherwood, Mary Elizabeth Wilson. "On Spying in Washington, in 1862–1863, When It Was a Civil War Camp." In *Epistle to Posterity: Being Rambling Recollections of Many Years of My Life*, by Mary Elizabeth Wilson Sherwood (New York: Harper & Brothers, 1897). http://education.yahoo.com/reference/quotations/quote/64069.

Shirer, William L. *The Rise and Fall of the Third Reich*. New York: Simon & Schuster, 1960.

Shitov, Andrey. "Agent Del'mar vykhodit na svyaz'" [Agent Delmar comes into contact]. *Rossiyskaya Gazeta*, January 30, 2008. www.rg.ru/2008/01/30/delmar.html.

Sibley, Katherine A. S. *Red Spies in America: Stolen Secrets and the Dawn of the Cold War*. Lawrence: University Press of Kansas, 2004.

Snow, John H. *The Case of Tyler Kent.* New York: Domestic and Foreign Affairs Press, 1946; New Canaan, CT: Long House, 1982.

Sparks, Jared. *The Writings of George Washington: Being His Correspondence, Addresses, Messages and Other Papers, Official and Private.* Boston: American Stationers Company, 1837.

Stern, Philip Van Doren. *Secret Missions of the Civil War.* New York: Wings, 1959.

Tanenhaus, Sam. *Whittaker Chambers: A Biography.* New York: Random House, 1997.

Taylor, J. G. *Some New Light on the Later Life and Resting Place of Benedict Arnold and His Wife, Peggy Shippen.* London: George White, 1931.

Theoharis, Athan. *The FBI and American Democracy.* Lawrence: University Press of Kansas, 2004.

Thompson, Edmund R., ed. *Secret New England: Spies of the Revolution.* Kennebunk, ME: Association of Former Intelligence Officers, 1991.

Thompson, Edmund R., and Kenneth J. Campbell. "General Gage's Spies." In *Secret New England: Spies of the Revolution,* edited by Edmund R. Thompson. Kennebunk, ME: Association of Former Intelligence Officers, 1991.

Tsu, Sun. *The Art of War,* translated by Denma Translation Group. Boston: Shambhala, 2001.

Tully, Andrew. *Inside the FBI.* New York: Dell, 1980.

Turrou, Leon. *Nazi Spies in America.* New York: Random House, 1938.

US Central Intelligence Agency. *Intelligence in the War for Independence.* Washington, DC: US Central Intelligence Agency, 1997.

Usdin, Steven T. *Engineering Communism: How Two Americans Spied for Stalin and Founded the Soviet Silicon Valley.* New Haven, CT: Yale University Press, 2005.

———. "Tracking Julius Rosenberg's Lesser Known Associates." *Studies in Intelligence* 49, no. 3 (2005): 13–24.

US Senate Select Committee to Study Governmental Operations with respect to Intelligence Activities. Final Report on the FBI's Covert Action Programs against American Citizens, April 23, 1976. www.icdc.com/~paulwolf/cointelpro/churchfinalreportIIIa.htm.

Vaillancourt, John P. "Edward Bancroft (@Edwd. Edwards), Estimable Spy." *Studies in Intelligence,* 5, no. 1 (Winter 1961): 53–67.

Van Doren, Carl. *Benjamin Franklin.* New York: Book of the Month Club, 1938/1980.

———. *Secret History of the American Revolution.* New York: Viking Press, 1941.

Varon, Elizabeth R. *Southern Lady, Yankee Spy: The True Story of Elizabeth Van Lew, a Union Agent in the Heart of the Confederacy.* New York: Oxford University Press, 2003.

Volkman, Ernest. *Espionage: The Greatest Spy Operations of the 20th Century.* New York: John Wiley and Sons, 1995.

———. *Spies: The Secret Agents Who Changed the Course of History.* New York: John Wiley and Sons, 1994.

Wallace, Willard. *Traitorous Hero: The Life and Fortunes of Benedict Arnold.* New York: Harper & Brothers, 1954.

Walsh, Michael. "George Koval: Atomic Spy Unmasked." *Smithsonian Magazine,* May 2009. www.smithsonianmag.com/history-archaeology/Iowa-Born-Soviet-Trained.html.

Warner, Michael. "Did Truman Know about Venona?" *Bulletin of the Center for the Study of Intelligence* 11 (Summer 2000): 2–4.

Warner, Michael. "The Kaiser Sows Destruction." *Studies in Intelligence* 46, no. 1 (2002): 3–9.

Webb, G. Gregg. "Friends Mighty in War: An Analysis of the Intelligence Liaison between Assistant Secretary of State Adolph Berle and FBI Director J. Edgar Hoover, 1940–1944." *Studies in Intelligence* 49, no. 3 (2005): 25–38.

Weiner, Timothy, David Johnston, and Neil A. Lewis. *Betrayal: The Story of Aldrich Ames, an American Spy.* New York: Random House, 1995.

Weinstein, Allen. *Perjury: The Hiss–Chambers Case.* New York: Alfred A. Knopf, 1978.

Weinstein, Allen, and Alexander Vassiliev. *The Haunted Wood: Soviet Espionage in America—the Stalin Era.* New York: Modern Library, 1999.

Weisband, William, Jr. Interview with William Weisband's Son by *Nova Online* "Family of Spies" Series. www.pbs.org/wgbh/nova/venona/fami_weisband.html.

West, Nigel. *Venona: The Greatest Secret of the Cold War.* New York: HarperCollins, 1999.

West, Rebecca. *The New Meaning of Treason.* New York: Viking Press, 1947; new edition, 1964.

White, G. Edward. *Alger Hiss's Looking-Glass Wars: The Covert Life of a Soviet Spy.* New York: Oxford University Press, 2004.

Wighton, Charles, and Gunter Peis. *Hitler's Spies and Saboteurs.* New York: Charter, 1958.

Willing, Richard. "William Colepaugh: American Citizen, Navy Veteran, Nazi Sympathizer, Spy." *Intelligencer* 15, no. 1 (Fall–Winter 2005): 49–58.

Winchell, Walter. *Winchell Exclusive.* Englewood Cliffs, NJ: Prentice Hall, 1975.

Winkler, H. Donald. *Stealing Secrets: How a Few Daring Women Deceived Generals, Impacted Battles and Altered the Course of the Civil War.* Naperville, IL: Cumberland House, 2010.

Winks, Robin. *Cloaks and Gowns: Scholars in the Secret War 1939–1961.* New York: Morrow, 1987.

Witcover, Jules. *Sabotage at Black Tom.* Chapel Hill, NC: Algonquin Books, 1989.

Zinn, Howard. *A People's History of the United States 1492–Present.* New York: HarperCollins, 2003.

About the Author

Michael Sulick is a retired intelligence operations officer who from 2007 to 2010 was director of the Central Intelligence Agency's National Clandestine Service, where he was responsible for supervising the CIA's covert collection operations and coordinating the espionage activities of the US intelligence community. During his twenty-eight-year career, his assignments also included chief of CIA counterintelligence (2002–4) and chief of the Central Eurasia Division (1999–2002). He also holds a PhD in comparative literature from the City University of New York.

INDEX

Note: Page numbers in italics indicate photographs.

Boston Tea Party, 22
Bowser, Mary, 281n12, 102–3
Boyd, Belle, 280n13
Boy-Ed, Karl, 113–18, *115*, 122
Brenner, Joel, 271
Bretton Woods Conference, 204
Browder, Earl, 188–89, 245
Brown, John, 58
Buchanan, James, 82
Bullitt, William, 165
Bureau of Investigation (US Justice
    Department), 119–22; and gangsterism
    during the 1920s, 127, 130; and Palmer
    raids, 124–25, 128; and World War I
    counterespionage, 119–22. *See also*
    Federal Bureau of Investigation (FBI)
Bureau of Military Information, 73–74
Burger, Peter, 144–45
Burgoyne, John, 45
Burke, John, 68
Burnside, Ambrose, 96, 104
Byrnes, James, 205

C
Calhoun, John, 81
Callan, John, 90–91
Canada: the Continental Army's plan to
    invade, 43–44; and Soviet defector
    Gouzenko, 182–83
Canaris, Wilhelm, 129, 135–36, 143, 145,
    283n1
Capone, Al, 130
Carleton, Guy, 43
Carnegie Endowment for International
    Peace, 196
Carranza, Ramon, 110
Carter, Jimmy, 268–69
CDDC. *See* Committee on Detecting and
    Defeating Conspiracies (CDDC)
Central Intelligence Agency (CIA), 18, 25,
    32; during the Cold War, 27–28, 33,
    265, 267–68; counterespionage, 267;
    failures to detect spies within ranks,
    27–28, 267–68; intelligence collection,
    267; and Venona Project, 176

Chamberlain, Neville, 152
Chambers, Whittaker, 193–200, *195*;
    allegations against Currie, 209–10;
    allegations against Hiss, 193, 195–98;
    allegations against White, 205;
    communist sympathies and CPUSA,
    193–94; and Hiss trials, 197–98; HUAC
    testimony, 193, 196–97, 205, 210;
    revelations of thirteen spies' identities,
    195–96, 209–10, 287n4; and Roosevelt,
    195–96, 287n4; and Ware Group, 194,
    202; and White in the Treasury
    Department, 202, 203, 205
Charles II, King, 49
Chicago Police Department, 71
Chin, Larry Wu Tai, 269–70
China: Cold War espionage against the
    US, 269–70; cyber espionage, 273–74
Church, Benjamin, 7, 9, 21–28, *23*, 174;
    access to secrets, 26; and Arnold, 41;
    arrest, 9, 26–27; exposure, 24–26;
    motivations, 7, 23, 26, 266; and
    Washington, 24–25, 26
Churchill, Winston, 150–53
City College of New York, 228, 244, 257,
    260
civil liberties and counterespionage:
    abuses of, 4–5, 87–91, 124–25, 271–72;
    Baker's National Detective Police,
    87–91, 271; the delicate balance of
    individual freedoms and liberties, 3–4;
    and war on terrorism, 271–72
Civil War espionage, 11, 63–105; access to
    secrets, 81–82, 95, 96; Baker's National
    Detective Police, 4, 5–6, 67, 72, 87–91,
    96, 97, 104–5; Confederate counteres-
    pionage, 66–67, 77–80, 96; Conrad,
    93–97, 105; damage inflicted, 82, 86,
    95–96; divided families and loyalties,
    65–66; doctor spies, 68–69, 97;
    Edmonds, 68, 103–4, 105; female spies,
    66, 68, 81–86, 93, 99–104, 105, 280n13;
    Greenhow, 68, 81–86, 93, 100; hunt for
    secessionist clerks in Union capital,
    88–91; ideological motivations, 66, 81,